T0122910

Get the eBook FREE!

(PDF, ePub, Kindle, and liveBook all included)

We believe that once you buy a book from us, you should be able to read it in any format we have available. To get electronic versions of this book at no additional cost to you, purchase and then register this book at the Manning website.

Go to https://www.manning.com/freebook and follow the instructions to complete your pBook registration.

That's it!
Thanks from Manning!

Swift in Depth

Swift in Depth

TJEERD IN 'T VEEN

MANNING

SHELTER ISLAND

For online information and ordering of this and other Manning books, please visit www.manning.com. The publisher offers discounts on this book when ordered in quantity. For more information, please contact

> Special Sales Department
> Manning Publications Co.
> 20 Baldwin Road
> PO Box 761
> Shelter Island, NY 11964
> Email: orders@manning.com

Manning Publications Co.
20 Baldwin Road
PO Box 761
Shelter Island, NY 11964

Development editor:	Helen Stergius
Technical development editor:	Alain Couniot
Review editor:	Aleks Dragosavljević
Project editor:	Deirdre Hiam
Copy editor:	Darren Meiss
Proofreaders:	Carol Shields and Melody Dolab
Technical proofreader:	Edwin Chun Wing Kwok
Typesetter:	Dennis Dalinnik
Cover designer:	Marija Tudor

ISBN: 9781617295188
Printed in the United States of America
1 2 3 4 5 6 7 8 9 10 – SP – 23 22 21 20 19 18

brief contents

contents

preface

I started as an iOS developer in 2011. I loved to make iPhone apps and still do to this day. Besides doing mobile development work, I also was involved in some web development while learning Ruby. I loved the short powerful language, and wished I could use a compile-time language like Objective-C, but with the elegance and expressive nature of Ruby.

Then Apple introduced Swift, and it seems like they listened. Swift was a fresh take on programming for me, combining the elegance of a dynamic language with the speed and safety of a static language. I never liked the Objective-C syntax. I used to say things like "Yeah, Objective-C is verbose, but it gets the job done." But with Swift, however, I find reading and writing code very pleasing again, like I did with Ruby. I could finally use a static language and keep producing work *while* loving the language I'm working with. It was a good combination for me.

However, it wasn't love at first sight. Before I truly enjoyed Swift, I struggled a lot with it. Swift looks very friendly, but boy, was it tough sometimes. Everything needs to be safe at compile-time, and I could not mix and match types in arrays anymore. Meanwhile, Swift was only an early version and kept changing; it was hard to keep up. "What are generators? Oh, they are called iterators now? And why use guard? Can't we use an if statement instead? Pfft, optionals are overrated; we can use simple nil checks?", and so on. I wouldn't even consider working with generics.

However, I persevered and started to embrace these Swift concepts. I realized they were older concepts from other programming languages but wearing a fresh new coat that truly helped me become a better programmer and deliver better work. Over time, I started to love the Swift language and its pretty syntax.

Since Swift 2, I had the luxury of working in a big company where we produced Swift code on a large scale, starting with about 20 developers and growing to over 40. After working with Swift with so many developers, and after being involved in hundreds of pull requests, I noticed that other developers had the same struggles as me. Or my fellow developers delivered code just fine, but didn't realize that a more elegant or robust alternative was hidden, waiting to be discovered. Even though our code was correct, sometimes it could be a bit cleaner, or more succinct, or just a bit safer. I also noticed that we all stayed away from powerful techniques—such as generics or `flatMap`—because they were hard to grasp. Or we used to love the idea of generics, but weren't sure why or when to apply it ourselves.

After these realizations I started to write. First, these scribbles would be notes for myself on how to cleanly unwrap optionals, how lazy properties work, how to deal with generics, and so on. Then, these notes matured, and before I knew it I had enough content for some chapters. It was time to turn these notes into something more elaborate: a programming book that could help others shorten their Swift journey.

With a few rough chapters in hand, I was wondering if I should throw an ebook online. However, with an "impressive" 200 people following me on Twitter and lacking a popular blog website, I figured I wouldn't find the audience I wanted. Moreover, I thought that I had to learn a lot of the unknowns about writing a book.

I decided to approach a publisher to help me turn these rough chapters into a great book. I approached Manning, and we've been working on this book together ever since. I believe these "small notes" have grown into something special. With the help of Manning and Swift friends, I have spent most of my free time for over a year writing and polishing and trying to make Swift's tough concepts more simple to understand.

By reading this book, I hope that it helps you on your path to becoming a Swift master. Also, I hope that you can tell I thoroughly enjoy sharing these concepts with you. I hope this book makes your Swift journey easy and fun.

TJEERD IN 'T VEEN

acknowledgements

Thank you, Manning, for helping me publish my first book.

I want to give special thanks to Mike Stephens for taking the chance by getting me on board. Thank you, Helen Stergius, for working with me during the whole process. Thank you, Alain Couniot, for the great technical reviews of my chapters; it's not an easy job to keep pointing out errors and possible improvements; still, I greatly appreciate it. And I also want to thank Alexander Pawlicki for his creative cartoon illustrations used throughout the book.

Also thank you to the rest of the Manning team: Aleksandar Dragosavljević, Candace Gillhoolley, Ana Romac, Cheryl Weisman, Deirdre Hiam, Dottie Marsico, Nichole Beard, Mary Piergies, Carol Shields, Darren Meiss, Melody Dolab, and Marija Tudor.

I want to give special thanks to friends, coworkers, and others who have been my guinea pigs and reviewed (parts of) the book: Bart den Hollander, Dimitar Gyurov, Dario de Rosa, Rein Spijkerman, Janina Kutyn, Sidney de Koning, Torben Schulz, and Edwin Chun Wing Kwok.

I knew writing a book was tough, but it was much harder than I imagined it to be. My fiancée Jenika and I just had a baby daughter, and it was quite the struggle to start a new family, have sleepless nights, maintain a full-time job, *and* write a programming book in a second language. I couldn't have done it if I didn't love writing this book while having the support of my fiancée. Thank you, Jenika, for being so patient with me.

about this book

Swift is a young language. At the time of writing, Swift has reached the fourth version and yet is not ABI-stable, meaning that there will be breaking changes when Swift 5 comes out. So why is this book in any position to tell you how to write your code?

You'd be right to be skeptical, but please bear with me. Even though Swift is relatively new, I think it's fair to say that some solutions work better than others, which is even more essential to understand if you're using Swift for real production apps.

Swift borrows a lot of important concepts from other programming languages, such as Haskell, Ruby, Rust, Python, C#, and others. Therefore, you'd be wise to keep an eye out for these concepts.

By mixing programming paradigms with real-world experience, this book shares some very fun and useful best practices you can instantly apply to your work.

Having programmed for over a decade in multiple languages and teams, I would like to share tips, tricks, and guidelines that helped my Swift career tremendously, and I want the same for you.

Why this book?

Honestly, a lot of software in this world runs on "ugly" code, and that is completely normal. If your product does what it needs to do, that is—like it or not—good enough for businesses.

As a developer, you have to make sure your product works and works well. But your users won't look under the hood and point out ugly if statements. Perfectionism is harmful to software development and the cause or large numbers of unfinished projects.

Still, there's a large gap between "It does what it needs to do" and a project where some excellent decisions were made that pay off in the long run.

Having worked on numerous projects, one thing I highly value is writing code that your coworkers and your future self will understand *clearly*—because elegant code means less chance of bugs, higher maintainability, better understanding for developers who inherit code, increased programmer happiness, and many other benefits.

Another aspect I value is the robustness of code, meaning how refactor-proof some pieces are. Will it break if you sneeze on it? Or can you change code without a hassle?

In this book, I share my tips, tricks, and guidelines that have worked well for me and companies I've worked for. On top of that, it fills in significant knowledge gaps that may arise while working with Swift.

Although this is a Swift book, a lot of the principles shared here are not Swift-centric and carry over to other programming languages as well; this is because Swift borrows a lot of ideas and paradigms from other languages. After you finish this book, you may find it easy to apply concepts in other languages. For instance, you'll learn a *lot* about optionals, or how to use the `reduce` method on arrays. Later, you may decide to learn Kotlin, where you may apply optionals and `reduce`—called `fold`—straight away. You may also find Rust—and its similar generics implementation—easier to learn.

Because of Swift's multi-paradigm nature, this book switches without preference between object-oriented programming, functional programming, and protocol-oriented programming paradigms—although admittedly, I do favor other techniques over subclassing. Switching between these paradigms offers you many tools and solutions to a problem, with insights as to *why* a certain solution works well or not. Whether you're stuck in a rut or open to many new programming insights, this book challenges you to solve problems in different ways.

Is this book for you?

This book does assume that you have made one or more applications in Swift. Do you work in a team? Even better—this book shows you how to write good, clear code that gets appreciated in teams, and helps you improve pull requests of others. Your code will be more robust and cause less maintenance for you and your team.

This book fills in knowledge gaps for both beginner and seasoned Swift developers. Perhaps you mastered protocols but still struggle with flatMapping on types or asynchronous error handling. Or maybe you create beautiful apps but stay away from generics because they can be hard to interpret. Or perhaps you sort-of know when to use a struct versus a class but aren't aware that enums are sometimes a better alternative. Either way, this book helps you with these topics. By the end, generics should come as naturally as for loops. You'll be confident calling `flatMap` on optionals, know how to work with associated types, and you'll gladly use `reduce` in your daily routine when working with iterators.

If you're aiming to get a programming interview for a new job in the future, you're in for a treat. You're going to be able to answer a lot of relevant questions in regard to

Swift development trade-offs and decisions. This book can even help you write elegant code in your code assignments.

If you just want an app in the app store, just keep doing what you're doing; no need to read this book! But if you want to write code that is more robust, easier to understand, and increases your chances of getting a job, getting better at your job, or giving qualitative comments on pull requests, you're at the right place.

What this book is not

This book is focused on Swift. It mostly uses framework-free examples because it isn't about teaching Cocoa, iOS, Kitura, or other platforms and frameworks.

What does happen in this book is I often make use of Apple's Foundation, which is hard to avoid if you want real-world examples. If you're on Linux, you can use swift.org's Foundation alternative to get similar results.

A big emphasis on practical scenarios

This book is very practical, showcasing tips and tricks you can apply straight away in your daily programming.

Don't worry: it's not a theory-dense book. You'll learn a lot of theory, but only via the use of real-world problems that any Swift developer runs into sooner or later. It doesn't, however, reach an academic level where it discusses Swift's LLVM representation or machine code.

Also, I made sure to avoid a personal pet peeve of mine: I do not subclass "Animal" with "Dog" or add a "Flyable" protocol to "Bird." I also don't add "Foo" to "Bar." You'll deal with real-world scenarios, such as talking to APIs, loading local data, and refactoring and creating functions, and you'll see useful bits and pieces of code you can implement in your projects.

Roadmap

The following sections provide an overview of the book, divided into chapters. The book is quite modular, and you can start with any chapter that interests you.

Some chapters I consider crucial chapters. Chapter 4, "Making optionals second nature," is key, because optionals are so prevalent in Swift and return over and over again in chapters.

To understand the abstract side of Swift, I highly recommend reading chapter 7, "Generics," chapter 8, "Putting the pro in protocol-oriented programming," and chapter 12, "Protocol extensions." Together, these chapters lay a solid foundation for key Swift skills. Be sure not to skip these!

As a bonus, if you're interested in learning functional programming techniques, direct your attention to chapter 2, "Modeling data with enums," chapter 10, "Understanding map, flatMap, and compactMap," and chapter 11, "Asynchronous error handling with Result."

CHAPTER 1: INTRODUCING SWIFT IN DEPTH

This warmup chapter shows the current state of Swift, what it's good at, what it's not so good at, and what you'll be doing in this book. It's not very technical, but it sets expectations and prepares you for what you'll learn.

CHAPTER 2: MODELING DATA WITH ENUMS

This chapter is excellent if you want to flex your brain and think differently about modeling data and see how far enums can go to help you.

You'll see how to model data with structs and enums, and how to reason about it so that you can turn structs into enums and back again.

You'll be challenged to step away from the usual class, subclass, and struct approach and see how to model data with enums instead, and why you would want to.

You'll also see other interesting uses for enums and how to use enums to write safer code.

By the end of this chapter, you may catch yourself writing enums a lot more.

CHAPTER 3: WRITING CLEANER PROPERTIES

Swift has a rich property system with many options to pick from. You'll learn to pick the right type of properties for the right types of situations. You'll also create clean computed properties and stored properties with behavior.

Then you'll discover when to use lazy properties, which can cause subtle bugs if they're not carefully handled.

CHAPTER 4: MAKING OPTIONALS SECOND NATURE

This chapter leaves no stone unturned regarding optionals.

Optionals are so pervasive that this chapter takes a very thorough look at them. Both for beginners and Swift masters, this chapter is riddled with best practices and tips and tricks that will boost your day-to-day Swift code.

It covers optionals in many scenarios, such as when handling optional Booleans, optional strings, optional enums, implicitly unwrapped optionals, and force unwrapping.

CHAPTER 5: DEMYSTIFYING INITIALIZERS

Life in the programming world starts with initializers. Avoiding them in Swift is impossible, and of course, you work with them already. Still, Swift has a lot of weird rules and gotchas regarding structs and classes and how their properties are initialized. This chapter uncovers these strange rules to help you avoid boxing matches with the compiler.

It isn't just theory either; you'll see how you can write less initialization code to keep your codebase clean, and you're going to gain an understanding of subclassing and how the initializer rules apply there.

CHAPTER 6: EFFORTLESS ERROR HANDLING

This book has two error handling chapters covering two different idioms: one for synchronous error handling, and one for asynchronous error handling.

This chapter deals with synchronous error handling. You'll discover best practices related to throwing errors, handling errors, and maintaining a good state in your programs. But it also touches on propagating, adding technical information, adding user-facing information, and bridging to NSError.

You'll also find out how to make your APIs a bit more pleasant by making them throw fewer errors while respecting the integrity of an application.

CHAPTER 7: GENERICS

Generics are a rite of passage for Swift developers. They can be hard to understand or work with at first. However, once you're comfortable with them, you'll be tempted to use them often. This chapter makes sure you know when and how to apply them by creating generics functions and types.

You'll see how you can make code polymorphic with generics so that you'll be able to write highly reusable components and shrink down your codebase at the same time.

Generics become even more interesting when you constrain them with protocols for specialized functionality. You'll discover core protocols, such as Equatable, Comparable, and Hashable, and see how to mix and match generics with them.

Generics won't be intimidating after you have read this chapter, I promise.

CHAPTER 8: PUTTING THE PRO IN PROTOCOL-ORIENTED PROGRAMMING

Protocols—similar to typeclasses in Haskell or traits in Rust—are the holy grail of Swift. Because Swift can be considered a protocol-oriented language, this chapter provides a look at applying protocols in useful ways.

It covers generics and shows how they fare against using protocols as types. You'll be able to clearly choose (or switch) between either. Protocols with associated types can be considered advanced protocols. This chapter makes sure that you understand why and how they work so that you don't have to refrain from using them. It models a piece of a program with protocols, and keeps running into shortcomings, which it ultimately solves with associated types.

Then you'll see how to pass protocols with associated types around in functions and types, so that you can create extremely flexible, yet abstract code.

This chapter puts a lot of focus on how to use protocols at compile time (static dispatch) and how to use them at runtime (dynamic dispatch) and their trade-offs. This chapter aims to provide a strong foundation for protocols so that you can tackle more difficult patterns in later chapters.

CHAPTER 9: ITERATORS, SEQUENCES, AND COLLECTIONS

It's not uncommon to create a data structure in Swift that isn't only using the core types, such as sets arrays and dictionaries. Perhaps you'll need to create a special caching storage, or maybe a pagination system when downloading a Twitter feed.

Data structures are often powered up by the Collection protocol and the Sequence protocol. You'll see how Sequence in turn is using the IteratorProtocol. With these combined, you'll be able to extend and implement core functionalities in your data types.

First, you'll take a look at how iteration works with the IteratorProtocol and Sequence protocols. You'll discover some useful iterator patterns, such as reduce(), reduce(into:), and zip, as well as how lazy sequences work.

You'll create a data structure called a bag, also known as a multiset, using the Sequence protocol.

Then you'll discover the Collection protocol and the landscape of all the collection protocols Swift offers.

At the end, you'll create another data structure and see how to make it conform to the Collection protocol. This part is highly practical, and you can apply the same techniques to your code straight away.

CHAPTER 10: UNDERSTANDING MAP, FLATMAP, AND COMPACTMAP

This chapter highlights key concepts commonly found not only in Swift but also other frameworks and programming languages.

Sooner or later you'll run into map, flatMap, and compactMap on arrays, optionals, error types, and perhaps even functional reactive programming such as RxSwift.

You'll get a proper look at how to clean up code by applying map and flatMap on optionals. But you'll also see how to map over dictionaries, arrays, and other collection types. You'll also learn the benefits of flatMapping over strings.

Lastly, you'll get to review compactMap and how it elegantly handles optionals in collections.

Understanding map, flatMap, and compactMap on a deeper level is a good base for understanding how to read and write more concise yet elegant code, and a good base for working with Result in chapter 11.

CHAPTER 11: ASYNCHRONOUS ERROR HANDLING WITH RESULT

Swift's error handling falls a bit short on asynchronous error handling. You're going to take a closer look and see how to get compile-time safety for asynchronous programming by making use of a so-called Result type, which is unofficially offered by Apple via the Swift Package Manager.

Perhaps you're using some version of Result already, found in multiple frameworks. But even if you're acquainted with Result, I'd wager that you'll see new and useful techniques in this chapter.

You'll start by learning the downsides of traditional Cocoa-style error handling and why Result can help with that. Then you'll see how to transform a traditional call to one that uses Result.

Also, you're going to take a look at transforming throwing functions to Result and back again. You'll be applying the special AnyError type to create more flexibility, avoiding NSError, and making sure that you get a *lot* of compile-time safety.

As a cool trick, you'll learn about the Never type, which is a unique way to tell the Swift compiler that a Result can never succeed or fail.

Lastly, you'll use what you learned from map and flatMap on optionals to understand how to map over values and errors, and even how to flatMap with Result. You'll end up with a so-called monadic style of error handling, which gives you the power to very cleanly and elegantly propagate an error up in the call stack with very little code while keeping a lot of safety.

CHAPTER 12: PROTOCOL EXTENSIONS

This chapter is all about modeling data in a decoupled way, offering default implementations via protocols, making use of clever overrides, and seeing how to extend types in interesting ways.

As a start, you'll learn about modeling data with protocols versus subclasses.

Then, you're going to model data two ways: one approach entails protocol inheritance, and the other uses protocol composition. Both have their pros and cons, which you'll discover when you go over the trade-offs.

Also, you'll see how protocol extensions work when overridden by protocol inheritance and concrete types. It's a little theoretical, but it's useful to understand protocols on a deeper level.

You'll also see how you can extend in two directions. One direction is extending a class to adhere to a protocol, and the other is extending a protocol and constraining it to a class. It's a subtle but important difference.

At the end of the chapter you're going to extend `Collection`, and then you'll dive deeper and extend `Sequence` to create highly reusable extensions. You'll get acquainted with `ContiguousArray` and functions that have the `rethrows` keyword, while you create useful methods you can directly apply in your projects.

CHAPTER 13: SWIFT PATTERNS

This may be the hardest chapter in the book, but it's a great mountain to climb.

This chapter's goal is to handle common obstacles that you may run into. The patterns described here are not a rehash of SOLID principles—plenty of books cover that! Instead, it focuses on modern approaches for a modern language.

You'll discover how to mock an API with protocols and associated types—something that comes in handy frequently—so that you can create an offline version of an API and a testing version of an API.

Then, you'll see how conditional conformance works in accordance with generic types and protocols with associated types. Next, you'll create a generic type, and power it up by using the powerful technique of conditional conformance, which is another way to deliver highly flexible code.

After that, you'll deal with an issue you may run into when trying to use a protocol as a concrete type. You'll use two techniques to combat it: one involves enums, and the other involves an advanced technique called type erasure.

Lastly, you're also going to examine whether protocols are a good choice. Contrary to popular belief, protocols are not always the answer. You'll look at an alternative way to create a flexible type, involving a struct and higher-order functions.

CHAPTER 14: DELIVERING QUALITY SWIFT CODE

This is the least code-centric chapter in the book, but it may be one of the most important ones.

It's about writing clean, easy-to-understand code that creates fewer headaches for everybody on your team (if you're on one). It challenges you about establishing naming conventions, adding documentation and comments, and cutting up large classes into small generic components. You'll also set up SwiftLint, a tool that adds style consistency and helps avoid bugs in your projects. Also you'll get a peek at architecture, and how to transform large classes with too many responsibilities into smaller generic types.

This chapter is a good check to see if your code is up to standards and styles, which will help when creating pull requests or finishing code assignments for a new job.

CHAPTER 15: WHERE TO SWIFT FROM HERE

At this point, your Swift skills will be seriously powered-up. I share some quick pointers on where to look next so you can continue your Swift journey.

About the code

This book contains many examples of source code, both in numbered listings and in line with normal text. In both cases, source code is formatted in a `fixed-width font` `like this` to separate it from ordinary text. Sometimes code is also **in bold** to highlight code that has changed from previous steps in the chapter, such as when a new feature adds to an existing line of code.

In many cases, the original source code has been reformatted; we've added line breaks and reworked indentation to accommodate the available page space in the book. In rare cases, even this was not enough, and listings include line-continuation markers (➡). Additionally, comments in the source code have often been removed from the listings when the code is described in the text. Code annotations accompany many of the listings, highlighting important concepts.

The source code for all listings in this book is available for download from the Manning website at https://www.manning.com/books/swift-in-depth and from GitHub at https://github.com/tjeerdintveen/manning-swift-in-depth. With the exception of chapters 14 and 15, every chapter has source code included.

Book forum

Purchase of *Swift in Depth* includes free access to a private web forum run by Manning Publications where you can make comments about the book, ask technical questions, and receive help from the authors and from other users. To access the forum, go to https://forums.manning.com/forums/swift-in-depth. You can also learn more about Manning's forums and the rules of conduct at https://forums.manning.com/forums/about. Manning's commitment to our readers is to provide a venue where a meaningful dialogue between individual readers and between readers and the authors can take place. It is not a commitment to any specific amount of participation on the part of the authors, whose contribution to the forum remains voluntary (and unpaid). We suggest you try asking the authors some challenging questions lest their interest stray! The forum and the archives of previous discussions will be accessible from the publisher's website as long as the book is in print.

About the author

Tjeerd in 't Veen is an avid Swift fan and a freelance iOS developer, having experience working for agencies, co-founding a small startup, and at time of writing, helping ING scale up their mobile development. Starting out as a Flash developer in 2001, his career progressed to iOS development with Objective-C, web development with Ruby, and some tinkering in other programming languages.

When he's not developing in Swift, he's busy spending time with his two daughters, making cringy dad jokes, and dabbling on an acoustic guitar.

You can find him on Twitter via @tjeerdintveen.

About the cover illustration

The figure on the cover of *Swift in Depth* is captioned "Man from Omišalj, island Krk, Croatia." The illustration is taken from the reproduction, published in 2006, of a nineteenth-century collection of costumes and ethnographic descriptions entitled *Dalmatia* by Professor Frane Carrara (1812–1854), an archaeologist and historian, and the first director of the Museum of Antiquity in Split, Croatia. The illustrations were obtained from a helpful librarian at the Ethnographic Museum (formerly the Museum of Antiquity), itself situated in the Roman core of the medieval center of Split: the ruins of Emperor Diocletian's retirement palace from around AD 304. The book includes finely colored illustrations of figures from different regions of Dalmatia, accompanied by descriptions of the costumes and of everyday life.

Dress codes have changed since the nineteenth century, and the diversity by region, so rich at the time, has faded away. It is now hard to tell apart the inhabitants of different continents, let alone different towns or regions. Perhaps we have traded cultural diversity for a more varied personal life—certainly for a more varied and fast-paced technological life.

At a time when it's hard to tell one computer book from another, Manning celebrates the inventiveness and initiative of the computer business with book covers based on the rich diversity of regional life of two centuries ago, brought back to life by illustrations from collections such as this one.

Introducing Swift in depth

In this chapter

- A brief overview of Swift's popularity and supported platforms
- The benefits of Swift
- A closer look at Swift's subtle downsides
- What we will learn in this book

It is no secret that Swift is supported on many platforms, such as Apple's iOS, macOS, watchOS, and tvOS. Swift is open source and also runs on Linux, and it's gaining popularity on the server side with web frameworks such as Vapor, Perfect, Zewo, and IBM's Kitura.

On top of that, Swift is slowly not only encompassing application programming (software for users) but also starting to enter systems programming (software for systems), such as SwiftNIO or command-line tools. Swift is maturing into a multi-platform language. By learning Swift, many doors open to you.

Swift was the most popular language on Stack overflow in 2015 and remains in the top five most-loved languages in 2017. In 2018, Swift bumped to number 6 (https://insights.stackoverflow.com/survey/2018).

Swift is clearly here to stay, and whether you love to create apps, web services, or other programs, I aim for you to get as much value as possible out of this book for both yourself and any team you're on.

What I love about Swift is that it's easy to learn, yet hard to master. There's always more to learn! One of the reasons is that Swift embraces many programming paradigms, allowing you to pick a suitable solution to a programming problem, which you're going to explore in this book.

1.1 *The sweet spot of Swift*

One thing I love about a dynamic language—such as Ruby—is its expressive nature. Your code tells you what you want to achieve without getting too much in the way of memory management and low-level technology. Writing in Ruby one day, and Objective-C the other, made me believe that I either had to pick between a compiled language that performed well or an expressive, dynamic language at the cost of lower performance.

Then Swift came out and broke this fallacy. Swift finds the right balance where it shares many benefits of dynamic languages—such as Ruby or Python—by offering a friendly syntax and strong polymorphism. Still, Swift avoids some of the downsides of dynamic languages, most notably the performance, because Swift compiles to native machine code via the LLVM compiler. Because Swift is compiled via LLVM, you get not only high performance, but also tons of safety checks, optimizations, and the guarantee that your code is okay before even running it. At the same time, Swift *reads* like an expressive dynamic language, making it pleasant to work with and effortless to express your intent.

Swift can't stop you from writing bugs or poor code, but it does help reduce program errors at compile time using various techniques, including, but not limited to, static typing and strong support for *algebraic data types* (enums, structs, and tuples). Swift also prevents null errors thanks to optionals.

A downside of some static languages is that you always need to define the types. Swift makes this easier via type inference and can deduce concrete types when it makes sense. This way, you don't need to explicitly spell out every single variable, constant, and generic.

Swift is a mixtape of different programming paradigms, because whether you take an object-oriented approach, functional programming approach, or are used to working with abstract code, Swift offers it all. As the major selling point, Swift has a robust system when it comes down to polymorphism, in the shape of generics and *protocol-oriented programming*, which gets pushed hard as a marketing tool, both by Apple and developers (see figure 1.1).

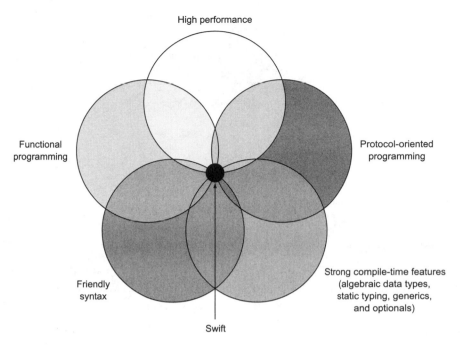

Figure 1.1   The sweet spot of Swift

1.2   *Below the surface*

Even though Swift reels you in with its friendly syntax and promises to build amazing apps, it's merely the tip of the iceberg. An enticing entry to learning Swift is to start with iOS development, because not only will you learn about Swift, you will also learn how to create beautiful apps that are composed of crucial components from Apple frameworks.

But as soon as you need to deliver components yourself and start building more elaborate systems and frameworks, you will learn that Swift works hard to hide many complexities—and does so successfully. When you need to learn these complexities, and you will, Swift's difficulty curve goes up exponentially. Even the most experienced developers are still learning new Swift tricks and tidbits every day!

Once Swift has you hooked, you'll likely hit speed bumps in the shape of generics and associated types, and something as "simple" as handling strings may cause more trouble than you might expect (see figure 1.2).

This book shines in helping you handle the most common complexities. You will cover and tackle any issues and shortcomings with Swift, and you'll be able to wield the powers that these complexities bring while having fun doing so.

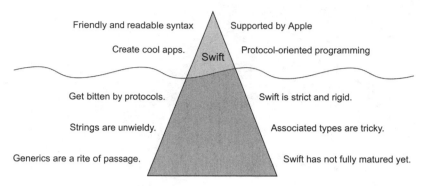

Figure 1.2   The tip of Swift's iceberg

1.3 *Swift's downsides*

Swift is my favorite programming language, but let's not look at it through rose-tinted glasses. Once you acknowledge both Swift's strong and weak points, you can adequately decide when and how you'd like to use it.

1.3.1 *ABI stability*

Swift is still moving fast and is not ABI-stable, which means that code written in Swift 4 will not be compatible with Swift 5, and vice versa. Imagine writing a framework for your application. As soon as Swift 5 comes out, an application written in Swift 5 can't use your framework until you've updated your framework to Swift 5. Luckily, Xcode offers plenty of help to migrate, so I expect that this migration won't be as painful.

1.3.2 *Strictness*

Swift is a strict and rigid language, which is a common criticism of static languages but even more so when working with Swift. Before getting comfortable with Swift, you may feel like you're typing with handcuffs on. In practice, you have to resolve many types at compile-time, such as using optionals, mixing values in collections, or handling enums.

I would argue that Swift's strict nature is one of its strong selling points. As soon as you try to compile, you learn of code that isn't working as opposed to having a customer run into a runtime error. Once you've made the initial investment to get comfortable with Swift, it will come naturally, and its restrictiveness will stop you less. This book helps you get over the hump, so that Swift becomes second nature.

1.3.3 *Protocols are tricky*

Protocols are the big selling point of Swift. But once you start working with protocols, you will hit sharp edges and cut yourself from time to time. Things that "should just work" somehow don't. Protocols are great in their current state and already good enough for creating quality software, but sometimes you hit a wall, and you'll have to use workarounds—of which this book shares plenty.

A common source of frustration: if you'd like to pass `Equatable` types to a function to see if they are equal, you get stopped. For instance, you might naively try checking if one value is equal to everything inside an array, as shown in the next listing. You will learn that this won't fly in Swift.

Listing 1.1 Trying to equate to types

```
areAllEqual(value: 2, values: [3,3,3,3])

func areAllEqual(value: Equatable, values: [Equatable]) -> Bool {
    guard !values.isEmpty else { return false }

    for element in values {
        if element != value {
            return false
        }
    }

    return true
}
```

Swift returns a cryptic error with a vague suggestion on what to do:

```
error: protocol 'Equatable' can only be used as a generic constraint
because it has Self or associated type requirements
```

You'll see why this happens and how to avoid these issues in chapters 7 and 8.

Swift's protocol extensions are another of its major selling points and are one of the most powerful features it has to offer. Protocols can act like interfaces; protocol extensions offer default implementations to types, helping you avoid rigid subclassing trees.

Protocols, however, are trickier than they may seem and may surprise even the seasoned developer. For instance, let's say you have a protocol called `FlavorType` representing a food or drink item that you can improve with flavor, such as coffee. If you extend this protocol with a default implementation that is *not* found inside the protocol declaration, you may get surprising results! Notice in the next listing how you have two `Coffee` types, yet they both yield different results when calling `addFlavor` on them. It's a subtle but significant detail.

Listing 1.2 Protocols can surprise us

```
protocol FlavorType{
//    func addFlavor() // You get different results if this method doesn't exist.
}

extension FlavorType {
    func addFlavor() { // Create a default implementation.
        print("Adding salt!")
    }
}
```

```
struct Coffee: FlavorType {
    func addFlavor() { // Coffee supplies its own implementation.
        print("Adding cocoa powder")
    }
}


let tastyCoffee: Coffee = Coffee() // tastyCoffee is of type 'Coffee'
tastyCoffee.addFlavor() // Adding cocoa powder

let grossCoffee: FlavorType = tastyCoffee // grossCoffee is of type FlavorType
grossCoffee.addFlavor() // Adding salt!
```

Even though you're dealing with the same coffee type, first you add cocoa powder, and then you accidentally add salt, which doesn't help anyone get up in the morning. As powerful as protocols are, they can introduce subtle bugs sometimes.

1.3.4 *Concurrency*

Our computers and devices are concurrent machines, utilizing multiple CPUs simultaneously. When working in Swift you are already able to express concurrent code via Apple's Grand Central Dispatch (GCD). But concurrency doesn't exist in Swift as a language feature.

Because you can already use GCD, it's not that big of a problem to wait a bit longer on a fitting concurrency model. Still, GCD in combination with Swift is not spotless.

First, working with GCD can create a so-called pyramid of doom—also known as deeply nested code—as showcased by a bit of unfinished code in the following listing.

Listing 1.3 A pyramid of doom

```
func loadMessages(completion: (result: [Message], error: Error?) -> Void) {
    loadResource("/user") { user, error in
        guard let data = data else {
            completion(nil, error)
            return
        }
        loadResource("/messages/", user.id) { messages, error in
            guard let messages = messages else {
                completion(nil, error)
                return
            }
            storeMessages(messages) { didSucceed, error in
                guard let error != nil else

{

                    completion(nil, error)
                    return
                }
                DispatchQueue.main.async { // Move code back to main queue
                    completion(messages)
                }
```

```
            }
         }
      }
   }
```

Second, you don't know on which queue asynchronous code gets called. If you were to call `loadMessages`, you could be in trouble if a small change moves the completion block to a background queue. You may be extra cautious and complete the callback on the main queue at the call site, but either way, there is a compromise.

Third, the error handling is suboptimal and doesn't fit the Swift model. Both the returned data and error can theoretically be filled or nil. The code doesn't express that it can only be one or the other. We cover this in chapter 11.

You can expect an async/await model in Swift later, perhaps version 7 or 8, which means a wait until these issues get solved. Luckily, GCD is more than enough for most of your needs, and you may find yourself turning to RxSwift as a reactive programming alternative.

1.3.5 *Venturing away from Apple's platforms*

Swift is breaking into new territory for the web and as a systems language, most notably with its support of IBM in the shape of the web server Kitura and in bringing Swift to the cloud. Moving away from Apple's platforms offers exciting opportunities, but be aware that you may find a lack of packages to help you out. For the xOS frameworks, such as iOS, watchOS, tvOS, and macOS, you can use CocoaPods or Carthage to handle your dependencies; outside of the xOS family, you can use the Swift Package Manager, offered by Apple. Many Swift developers are focused on iOS, however, and you may run into an alluring package with a lack of support for the Swift Package Manager.

Although it's hard to match existing ecosystems, such as thousands of Python's packages, npm from Node.js, and Ruby gems, it also depends on your perspective. A lack of packages can also be a signal that you can contribute to the community and ecosystem while learning Swift along the way.

Even though Swift is open source, Apple is holding the wheel. You don't have to worry about Apple stopping support of Swift, but you may not always agree with the direction or speed of Swift's updates. You still have to depend on third-party tools to get dependencies working for iOS and macOS, and Xcode doesn't yet integrate well with the Swift Package Manager; unfortunately, both issues appear to be a low priority for Apple.

1.3.6 *Compile times*

Swift is a high-performing language. But the compilation process can be quite slow and suck up plenty of developer time. Swift is compiled into multiple steps via the LLVM compiler. Although this gives you optimizations when you run your code, in day-to-day programming you may run into slow build times, which can be a bit tedious if you're trying to quickly test a running piece of code. Not every Swift project is a single project, either; as soon as you incorporate multiple frameworks, you'll be compiling a lot of code to create a build, slowing down your process.

In the end, every programming language has pros and cons—it's a matter of picking the right tool for the job. I believe that Swift has a bright future ahead to help you create beautiful software with clean, succinct, and high-performing code!

1.4   What you will learn in this book

This book aims to show you how to solve problems in elegant ways while applying best practices.

Even though this book has Swift on the cover, I think one of its strong points is that you'll learn concepts that seamlessly transfer to other languages.

You'll learn

- Functional programming concepts, such as `reduce`, `flatMap`, `Optional`, and `Result`, but also how to think in algebraic data types with structs, tuples, and enums
- Many real-world scenarios that you approach from different angles while considering the pros and cons of each approach
- Generics, covering compile-time polymorphism
- How to write more robust, concise, easy-to-read code
- Protocol-oriented programming, including thoroughly understanding associated types, which are considered the hardest part of protocols
- How Swift works at runtime and compile-time via the use of generics, enums, and protocols
- How to make trade-offs in functional programming, object-oriented programming, and protocol-oriented programming

At the end of this book, your tool belt will be heavy from all the options you have to tackle programming problems. After you internalize these concepts, you may find that learning other languages—such as Kotlin, Rust, and others that share similar ideas and functionality—is much easier.

1.5   How to make the most of this book

An excellent way to learn a programming language is to do exercises before reading a chapter. Be honest and see if you can *truly* finish them, as opposed to glancing over them and thinking you already know the answer. Some exercises may have some tricky situations hidden in there, and you will see it once you start working on them.

After doing the exercises for a chapter, decide if you want to read the chapter to learn new matter.

This book does have a flow that amps up the difficulty the further you read. Still, the book is set up in a modular way. Reading the chapters out of order is okay.

1.6 *Minimum qualifications*

This is not an absolute beginner's book; it assumes that you have worked a bit with Swift before.

If you consider yourself an advanced beginner or at intermediate level, most chapters will be valuable to you. If you consider yourself an experienced developer, I still believe many chapters are good to fill in your knowledge gaps. Because of this book's modularity, you can pick and choose the chapters you'd like to read without having to read earlier chapters.

1.7 *Swift version*

This book is written for Swift version 4.2. All the examples will run on that version either in the command line, or in combination with Xcode 10.

Summary

- Swift is supported on many platforms.
- Swift is frequently used for iOS, watchOS, tvOS, and macOS development and more and more every day for web development, systems programming, command-line tools, and even machine learning.
- Swift walks a fine line between high performance, readability, and compile-time safety.
- Swift is easy to learn but hard to master.
- Swift is a safe and high-performing language.
- Swift does not have built-in concurrency support.
- Swift's Package Manager doesn't work yet for iOS, watchOS, tvOS, or macOS.
- Swift entails multiple programming styles, such as functional programming, object-oriented programming, and protocol programming.

Modeling data with enums

This chapter covers

- How enums are an alternative to subclassing
- Using enums for polymorphism
- Learning how enums are "or" types
- Modeling data with enums instead of structs
- How enums and structs are algebraic types
- Converting structs to enums
- Safely handling enums with raw values
- Converting strings to enums to create robust code

Enumerations, or enums for short, are a core tool used by Swift developers. Enums allow you to define a type by *enumerating* over its values, such as whether an HTTP method is a *get, put, post,* or *delete* action, or denoting if an IP-address is either in *IPv4* or *IPv6* format.

Many languages have an implementation of enums, with a different type of implementation per language. Enums in Swift, unlike in C and Objective-C, aren't *only* representations of integer values. Instead, Swift borrows many concepts from the functional programming world, which bring plenty of benefits that you'll explore in this chapter.

In fact, I would argue that enums are a little underused in Swift-land. I hope to change that and help you see how enums can be surprisingly useful in many ways. My goal is to expand your enum-vocabulary so that you can directly use these techniques in your projects.

First, you'll see multiple ways to model your data with enums and how they fare against structs and classes.

Enums are a way to offer polymorphism, meaning that you can work with a single type, representing more types. We shed some light on how we can store multiple types into a single collection, such as an array.

Then, you'll see how enums are a suitable alternative to subclassing.

We dive a little into some algebraic theory to understand enums on a deeper level; then you'll see how you can apply this theory and convert structs to enums and back again.

As a cherry on top, we explore raw value enums and how you can use them to handle strings cleanly.

After reading this chapter, you may find that you're modeling data better, writing enums just a bit more often, and ending up with safer and cleaner code in your projects.

2.1   Or vs. and

Enums can be thought of as an "or" type. Enums can only be one thing at once—for example, a traffic light can either be green *or* yellow *or* red. Alternatively, a die can either be six-sided *or* twenty-sided, but not both at the same time.

> **JOIN ME!**   All code from this chapter is online. It's more educational and fun if you follow along. You can download the source code at https://mng.bz/gNre.

2.1.1   *Modeling data with a struct*

Let's start off with an example that shows how to think about "or" and "and" types when modeling data.

In the upcoming example, you're modeling message data in a chat application. A message could be text that a user may send, but it could also be a join message or leave message. A message could even be a signal to send balloons across the screen (see figure 2.1). Because why not? Apple does it, too, in their Messages app.

Here are some types of messages that your application might support:

- Join messages, such as "Mother in law has joined the chat"
- Text messages that someone can write, such as "Hello everybody!"

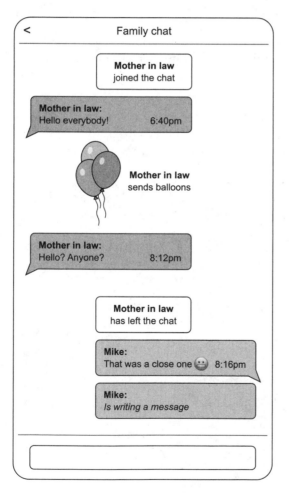

Figure 2.1   A chat application

- Send balloons messages, which include some animations and annoying sounds that others can see and hear
- Leave messages, such as "Mother in law has left the chat"
- Draft messages, such as "Mike is writing a message"

Let's create a data model to represent messages. Your first idea might be to use a struct to model your `Message`. You'll start by doing that and showcase the problems that come with it. Then you'll solve these problems by using an enum.

You can create multiple types of messages in code, such as a join message when someone enters a chatroom.

Listing 2.1   A join chatroom message

```
import Foundation // Needed for the Date type.

let joinMessage = Message(userId: "1",
                          contents: nil,
                          date: Date(),
                          hasJoined: true, // Set the joined Boolean
                          hasLeft: false,
                          isBeingDrafted: false,
                          isSendingBalloons: false)
```

You can also create a regular text message.

Listing 2.2   A text message

```
let textMessage = Message(userId: "2",
                          contents: "Hey everyone!", // Pass a message
                          date: Date(),
                          hasJoined: false,
                          hasLeft: false,
                          isBeingDrafted: false,
                          isSendingBalloons: false)
```

In your hypothetical messaging app, you can pass this message data around to other users.

The `Message` struct looks as follows.

Listing 2.3   The `Message` struct

```
import Foundation

struct Message {
    let userId: String
    let contents: String?
    let date: Date

    let hasJoined: Bool
    let hasLeft: Bool
```

```
    let isBeingDrafted: Bool
    let isSendingBalloons: Bool
}
```

Although this is one small example, it highlights a problem. Because a struct can contain multiple values, you can run into bugs where the Message struct can be a text message, a hasLeft command, and an isSendingBalloons command. An invalid message state doesn't bode well because a message can only be one *or* another in the business rules of the application. The visuals won't support an invalid message either.

To illustrate, you can have a message in an invalid state. It represents a text message, but also a join and a leave message.

Listing 2.4   An invalid message with conflicting properties

```
let brokenMessage = Message(userId: "1",
                            contents: "Hi there", // Have text to show
                            date: Date(),
                            hasJoined: true, // But this message also signals
          a joining state
                            hasLeft: true, // ... and a leaving state
                            isBeingDrafted: false,
                            isSendingBalloons: false)
```

In a small example, running into invalid data is harder, but it inevitably happens often enough in real-world projects. Imagine parsing a local file to a Message, or some function that combines two messages into one. You don't have any compile-time guarantees that a message is in the right state.

You can think about validating a Message and throwing errors, but then you're catching invalid messages at runtime (if at all). Instead, you can enforce correctness at compile time if you model the Message using an enum.

2.1.2   *Turning a struct into an enum*

Whenever you're modeling data, see if you can find *mutually exclusive* properties. A message can't be both a join and a leave message at the same time. A message can't also send balloons and be a draft at the same time.

But a message can be a join message *or* a leave message. A message can also be a draft, *or* it can represent the sending of balloons. When you detect "or" statements in a model, an enum could be a more fitting choice for your data model.

Using an enum to group the properties into cases makes the data much clearer to grasp.

Let's improve the model by turning it into an enum.

Listing 2.5   Message as an enum (lacking values)

```
import Foundation

enum Message {
    case text
```

```
    case draft
    case join
    case leave
    case balloon
}
```

But you're not done yet because the cases have no values. You can add values by adding a tuple to each case. A tuple is an ordered set of values, such as (userId: String, contents: String, date: Date).

By combining an enum with tuples, you can build more complex data structures. Let's add tuples to the enum's cases now.

Listing 2.6 `Message` **as an enum (with values)**

```
import Foundation

enum Message {
    case text(userId: String, contents: String, date: Date)
    case draft(userId: String, date: Date)
    case join(userId: String, date: Date)
    case leave(userId: String, date: Date)
    case balloon(userId: String, date: Date)
}
```

By adding tuples to cases, these cases now have so-called *associated values* in Swift terms. Also, you can clearly see which properties belong together and which properties don't.

Whenever you want to create a Message as an enum, you can pick the proper case with related properties, without worrying about mixing and matching the wrong values.

Listing 2.7 Creating enum messages

```
let textMessage = Message.text(userId: "2", contents: "Bonjour!", date: Date())
let joinMessage = Message.join(userId: "2", date: Date())
```

When you want to work with the messages, you can use a switch case on them and unwrap its inner values.

Let's say that you want to log the sent messages.

Listing 2.8 Logging messages

```
logMessage(message: joinMessage) // User 2 has joined the chatroom
logMessage(message: textMessage) // User 2 sends message: Bonjour!

func logMessage(message: Message) {
    switch message {
    case let .text(userId: id, contents: contents, date: date):
        print("[\(date)] User \(id) sends message: \(contents)")
    case let .draft(userId: id, date: date):
        print("[\(date)] User \(id) is drafting a message")
```

```
      case let .join(userId: id, date: date):
         print("[\(date)] User \(id) has joined the chatroom")
      case let .leave(userId: id, date: date):
         print("[\(date)] User \(id) has left the chatroom")
      case let .balloon(userId: id, date: date):
         print("[\(date)] User \(id) is sending balloons")
      }
   }
```

Having to switch on all cases in your entire application just to read a value from a single message may be a deterrent. You can save yourself some typing by using the `if case let` combination to match on a single type of `Message`.

```
if case let Message.text(userId: id, contents: contents, date: date) =
   textMessage {
   print("Received: \(contents)") // Received: Bonjour!
}
```

If you're not interested in specific properties when matching on an enum, you can match on these properties with an underscore, called a *wild card*, or as I like to call it, the "I don't care" operator.

```
if case let Message.text(_, contents: contents, _) = textMessage {
   print("Received: \(contents)") // Received: Bonjour!
}
```

2.1.3   *Deciding between structs and enums*

Getting compiler benefits with enums is a significant benefit. But if you catch yourself pattern matching often on a single case, a struct might be a better approach.

Also, keep in mind that the associated values of an enum are containers without additional logic. You don't get free initializers of properties; with enums, you'd have to manually add these.

Next time you write a struct, try to group properties. Your data model might be a good candidate for an enum!

2.2   *Enums for polymorphism*

Sometimes you need some flexibility in the shape of *polymorphism*. Polymorphism means that a single function, method, array, dictionary—you name it—can work with different types.

If you mix types in an array, however, you end up with an array of type `[Any]` (as shown in the following listing), such as when you put a `Date`, `String`, and `Int` into one array.

Listing 2.11 Filling an array with multiple values

```
let arr: [Any] = [Date(), "Why was six afraid of seven?", "Because...", 789]
```

Arrays explicitly want to be filled with the same type. In Swift, what these mixed types have in common is that they are an Any type.

Handling Any types are often not ideal. Since you don't know what Any represents at compile time, you have to check against the Any type at runtime to see what it presents. For instance, you could match on any types via pattern matching, using a *switch* statement.

Listing 2.12 Matching on Any values at runtime

```
let arr: [Any] = [Date(), "Why was six afraid of seven?", "Because...", 789]

for element: Any in arr {
  // element is "Any" type
  switch element {
    case let stringValue as String: "received a string: \(stringValue)"
    case let intValue as Int: "received an Int: \(intValue)"
    case let dateValue as Date: "received a date: \(dateValue)"
    default: print("I am not interested in this value")
  }
}
```

You can still figure out what Any is at runtime. But you don't know what to expect when matching on an Any type; therefore, you must also implement a default case to catch the values in which you're not interested.

Working with Any types is sometimes needed when you can't know what something is at compile time, such as when you're receiving unknown data from a server. But if you know beforehand the types that you're dealing with, you can get compile-time safety by using an enum.

2.2.1 *Compile-time polymorphism*

Imagine that you'd like to store two different types in an array, such as a Date and a range of two dates of type Range<Date>.

> **WHAT ARE THESE <DATE> BRACKETS?** Range is a type that represents a lower and upper bound. The <Date> notation indicates that Range is storing a *generic type*, which you'll explore deeply in chapter 7.
>
> The Range<Date> notation tells you that you're working with a range of two Date types.

You can create a DateType representing either a single date *or* a range of dates. Then you can fill up an array of both a Date and Range<Date>, as shown next.

Listing 2.13 Adding multiple types to an array via an enum

```
let now = Date()
let hourFromNow = Date(timeIntervalSinceNow: 3600)

let dates: [DateType] = [
    DateType.singleDate(now),
    DateType.dateRange(now..<hourFromNow)
]
```

The enum itself merely contains two cases, each with its associated value.

Listing 2.14 Introducing a `DateType` enum

```
enum DateType {
  case singleDate(Date)
  case dateRange(Range<Date>)
}
```

The array itself consists only of `DateType` instances. In turn, each `DateType` harbors one of the multiple types (see figure 2.2).

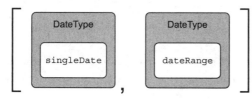

Figure 2.2 Array enums

Thanks to the enum, you end up with an array containing multiple types, while maintaining compile-time safety. If you were to read values from the array, you could switch on each value.

Listing 2.15 Matching on the `dateType` enum

```
for dateType in dates {
    switch dateType {
    case .singleDate(let date): print("Date is \(date)")
    case .dateRange(let range): print("Range is \(range)")
    }
}
```

The compiler also helps if you modify the enum. By way of illustration, if you add a year case to the enum, the compiler tells you that you forgot to handle a case.

Listing 2.16 Adding a year case to `DateType`

```
enum DateType {
  case singleDate(Date)
```

```
case dateRange(Range<Date>)
case year(Int)                    ⟵┤  Year is newly
}                                         added.
```

The compiler is now throwing the following.

Listing 2.17 Compiler notifies you of an error

```
error: switch must be exhaustive
    switch dateType {
    ^

add missing case: '.year(_)'
    switch dateType {
```

Thanks to enums, you can bring back compile-time safety when mixing types inside arrays and other structures such as dictionaries.

Of course, you must know beforehand what kind of cases you expect. When you know what you're working with, the added compile-time safety is a nice bonus.

2.3 *Enums instead of subclassing*

Subclassing allows you to build a hierarchy of your data. For example, you could have a fast food restaurant selling burgers, fries, the usual. For that, you'd create a super-class of FastFood, with subclasses like Burger, Fries, and Soda.

One of the limitations of modeling your software with hierarchies (subclassing) is that doing so constrains you in a specific direction that won't always match your needs.

For example, the aforementioned restaurant has been getting complaints from customers wanting authentic Japanese sushi with their fries. They intend to accommodate the customers, but their subclassing model doesn't fit this new requirement.

In an ideal world, modeling your data hierarchically makes sense. But in practice, you'll sometimes hit edge cases and exceptions that may not fit your model.

In this section, we explore these limitations of modeling your data via subclassing in more of a real-world scenario and solve these with the help of enums.

2.3.1 *Forming a model for a workout app*

Next up, you're building a model layer for a workout app, which tracks running and cycling sessions for someone. A workout includes the start time, end time, and a distance.

You'll create both a Run and a Cycle struct that represent the data you're modeling.

Listing 2.18 The Run struct

```
import Foundation          ⟵┐  Need Foundation
                              │  for the Date type
struct Run {
    let id: String
    let startTime: Date
```

```
        let endTime: Date
        let distance: Float
        let onRunningTrack: Bool
}
```

Listing 2.19   The `Cycle` struct

```
struct Cycle {

    enum CycleType {
        case regular
        case mountainBike
        case racetrack
    }

    let id: String
    let startTime: Date
    let endTime: Date
    let distance: Float
    let incline: Int
    let type: CycleType
}
```

These structs are a good starting point for your data layer.

Admittedly, having to create separate logic in your application for both the `Run` and `Cycle` types can be cumbersome. Let's try to solve this via subclassing. Then you'll quickly learn which problems accompany subclassing, after which you'll see how enums can solve some of these problems.

2.3.2 *Creating a superclass*

Many similarities exist between `Run` and `Cycle`, which at first look make a good candidate for a superclass. The benefit of a superclass is that you can pass the superclass around, such as in your methods and arrays. A superclass saves you from creating specific methods and arrays for each workout subclass.

You could create a superclass called `Workout`; then you can turn `Run` and `Cycle` into classes and make them subclass `Workout`, which inherits from `Workout` (see figure 2.3).

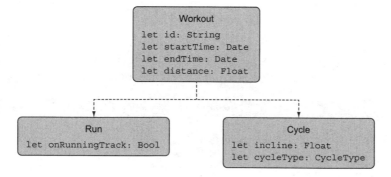

Figure 2.3   A subclassing hierarchy

Hierarchically, the subclassing structure makes a lot of sense because workouts share so many values.

The new `Workout` superclass contains the properties that both `Run` and `Cycle` share, specifically `id`, `startTime`, `endTime`, and `distance`.

2.3.3 The downsides of subclassing

Here we quickly touch upon issues related to subclassing. First of all, you're forced to use classes. Classes can be favorable, but having the choice between classes, structs, or other enums disappears when you use subclassing.

Being forced to use classes, however, isn't the biggest problem. Let's showcase another limitation by adding a new type of workout, called `Pushups`, which stores multiple repetitions and a single date.

Listing 2.20 The `Pushups` class

```
class Pushups: Workout {          ◁──┐  Pushups subclasses
    let repetitions: [Int]           │  Workout
    let date: Date
}
```

Subclassing `Workout` doesn't work properly because some properties of `Workout` don't apply to `Pushups`. `Workout` requires a `startTime`, `endTime`, and `distance` value, none of which `Pushups` needs.

To allow `Pushups` to subclass `Workout`, you'd have to refactor the superclass and all its subclasses. You would do this by moving `startTime`, `endTime`, and `distance` from `Workout` to the `Cycle` and `Run` classes because these properties aren't part of a `Pushups` class (see figure 2.4).

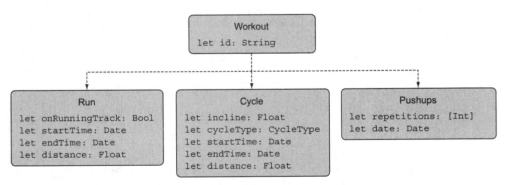

Figure 2.4 A refactored subclassing hierarchy

Refactoring an entire data model shows the issue when subclassing. As soon as you introduce a new subclass, you risk needing to refactor the superclass and all its subclasses, which is a significant impact on existing architecture.

Let's consider another approach involving enums.

2.3.4 *Refactoring a data model with enums*

By using enums, you stay away from a hierarchical structure, yet you can still keep the option of passing a single `Workout` around in your application. You'll also be able to add new workouts without needing to refactor the existing workouts.

You do this by creating a `Workout` enum instead of a superclass. You can contain different workouts inside the `Workout` enum.

Listing 2.21 Workout as an enum

```
enum Workout {
    case run(Run)
    case cycle(Cycle)
    case pushups(Pushups)
}
```

Now `Run`, `Cycle`, and `Pushups` won't subclass `Workout` anymore. In fact, all the workouts can be any type, such as a struct, class, or even another enum.

You can create a `Workout` by passing it a `Run`, `Cycle`, or `Pushups` workout. For example, you can convert `Pushups` to a struct, initialize it, and pass it to the `pushups` case inside the `Workout` enum.

Listing 2.22 Creating a workout

```
let pushups = Pushups(repetitions: [22,20,10], date: Date())
let workout = Workout.pushups(pushups)
```

Now you can pass a `Workout` around in your application. Whenever you want to extract the workout, you can pattern match on it.

Listing 2.23 Pattern matching on a workout

```
switch workout {
case .run(let run):
    print("Run: \(run)")
case .cycle(let cycle):
    print("Cycle: \(cycle)")
case .pushups(let pushups):
    print("Pushups: \(pushups)")
}
```

The benefit of this solution is that you can add new workouts without refactoring existing ones. For example, if you introduce an `Abs` workout, you can add it to `Workout` without touching `Run`, `Cycle`, or `Pushups`.

Listing 2.24 Adding a new workout to the `Workout` enum

```
enum Workout {
    case run(Run)
    case cycle(Cycle)
```

```
        case pushups(Pushups)
        case abs(Abs)            ⊲──┤  New workout is
    }                                 introduced
```

Not having to refactor other workouts to add a new one is a significant benefit and worth considering using enums over subclassing.

2.3.5 *Deciding on subclassing or enums*

Trying to determine when enums or subclasses fit your data model isn't always easy.

When types share many properties, and you predict that won't change in the future, you can get very far with classic subclassing. But subclassing steers you into a more rigid hierarchy. On top of that, you're forced to use classes.

When similar types start to diverge, or if you want to keep using enums and structs (as opposed to classes only), creating an encompassing enum offers more flexibility and could be the better choice.

The downside of enums is that now your code needs to match all cases in your entire application. Although this may require extra work when adding new cases, it also is a safety net where the compiler makes sure you haven't forgotten to handle a case somewhere in your application.

Another downside of enums is that at the time of writing, enums can't be extended with new cases. Enums lock down a model to a fixed number of cases, and unless you own the code, you can't change this rigid structure. For example, perhaps you're offering an enum via a third-party library, and now its implementers can't expand on it.

These are trade-offs you'll have to make. If you can lock down your data model to a fixed, manageable number of cases, enums can be a good choice.

2.3.6 *Exercises*

1 Can you name two benefits of using subclassing instead of enums with associated types?
2 Can you name two benefits of using enums with associated types instead of subclassing?

2.4 *Algebraic data types*

Enums are based on something called *algebraic data types*, which is a term that comes from functional programming. Algebraic data types commonly express composed data via something called sum types and product types.

Enums are *sum types*; an enum can be only one thing at once, hence the "or" way of thinking covered earlier.

On the other end of the spectrum are *product types*, types that contains multiple values, such as a tuple or struct. You can think of a product type as an "and" type—for example, a User struct can have both a name *and* an id. Alternatively, an address class can have a street *and* a house number *and* a zip code.

Let's use this section to cover a bit of theory so that you can reason about enums better. Then we move on to some practical examples where you'll turn an enum into a struct and vice versa.

2.4.1   Sum types

Enums are sum types, which have a fixed number of values they can represent. For instance, the following enum called `Day` represents any day in the week. There are seven possible values that `Day` can represent.

Listing 2.25   The `Day` enum

```
enum Day {
    case sunday
    case monday
    case tuesday
    case wednesday
    case thursday
    case friday
    case saturday
}
```

To know the number of possible values of an enum, you *add* (sum) the possible values of the types inside. In the case of the `Day` enum, the total sum is seven.

Another way to reason about possible values is the `UInt8` type. Ranging from 0 to 255, the total number of possible values is 256. It isn't modeled this way, but you can think of an `UInt8` as if it's an enum with 256 cases.

If you were to write an enum with two cases, and you added an `UInt8` to one of the cases, this enum's possible variations jump from 2 to 257.

For instance, you can have an `Age` enum—representing someone's age—where the age can be unknown, but if it is known, it contains an `UInt8`.

Listing 2.26   The `Age` enum

```
enum Age {
  case known(UInt8)
  case unknown
}
```

`Age` now represents 257 possible values, namely, the unknown case(1) + known case(256).

2.4.2   Product types

On the other end of the spectrum are product types. A product type multiplies the possible values it contains. As an example, if you were to store two Booleans inside a struct, the total number of variations is the product (multiplication) of these two enums.

Listing 2.27 A struct containing two Booleans

```
struct BooleanContainer {
  let first: Bool
  let second: Bool
}
```

The first Boolean (two possible values) *times* the second Boolean (two possible values) is four possible states that this struct may have.

In code, you can prove this by revealing all the variations.

Listing 2.28 `BooleanContainer` has four possible variations

```
BooleanContainer(first: true, second: true)
BooleanContainer(first: true, second: false)
BooleanContainer(first: false, second: true)
BooleanContainer(first: false, second: false)
```

When you're modeling data, the number of variations is good to keep in mind. The higher the number of possible values a type has, the harder it is to reason about a type's possible states.

As hyperbole, having a struct with 1,000 strings for properties has a lot more possible states than a struct with a single Boolean property.

2.4.3 Distributing a sum over an enum

I won't focus only on theory regarding sum and product types, either. You're not here to write a dry, theoretically based graduate paper, but to produce beautiful work.

Imagine that you have a `PaymentType` enum containing three cases, which represent the three ways a customer can pay.

Listing 2.29 Introducing `PaymentType`

```
enum PaymentType {
  case invoice
  case creditcard
  case cash
}
```

Next, you're going to represent the status of a payment. A struct is a suitable candidate to store some auxiliary properties besides the `PaymentType` enum, such as when a payment is completed and whether or not it concerns a recurring payment.

Listing 2.30 A `PaymentStatus` struct

```
struct PaymentStatus {
  let paymentDate: Date?
  let isRecurring: Bool
  let paymentType: PaymentType
}
```

The product of all the variations would be all possible dates *times* 2 (Boolean) *times* 3 (enum with three cases). You'd have a high number of variations because the struct can store many date variations.

Like cream cheese on a bagel, you're smearing the properties of the struct out over the cases of the enum by following the rules of algebraic data types (see figure 2.5).

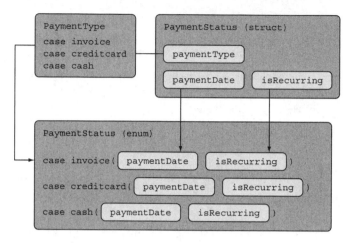

Figure 2.5   Turning a struct into an enum

You end up with an enum taking the same name as the struct. Each case represents the original enum's cases with the struct's properties inside.

Listing 2.31   `PaymentStatus` containing cases

```
enum PaymentStatus {
  case invoice(paymentDate: Date?, isRecurring: Bool)
  case creditcard(paymentDate: Date?, isRecurring: Bool)
  case cash(paymentDate: Date?, isRecurring: Bool)
}
```

All the information is still there, and the number of possible variations is still the same. Except this time you flipped the types inside out!

As a benefit, you're only dealing with a single type; the price is that you have some repetition inside each case. There's no right or wrong; it is merely a different approach to model the same data while leaving the same number of possible variations intact. It's a neat trick that displays the algebraic nature of types and helps you model enums in multiple ways. Depending on your needs, an enum might be a fitting alternative to a struct containing an enum, or vice versa.

2.4.4 Exercise

Given this data structure

```
enum Topping {
    case creamCheese
    case peanutButter
    case jam
}

enum BagelType {
    case cinnamonRaisin
    case glutenFree
    case oatMeal
    case blueberry
}

struct Bagel {
    let topping: Topping
    let type: BagelType
}
```

3 What is the number of possible variations of `Bagel`?

4 Turn `Bagel` into an enum while keeping the same amount of possible variations.

5 Given the following enum representing a puzzle game for a specific age range (such as baby, toddler, or teenager) and containing some puzzle pieces

```
enum Puzzle {
    case baby(numberOfPieces: Int)
    case toddler(numberOfPieces: Int)
    case preschooler(numberOfPieces: Int)
    case gradeschooler(numberOfPieces: Int)
    case teenager(numberOfPieces: Int)
}
```

How would this enum be represented as a struct instead?

2.5 A safer use of strings

Dealing with strings and enums is quite common. Let's go ahead and pay some extra attention to them so that you'll do it correctly. This section highlights some dangers when dealing with enums that hold a `String` raw value.

When an enum is defined as a raw value type, all cases of that enum carry some value inside them.

Enums with raw values are defined by having a type added to an enum's declaration.

Listing 2.32 Enums with raw values and string values

```
enum Currency: String {          ◁――――    String is the raw
    case euro = "euro"           ◁―――|     value type.
    case usd = "usd"                 |
    case gbp = "gbp"             All cases contain
}                                string values.
```

The raw values that an enum can store are only reserved for `String`, `Character`, and integer and floating-point number types.

An enum with raw values means each case has a value that's defined at compile-time. In contrast, enums with associated types—which you've used in the previous sections—store their values at runtime.

When creating an enum with a `String` raw type, each raw value takes on the name of the case. You don't need to add a string value if the `rawValue` is the same as the case name, as shown here.

> **Listing 2.33   Enum with raw values, with string values omitted**

```
enum Currency: String {
    case euro
    case usd
    case gbp
}
```

Since the enum still has a raw value type, such as `String`, each case still carries the raw values inside them.

2.5.1   Dangers of raw values

Use some caution when working with raw values, because once you read an enum's raw values, you lose some help from the compiler.

For instance, you're going to set up parameters for a hypothetical API call. You'd use these parameters to request transactions in the currency you supply.

You'll use the `Currency` enum to construct parameters for your API call. You can read the enum's raw value by accessing the raw value property, and set up your API parameters that way.

> **Listing 2.34   Setting a raw value inside parameters**

```
let currency = Currency.euro
print(currency.rawValue) // "euro"

let parameters = ["filter": currency.rawValue]
print(parameters) // ["filter": "euro"]
```

To introduce a bug, change the `rawValue` of the euro case, from "euro" to "eur" (dropping the "o"), since *eur* is the currency notation of the euro.

> **Listing 2.35   Renaming a string**

```
enum Currency: String {
    case euro = "eur"
    case usd
    case gbp
}
```

Because the API call relied on the `rawValue` to create your parameters, the parameters are now affected for the API call.

The compiler won't notify you, because the raw value is still valid code.

```
let parameters = ["filter": currency.rawValue]
// Expected "euro" but got "eur"
print(parameters) // ["filter": "eur"]
```

Everything still compiles. Unfortunately, you silently introduced a bug in part of your application.

Always make sure to update a string everywhere, which may sound obvious. But imagine that you're working on a big project where this enum was created in a completely different part of the application, or perhaps offered from a framework. An innocuous change on the enum may be damaging elsewhere in your application. These issues can sneak up on you, and they're easy to miss because you don't get notified at compile time.

You can play it safe and ignore an enum's raw values and match on the enum cases. As shown in the following code, when you set the parameters this way, you'll know at compile time when a case changes.

```
let parameters: [String: String]
switch currency {
    case .euro: parameters = ["filter": "euro"]
    case .usd: parameters = ["filter": "usd"]
    case .gbp: parameters = ["filter": "gbp"]
}

// Back to using "euro" again
print(parameters) // ["filter": "euro"]
```

You're recreating strings and ignoring the enum's raw values. It may be redundant code, but at least you'll have precisely the values you need. Any changes to the raw values won't catch you off guard because the compiler will now help you. You could even consider dropping the raw values altogether if your application allows.

Perhaps even better is that you *do* use the raw values, but you add safety by writing unit tests to make sure that nothing breaks. This way you'll have a safety net and the benefits of using raw values.

These are all trade-offs you'll have to make. But it's good to be aware that you lose help from the compiler once you start using raw values from an enum.

2.5.2   *Matching on strings*

Whenever you pattern match on a string, you open the door to missed cases. This section covers the downsides of matching on strings and showcases how to make an enum out of it for added safety.

In the next example, you're modeling a user-facing image management system in which customers can store and group their favorite photos, images, and gifs. Depending on the file type, you need to know whether or not to show a particular icon, indicating it's a jpeg, bitmap, gif, or an unknown type.

In a real-world application, you'd also check real metadata of an image; but for a quick and dirty approach, you'll look only at the extension.

The `iconName` function gives your application the name of the icon to display over an image, based on the file extension. For example, a jpeg image has a little icon shown on it; this icon's name is `"assetIconJpeg"`.

Listing 2.38   Matching on strings

```
func iconName(for fileExtension: String) -> String {
    switch fileExtension {
    case "jpg": return "assetIconJpeg"
    case "bmp": return "assetIconBitmap"
    case "gif": return "assetIconGif"
    default: return "assetIconUnknown"
    }
}

iconName(for: "jpg") // "assetIconJpeg"
```

Matching on strings works, but a couple of problems arise with this approach (versus matching on enums). Making a typo is easy, and thus harder to make it match—for example, expecting "jpg" but getting "jpeg" or "JPG" from an outside source.

The function returns an unknown icon as soon as you deviate only a little—for example, by passing it a capitalized string.

Listing 2.39   Unknown icon

```
iconName(for: "JPG") // "assetIconUnknown", not favorable
```

Sure, an enum doesn't solve all problems right away, but if you repeatedly match on the same string, the chances of typos increase.

Also, if any bugs are introduced by matching on strings, you'll know it at runtime. But switching on enums are exhaustive. If you were to switch on an enum instead, you'd know about bugs (such as forgetting to handle a case) at compile time.

Let's create an enum out of it! You do this by introducing an enum with a `String` raw type.

Listing 2.40 Creating an enum with a `String` raw value

```
enum ImageType: String {        ◁─┐   Introducing
    case jpg                      │   the enum
    case bmp
    case gif
}
```

This time when you match in the `iconName` function, you turn the string into an enum first by passing a `rawValue`. This way you'll know if `ImageType` gets another case added to it. The compiler will tell you that `iconName` needs to be updated and handle a new case.

Listing 2.41 `iconName` creates an enum

```
func iconName(for fileExtension: String) -> String {
    guard let imageType = ImageType(rawValue: fileExtension) else {
        return "assetIconUnknown"        ◁─   The function tries to convert the
    }                                         string to ImageType; it returns
    switch imageType {                   ◁─   "assetIconUnknown" if this fails.
    case .jpg: return "assetIconJpeg"
    case .bmp: return "assetIconBitmap"
    case .gif: return "assetIconGif"          iconName now matches on
    }                                         the enum, giving you compiler
}                                             benefits if you missed a case.
```

But you still haven't solved the issue of slightly differing values, such as "jpeg" or "JPEG." If you were to capitalize "jpg," the `iconName` function would return `"asset-IconUnknown"`.

Let's take care of that now by matching on multiple strings at once. You can implement your initializer, which accepts a raw value string.

Listing 2.42 Adding a custom initializer to `ImageType`

```
enum ImageType: String {
    case jpg
    case bmp
    case gif
                                              The string matching is
    init?(rawValue: String) {                 now case-insensitive,
        switch rawValue.lowercased() {   ◁─   making it more forgiving.
        case "jpg", "jpeg": self = .jpg
        case "bmp", "bitmap": self = .bmp ◁─  The initializer matches on
        case "gif", "gifv": self = .gif       multiple strings at once,
        default: return nil                   such as "jpg" and "jpeg."
        }
    }
}
```

OPTIONAL INIT?   The initializer from `ImageType` returns an optional. An optional initializer indicates that it can fail. When the initializer does fail—when you give it an unusable string—the initializer returns a nil value. Don't worry if this isn't clear yet; you'll handle optionals in depth in chapter 4.

Note a couple of things here. You set the `ImageType` case depending on its passed `rawValue`, but not before turning it into a lowercased string so you make the pattern matching case-insensitive. Next, you give each case multiple options to match on—such as case `"jpg"`, `"jpeg"`—so that it can catch more cases. You could have written it out by using more cases, but this is a clean way to group pattern matching.

Now your string matching is more robust, and you can match on variants of the strings.

Listing 2.43   Passing different strings

```
iconName(for: "jpg") // "Received jpg"
iconName(for: "jpeg") // "Received jpg"
iconName(for: "JPG") // "Received a jpg"
iconName(for: "JPEG") // "Received a jpg"
iconName(for: "gif") // "Received a gif"
```

If you do have a bug in the conversion, you can write a test case for it and only have to fix the enum in one location, instead of fixing multiple string-matching sprinkled around in the application.

Working with strings this way is now more idiomatic; the code has been made safer and more expressive. The trade-off is that a new enum has to be created, which may be redundant if you pattern-match on a string only once.

But as soon as you see code matching on a string repeatedly, converting it to an enum is a good choice.

2.5.3   Exercises

6 Which raw types are supported by enums?

7 Are an enum's raw values set at compile time or runtime?

8 Are an enum's associated values set at compile time or runtime?

9 Which types can go inside an associated value?

2.6   *Closing thoughts*

As you can see, enums are more than a list of values. Once you start "thinking in enums," you'll get a lot of safety and robustness in return, and you can turn structs to enums and back again.

I hope that this chapter inspired you to use enums in surprisingly fun and useful ways. Perhaps you'll use enums more often to combine them with, or substitute for, structs and classes.

In fact, perhaps next time as a pet project, see how far you can get by using only enums and structs. Limiting yourself to enums and structs is an excellent workout to help you think in sum and product types!

Summary

- Enums are sometimes an alternative to subclassing, allowing for a flexible architecture.
- Enums give you the ability to catch problems at compile time instead of runtime.
- You can use enums to group properties together.
- Enums are sometimes called sum types, based on algebraic data types.
- Structs can be distributed over enums.
- When working with enum's raw values, you forego catching problems at compile time.
- Handling strings can be made safer by converting them to enums.
- When converting a string to an enum, grouping cases and using a lowercased string makes conversion easier.

Answers

1 Can you name two benefits of using subclassing instead of enums with associated types?

  A superclass prevents duplication; no need to declare the same property twice. With subclassing, you can also override existing functionality.

2 Can you name two benefits of using enums with associated types instead of subclassing?

  No need to refactor anything if you add another type, whereas with subclassing you risk refactoring a superclass and its existing subclasses. Second, you're not forced to use classes.

3 Given the data structure, what is the number of possible variations of `Bagel`?

  Twelve (3 toppings times 4 bagel types)

4 Given the data structure, turn `Bagel` into an enum while keeping the same amount of possible variations.

  Two ways, because `Bagel` contains two enums. You can store the data in either enum:

```
// Use the Topping enum as the enum's cases.
enum Bagel {
    case creamCheese(BagelType)
    case peanutButter(BagelType)
    case jam(BagelType)
}

// Alternatively, use the BagelType enum as the enum's cases.
enum Bagel {
    case cinnamonRaisin(Topping)
```

```
        case glutenFree(Topping)
        case oatMeal(Topping)
        case blueberry(Topping)
    }
```

5 Given the enum representing a puzzle game for a specific age range, how would this enum be represented as a struct instead?

```
enum AgeRange {
    case baby
    case toddler
    case preschooler
    case gradeschooler
    case teenager
}

struct Puzzle {
    let ageRange: AgeRange
    let numberOfPieces: Int
}
```

6 Which raw types are supported by enums?

　　String, character, and integer and floating-point types

7 Are an enum's raw values set at compile time or runtime?

　　Raw type values are determined at compile time.

8 Are an enum's associated values set at compile time or runtime?

　　Associated values are set at runtime.

9 Which types can go inside an associated value?

　　All types fit inside an associated value.

Writing cleaner properties

This chapter covers

- How to create getter and setter computed properties
- When (not) to use computed properties
- Improving performance with lazy properties
- How lazy properties behave with structs and mutability
- Handling stored properties with behavior

Cleanly using properties can thoroughly simplify the interface of your structs, classes, and enums, making your code safer and easier to read and use for others (and your future self). Because properties are a core part of Swift, following the pointers in this chapter can help the readability of your code straight away.

First, we cover *computed* properties, which are functions that look like properties. Computed properties can clean up the interface of your structs and classes. You'll see how and when to create them, but also when it's better to avoid them.

Then we explore *lazy* properties, which are properties that you can initialize at a later time or not at all. Lazy properties are convenient for some reasons, such as when you want to optimize expensive computations. You'll also witness the different behaviors lazy properties have in structs versus classes.

Moreover, you'll see how you can trigger custom behavior on properties via so-called property observers and the rules and quirks that come with them.

By the end of this chapter, you'll be able to accurately choose between lazy properties, stored properties, and computed properties so that you can create clean interfaces for your structs and classes.

3.1   Computed properties

Computed properties are functions *masquerading* as properties. They do not store any values, but on the outside, they look the same as stored properties.

For instance, you could have a countdown timer in a cooking app and you could check this timer to see if your eggs are boiled, as shown in the following listing.

Listing 3.1   A countdown timer

```
cookingTimer.secondsRemaining  // 411
```

However, this value changes over time as shown here.

Listing 3.2   Value changes over time with computed properties

```
cookingTimer.secondsRemaining  // 409
// wait a bit
cookingTimer.secondsRemaining  // 404
// wait a bit
cookingTimer.secondsRemaining  // 392
```

Secretly, this property is a function because the value keeps dynamically changing.

The remainder of this section explores the benefits of computed properties. You'll see how they can clean up the interface of your types. You'll also see how computed properties run code each time a property is accessed, giving your properties a dynamic "always up to date" nature.

Then section 3.2 highlights when *not* to use computed properties and how lazy properties are sometimes the better choice.

3.1.1   Modeling an exercise

Let's examine a running exercise for a workout app. Users would be able to start a run and keep track of their current progress over time, such as the elapsed time in seconds.

> **JOIN ME!** It's more educational and fun if you check out the code and follow along with the chapter. You can download the source code at http://mng.bz/5N4q.

The type that represents an exercise is called Run, which benefits from computed properties. A run has an elapsedTime() function that shows how much time has passed since the start of a run. Once a run is finished, you can call the setFinished()

function to round up the exercise. You check to confirm a running exercise is completed by checking that the isFinished() function returns true. The lifecycle of a running exercise is shown in the following example.

Listing 3.3   The lifecycle of a running exercise

```
var run = Run(id: "10", startTime: Date())
// Check the elapsed time.
print(run.elapsedTime()) // 0.0053200125694749
// Check the elapsed time again.
print(run.elapsedTime()) // 14.00762099027634
run.setFinished() // Finish the exercise.
print(run.isFinished()) // true
```

After introducing Run, you'll see how to clean it up by transforming its function into computed properties.

3.1.2   *Converting functions to computed properties*

Let's take a peek at the Run type in the following listing to see how it is composed; then, you'll determine how to refactor it so that it uses computed properties.

Listing 3.4   The Run struct

```
import Foundation

struct Run {
    let id: String
    let startTime: Date
    var endTime: Date?

    func elapsedTime() -> TimeInterval {        ◁——  elapsedTime calculates the
        return Date().timeIntervalSince(startTime)     duration of the exercise,
    }                                                   measured in seconds.

    func isFinished() -> Bool {        ◁——┐  Check if the endTime is
        return endTime != nil                nil to determine if the
    }                                        exercise is finished.

    mutating func setFinished() {
        endTime = Date()
    }

    init(id: String, startTime: Date) {
        self.id = id
        self.startTime = startTime
        self.endTime = nil
    }
}
```

By looking at the signatures of the elapsedTime() and isFinished() functions shown in the following listing, you can see that both functions are not accepting a parameter but are returning a value.

Listing 3.5   Candidates for computed properties

```
func isFinished() -> Bool { ... }
func elapsedTime() -> TimeInterval { ... }
```

The lack of parameters and the fact that the functions return a value show that these functions are candidates for computed properties.

Next, let's convert isFinished() and elapsedTime() into computed properties.

Listing 3.6   Run with computed properties

```
struct Run {
    let id: String
    let startTime: Date
    var endTime: Date?                          ⎫ elapsedTime is
                                                ⎬ now a computed
                                                ⎭ property.
    var elapsedTime: TimeInterval {      ⟵─┐
        return Date().timeIntervalSince(startTime)
    }

    var isFinished: Bool {            ⟵─┐  isFinished is
        return endTime != nil            ⎬  now a computed
    }                                     ┘  property as well.

    mutating func setFinished() {
        endTime = Date()
    }

    init(id: String, startTime: Date) {
        self.id = id
        self.startTime = startTime
        self.endTime = nil
    }
}
```

You converted the functions into properties by giving a property a closure that returns a value.

This time, when you want to read the value, you can call the computed properties, as shown in the following example.

Listing 3.7   Calling computed properties

```
var run = Run(id: "10", startTime: Date())
print(run.elapsedTime) // 30.00532001256942749
print(run.elapsedTime) // 34.00822001332744283
print(run.isFinished) // false
```

Computed properties can change value dynamically and are thus *calculated*; this is in contrast to stored properties, which are fixed and have to be updated explicitly.

As a check before delivering a struct or class, do a quick scan to see if you can convert any functions to computed properties for added readability.

3.1.3 Rounding up

By turning functions into properties, you can clean up a struct or class interface. To outsiders, some values communicate better as properties to broadcast their intention. Your coworkers, for instance, don't always need to know that some properties can secretly be a function.

Converting lightweight functions to properties hides implementation details to users of your type, which is a small win, but it can add up in large codebases.

Let's continue and see how computed properties may *not* be the best choice and how lazy properties can help.

3.2 Lazy properties

Computed properties are not always the best choice to add a dynamic nature to your types. When a computed property becomes computationally expensive, you'll have to resort to other means, such as lazy properties.

In a nutshell, lazy properties make sure properties are calculated at a later time (if at all) and only once.

In this section, you'll discover how lazy properties can help when you're dealing with expensive computations or when a user has to wait for a long time.

3.2.1 Creating a learning plan

Let's go over an example where computed properties are not always the best choice and see how lazy properties are a better fit.

Imagine that you're creating an API that can serve as a mentor to learn new languages. Using a fancy algorithm, it gives customers a tailor-made daily routine for studying a language. LearningPlan will base its schedule on each customer's level, first language, and the language a customer wants to learn. The higher the level, the more effort is required of a customer. For simplicity, you'll focus on a learning plan that produces plans related to learning English.

This section won't implement an actual algorithm, but what is important to note is that this hypothetical algorithm takes a few seconds to process, which keeps customers waiting. A few seconds may not sound like much for a single occurrence, but it doesn't scale well when creating many schedules, especially if these schedules are expected to load quickly on a mobile device.

Because this algorithm is expensive, you only want to call it once when you need to.

3.2.2 When computed properties don't cut it

Let's discover why computed properties are not the best choice for expensive computations.

You can initialize a LearningPlan with a description and a level parameter, as shown in the following listing. Via the contents property, you can read the plan that the fancy algorithm generates.

Listing 3.8   Creating a `LearningPlan`

```
var plan = LearningPlan(level: 18, description: "A special plan for today!")

print(Date()) // 2018-09-30 18:04:43 +0000
print(plan.contents) // "Watch an English documentary."
print(Date()) // 2018-09-30 18:04:45 +0000
```

Notice how calling `contents` takes two seconds to perform, which is because of your expensive algorithm.

In the next listing, let's take a look at the `LearningPlan` struct; you can see how it's built with computed properties. This is a naïve approach that you'll improve with a lazy property.

Listing 3.9   A `LearningPlan` struct

```
struct LearningPlan {

    let level: Int

    var description: String                       The contents are where
                                                  the algorithm calculates
    // contents is a computed property.           a custom plan.
    var contents: String {
        // Smart algorithm calculation simulated here
        print("I'm taking my sweet time to calculate.")
        sleep(2)                              Simulate a two-second
                                              delay for the algorithm.
        switch level {
        case ..<25: return "Watch an English documentary."
        case ..<50: return "Translate a newspaper article to English and
        transcribe one song."
            case 100...: return "Read two academic papers and translate them
        into your native language."
            default: return "Try to read English for 30 minutes."
        }
    }
}
```

After the calculation is performed, you return a custom-made learning plan for the customer, depending on the level.

> **PATTERN MATCHING** You can pattern match on so-called *one-sided ranges*, meaning there is no start range. For example, `..<25` means "anything below 25, and `100...` means "100 and higher."

Notice how every time `contents` is called it takes two seconds to calculate.

As shown next, if you were to call it only five times (such as in a loop, shown in the following listing), the application would take ten seconds to perform—not very fast!

Listing 3.10   Calling contents five times

```
var plan = LearningPlan(level: 18, description: "A special plan for today!")
print(Date()) // A start marker
```

```
for _ in 0..<5 {
    plan.contents
}
print(Date()) // An end marker
```

This prints the following listing.

Listing 3.11 Taking ten seconds

```
2018-10-01 06:39:37 +0000
I'm taking my sweet time to calculate.
I'm taking my sweet time to calculate.
I'm taking my sweet time to calculate.
I'm taking my sweet time to calculate.
I'm taking my sweet time to calculate.
2018-10-01 06:39:47 +0000
```

Notice how the start and end date markers are ten seconds apart. Because a computed property runs whenever it's called, using computed properties for expensive operations is highly discouraged.

Next you'll replace the computed property with a lazy property to make your code more efficient.

3.2.3 *Using lazy properties*

You can use lazy properties to make sure a computationally expensive or slow property is performed only once, and only when you call it (if at all). Refactor the computed property into a lazy property in the following listing.

Listing 3.12 `LearningPlan` with a lazy property

```
struct LearningPlan {

    let level: Int

    var description: String
                                          contents is now a
                                          lazy property.
    lazy var contents: String = {   <——
        // Smart algorithm calculation simulated here
        print("I'm taking my sweet time to calculate.")
        sleep(2)

        switch level {
        case ..<25: return "Watch an English documentary."
        case ..<50: return "Translate a newspaper article to English and
    transcribe one song."
        case 100...: return "Read two academic papers and translate them
    into your native language."
        default: return "Try to read English for 30 minutes."
        }
    }()   <——  The property closure now
                needs parentheses, "()".
}
```

REFERRING TO PROPERTIES You can refer to other properties from inside a lazy property closure. Notice how `contents` can refer to the `level` property.

Still, this isn't enough; a lazy property is considered a regular property that the compiler wants to be initialized. You can circumvent this by adding a custom initializer, as shown in the following listing, where you elide `contents`, satisfying the compiler.

Listing 3.13 Adding a custom initializer

```
struct LearningPlan {
    // ... snip
    init(level: Int, description: String) { // no contents to be found here!
        self.level = level
        self.description = description
    }
}
```

Everything compiles again. Moreover, the best part is that when you repeatedly call `contents`, the expensive algorithm is used only once! Once a value is computed, it's stored. Notice in the following listing that even though `contents` is accessed five times, the lazy property is only initialized once.

Listing 3.14 Contents loaded only once

```
print(Date())
for _ in 0..<5 {
    plan.contents
}
print(Date())

// Will print:
2018-10-01 06:43:24 +0000
I'm taking my sweet time to calculate.
2018-10-01 06:43:26 +0000
```

Reading the contents takes two seconds the first time you access it, but the second time `contents` returns instantly. The total time spent by the algorithm is now two seconds instead of ten!

3.2.4 *Making a lazy property robust*

A lazy property on its own is not particularly robust; you can easily break it. Witness the following scenario where you set the `contents` property of `LearningPlan` to a less desirable plan.

Listing 3.15 Overriding the contents of `LearningPlan`

```
var plan = LearningPlan(level: 18, description: "A special plan for today!")
plan.contents = "Let's eat pizza and watch Netflix all day."
print(plan.contents) // "Let's eat pizza and watch Netflix all day."
```

As you can see, you can bypass the algorithm by setting a lazy property, which makes the property a bit brittle.

But not to worry—you can limit the access level of properties. By adding the `private(set)` keyword to a property, as shown in the following listing, you can indicate that your property is readable, but can only be set (mutated) by its owner, which is `LearningPlan` itself.

Listing 3.16 Making `contents` a `private(set)` property

```
struct LearningPlan {
    lazy private(set) var contents: String = {
    // ... snip
}
```

Now the property can't be mutated from outside the struct; `contents` is read-only to the outside world. The error, given by the compiler, confirms this, as the following listing shows.

Listing 3.17   `contents` property can't be set

```
error: cannot assign to property: 'contents' setter is inaccessible
plan.contents = "Let's eat pizza and watch Netflix all day."
~~~~~~~~~~~~~~ ^
```

This way you can expose a property as read-only to the outside and mutable to the owner only, making the lazy property a bit more robust.

3.2.5   *Mutable properties and lazy properties*

Once you initialize a lazy property, you cannot change it. You need to use extra caution when you use mutable properties—also known as `var` properties—in combination with lazy properties. This holds even truer when working with structs.

Let's go over a scenario where a seemingly innocent chance can introduce subtle bugs.

To demonstrate, in the following listing, `level` turns from a `let` to a `var` property so it can be mutated.

Listing 3.18 `LearningPlan` level now mutable

```
struct LearningPlan {
  // ... snip
  var level: Int
}
```

You create a copy by referring to a struct. Structs have so-called *value semantics*, which means that when you refer to a struct, it gets copied.

You can, as an example, create an intense learning plan, copy it, and lower the level, leaving the original learning plan intact, as the following listing shows.

Listing 3.19 Copying a struct

```
var intensePlan = LearningPlan(level: 138, description: "A special plan for
    today!")
intensePlan.contents                    ◄─┐  Populate the
var easyPlan = intensePlan              ◄─┤  lazy property.
easyPlan.level = 0                      ◄─┐
 // Quiz: What does this print?            │  A copy is made.
print(easyPlan.contents)                   │
                                        Lower the copy's level.
```

Now you've got a copy, but here's a little quiz: What do you get when you print easy-Plan.contents?

The answer is the intense plan: *"Read two academic papers and translate them into your native language."*

When easyPlan was created, the contents were already loaded before you made a copy, which is why easyPlan is copying the intense plan (see figure 3.1).

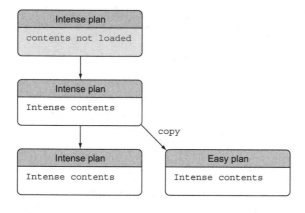

Figure 3.1   Copying after initializing a lazy description

Alternatively, you can call contents after making a copy, in which case both plans can individually lazy load their contents (see figure 3.2).

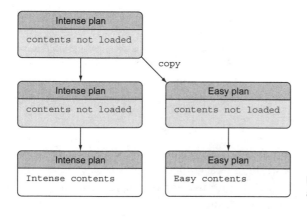

Figure 3.2   Copying before initializing a lazy description

In the next listing you see how both learning plans calculate their plans because the copy happens *before* the lazy properties are initialized.

Listing 3.20 Copying before lazy loading

```
var intensePlan = LearningPlan(level: 138, description: "A special plan for
    today!")
var easyPlan = intensePlan          ←——— A copy is made.
 easyPlan.level = 0                 ←
                                     | easyPlan gets a
// Now both plans have proper contents. lower level.
print(intensePlan.contents) // Read two academic papers and translate them
    into your native language.
print(easyPlan.contents) // Watch an English documentary.
```

The previous examples highlight that complexity surges as soon as you start mutating variables, used by lazy loading properties. Once a property changes, it's out of sync with a lazy-loaded property.

Therefore, make sure you keep properties immutable when a lazy property depends on it. Since structs are copied when you reference them, it becomes even more important to take extra care when mixing structs and lazy properties.

3.2.6 Exercises

In this exercise, you're modeling a music library (think Apple Music or Spotify):

```
//: Decodable allows you to turn raw data (such as plist files) into songs
struct Song: Decodable {
    let duration: Int
    let track: String
    let year: Int
}

struct Artist {

    var name: String
    var birthDate: Date
    var songsFileName: String

    init(name: String, birthDate: Date, songsFileName: String) {
        self.name = name
        self.birthDate = birthDate
        self.songsFileName = songsFileName
    }

    func getAge() -> Int? {
        let years = Calendar.current
            .dateComponents([.year], from: Date(), to: birthDate)
            .day

        return years
    }
```

```
func loadSongs() -> [Song] {
    guard
        let fileURL = Bundle.main.url(forResource: songsFileName,
withExtension: "plist"),
        let data = try? Data(contentsOf: fileURL),
        let songs = try? PropertyListDecoder().decode([Song].self, from:
data) else {
            return []
    }
    return songs
}

mutating func songsReleasedAfter(year: Int) -> [Song] {
    return loadSongs().filter { (song: Song) -> Bool in
        return song.year > year
    }
}
```

1 See if you can clean up the Artist type by using lazy and/or computed properties.

2 Assuming loadSongs is turned into a lazy property called songs, make sure the following code doesn't break it by trying to override the property data:

```
// billWithers.songs = []
```

3 Assuming loadSongs is turned into a lazy property called songs, how can you make sure that the following lines won't break the lazily loaded property? Point out two ways to prevent a lazy property from breaking:

```
billWithers.songs // load songs
billWithers.songsFileName = "oldsongs" // change file name
billWithers.songs.count // Should be 0 after renaming songsFileName,
    but is 2
```

3.3   *Property observers*

Sometimes you want the best of both worlds: you want to store a property, but you'd still like custom behavior on it. In this section, you'll explore the combination of storage and behavior via the help of *property observers*. It wouldn't be Swift if it didn't come with its own unique rules, so let's see how you can best navigate property observers.

Property observers are actions triggered when a stored property changes value, which is an ideal candidate for when you want to do some cleanup work after setting a property, or when you want to notify other parts of your application of property changes.

3.3.1   *Trimming whitespace*

Imagine a scenario where a player can join an online multiplayer game; the only thing a player needs to enter is a name containing a minimum number of characters.

However, people who want short names may fill up the remaining characters with spaces to meet the requirements.

You're going to see how you can clean up a name automatically after you set it. The property observer removes unnecessary whitespace from a name.

In the following example, you can see how the name automatically gets rid of trailing whitespace after a property is updated. Note that the initializer doesn't trigger the property observer.

Listing 3.21 Trimming whitespace

```
let jeff = Player(id: "1", name: "SuperJeff        ")    The whitespace in a player's
print(jeff.name) // "SuperJeff        "              ◁───  name isn't trimmed when you
print(jeff.name.count) // 13                               initialize a Player type.

jeff.name = "SuperJeff      "               The whitespace does get
print(jeff.name) // "SuperJeff"      ◁───┤  trimmed when you update
print(jeff.name.count) // 9                 the player's name again.
```

The name property automatically trims its whitespace, but *only* when updated, not when you initially set it. Before you solve this issue, look at the Player class to see how the property observer works, as shown in the following listing.

Listing 3.22 The `Player` class

```
import Foundation                Make sure the name
                                 is a var because it
class Player {                   mutates itself.

    let id: String                     A didSet property observer,            Refer to the
                                       which is triggered after a             previous value
    var name: String {   ◁───┘         property is set                        via the oldValue
        didSet {               ◁───                                           constant.
            print("My previous name was \(oldValue)")    ◁───┘
            name = name.trimmingCharacters(in: .whitespaces)    ◁───┐
        }
    }                                   The name property is trimmed
}                                       when it's set; this won't cause an
                                        infinite loop—you are modifying
    init(id: String, name: String) {   the stored name in this scope.
        self.id = id
        self.name = name
    }
}
```

DIDSET WILLSET   Besides didSet, you can also use willSet observers, which are triggered right before a property is changed. If you use willSet, you can use the newValue constant.

3.3.2 *Trigger property observers from initializers*

The name property got cleaned up after you updated the property, but initially name still contained its whitespace, as shown in the next listing.

Listing 3.23 **Property observer isn't triggered from initializer**

```
let jeff = Player(id: "1", name: "SuperJeff        ")
print(jeff.name) // "SuperJeff       "
print(jeff.name.count) // 13
```

Create a defer closure, which will be called right after initialization.

Property observers are unfortunately *not* triggered from initializers, which is intentional, but you have to be aware of this Swift gotcha. Luckily, there's a workaround.

Officially, the recommended technique is to separate the didSet closure into a function, then you can call this function from an initializer. However, another trick is to add a defer closure to the initializer method.

When a function finishes, the defer closure is called. You can put the defer closure anywhere in the initializer, but it will only be called after a function reaches the end, which is handy when you want to run cleanup code at the end of functions.

Add a defer closure to the initializer that sets the title in the next listing.

Listing 3.24 **Adding a** `defer` **closure to the initializer**

```
class Player {

    // ... snip

    init(id: String, name: String) {
        defer { self.name = name }
        self.id = id
        self.name = name
    }
}
```

Create a defer closure, which will be called right after initialization.

Because the title is ultimately set by defer, it doesn't really matter what you set it to here.

The defer closure is called right after Player is initialized, triggering the property observer as shown in the following listing.

Listing 3.25 **Trimming whitespace**

```
let jeff = Player(id: "1", name: "SuperJeff      ")
print(jeff.name) // "SuperJeff"
print(jeff.name.count) // 9

jeff.name = "SuperJeff      "
print(jeff.name) // "SuperJeff"
print(jeff.name.count) // 9
```

You get the best of both worlds. You can store a property, you can trigger actions on it, *and* there is no distinction between setting the property from the initializer or property accessor.

One caveat is that the defer trick isn't officially intended to be used this way, which means that the defer method may not work in the future. However, until then, this solution is a neat trick you can apply.

3.3.3 Exercises

4 If you need a property with both behavior and storage, what kind of property would you use?

5 If you need a property with only behavior and no storage, what kind of property would you use?

6 Can you spot the bug in the following code?

```
struct Tweet {
    let date: Date
    let author: String
    var message: String {
        didSet {
            message = message.trimmingCharacters(in: .whitespaces)
        }
    }
}

let tweet = Tweet(date: Date(),
                  author: "@tjeerdintveen",
                  message: "This has a lot of unnecessary whitespace    ")
```

7 How can you fix the bug?

3.4 Closing thoughts

Even though you have been using properties already, I hope that taking a moment to understand them on a deeper level was worthwhile.

You saw how to choose between a computed property, lazy property, and stored properties with behaviors. Making the right choices makes your code more predictable, and it cleans up the interface and behaviors of your classes and structs.

Summary

- You can use computed properties for properties with specific behavior but *without* storage.
- Computed properties are functions masquerading as properties.
- You can use computed properties when a value can be different each time you call it.
- Only lightweight functions should be made into computed properties.
- Lazy properties are excellent for expensive or time-consuming computations.
- Use lazy properties to delay a computation or if it may not even run at all.
- Lazy properties allow you to refer to other properties inside classes and structs.
- You can use the private(set) annotation to make properties read-only to outsiders of a class or struct.
- When a lazy property refers to another property, make sure to keep this other property immutable to keep complexity low.

- You can use property observers such as `willSet` and `didSet` to add behavior on stored properties.
- You can use `defer` to trigger property observers from an initializer.

Answers

1 See if you can clean up the `Artist` type by using lazy and/or computed properties:

```
struct Artist {

    var name: String
    var birthDate: Date
    let songsFileName: String

    init(name: String, birthDate: Date, songsFileName: String) {
        self.name = name
        self.birthDate = birthDate
        self.songsFileName = songsFileName
    }

    // Age is now computed (calculated each time)
    var age: Int? {
        let years = Calendar.current
            .dateComponents([.year], from: Date(), to: birthDate)
            .day

        return years
    }

    // loadSongs() is now a lazy property, because it's expensive to
    load a file on each call.
    lazy private(set) var songs: [Song] = {
        guard
            let fileURL = Bundle.main.url(forResource: songsFileName,
    withExtension: "plist"),
            let data = try? Data(contentsOf: fileURL),
            let songs = try? PropertyListDecoder().decode([Song].self,
    from: data) else {
                return []
        }
        return songs
    }()

    mutating func songsReleasedAfter(year: Int) -> [Song] {
        return songs.filter { (song: Song) -> Bool in
            return song.year > year
        }
    }

}
```

2 Assuming `loadSongs` is turned into a lazy property called `songs`, make sure the following code doesn't break it by overriding the property data:

```
// billWithers.songs = []
```

You can achieve this by making songs a private(set) property.

3 Assuming `loadSongs` is turned into a lazy property called `songs`, how can you make sure that the following lines won't break the lazily loaded property? Point out two ways:

```
billWithers.songs
billWithers.songsFileName = "oldsongs"
billWithers.songs.count // Should be 0 after renaming songsFileName,
   but is 2
```

The lazy property `songs` points to a var called `songsFileName`. To prevent mutation after lazily loading songs, you can make `songsFileName` a constant with `let`. Alternatively, you can make `Artist` a class to prevent this bug.

4 If you need a property with both behavior and storage, what kind of property would you use?

A stored property with a property observer

5 If you need a property with only behavior and no storage, what kind of property would you use?

A computed property, or lazy property if the computation is expensive

6 Can you spot the bug in the code?

The whitespace isn't trimmed from the initializer.

7 How can you fix the bug?

By adding an initializer to the struct with a `defer` clause

```
struct Tweet {
    let date: Date
    let author: String
    var message: String {
        didSet {
            message = message.trimmingCharacters(in: .whitespaces)
        }
    }

    init(date: Date, author: String, message: String) {
        defer { self.message = message }
        self.date = date
        self.author = author
        self.message = message
    }
}

let tweet = Tweet(date: Date(),
                  author: "@tjeerdintveen",
                  message: "This has a lot of unnecessary whitespace    ")

tweet.message.count
```

Making optionals
second nature

4

This chapter covers

- Best practices related to optionals
- Handling multiple optionals with guards
- Properly dealing with optional strings versus empty strings
- Juggling various optionals at once
- Falling back to default values using the nil-coalescing operator
- Simplifying optional enums
- Dealing with optional Booleans in multiple ways
- Digging deep into values with optional chaining
- Force unwrapping guidelines
- Taming implicitly unwrapped optionals

This chapter helps you acquire many tools to take you from optional frustration to *optional nirvana* while applying best practices along the way. Optionals are so pervasive in Swift that we spend some extra pages on them to leave no stone unturned. Even if you are adept at handling optionals, go through this chapter and fill in any knowledge gaps.

The chapter starts with what optionals are and how Swift helps you by adding syntactic sugar. Then we go over style tips paired with bite-sized examples that you regularly encounter in Swift. After that, you'll see how to stop optionals from propagating inside a method via a guard. We also cover how to decide on returning empty strings versus optional strings. Next, we show how to get more granular control over multiple optionals by pattern matching on them. Then, you'll see that you can fall back on default values with the help of the *nil-coalescing operator.*

Once you encounter optionals containing other optionals, you'll see how optional chaining can be used to dig deeper to reach nested values. Then we show how to pattern match on optional enums. You'll be able to shed some weight off your switch statements after reading this section. You'll also see how optional Booleans can be a bit awkward; we show how to correctly handle them, depending on your needs.

Force unwrapping, a technique to bypass the safety that optionals offer, gets some personal attention. This section shares when it is acceptable to force unwrap optionals. You'll also see how you can supply more information if your application unfortunately crashes. This section has plenty of heuristics that you can use to improve your code. Following force unwrapping, we cover implicitly unwrapped optionals, which are optionals that have different behavior depending on their context. You'll explicitly see how to handle them properly.

This chapter is definitely "big-boned." On top of that, optionals keep returning to other chapters with nifty tips and tricks, such as applying map and flatMap on optionals, and compactMap on arrays with optionals. The goal is that at the end of this chapter you'll feel adept and confident in being able to handle any scenario involving optionals.

4.1 The purpose of optionals

Simply put, an optional is a "box" that *does* or *does not* have a value. You may have heard of optionals, such as the Option type in Rust or Scala, or the Maybe type in Haskell.

Optionals help you prevent crashes when a value is empty; they do so by asking you to explicitly handle each case where a variable or constant could be nil. An optional value needs to be *unwrapped* to get the value out. If there is a value, a particular piece of code can run. If there isn't a value present, the code takes a different path.

Thanks to optionals you'll always know at compile time if a value can be nil, which is a luxury not found in specific other languages. As a case in point, if you obtain a nil value in Ruby and don't check for it, you may get a runtime error. The downside of handling optionals is that it may slow you down and cause some frustration up front because Swift makes you explicitly handle each optional when you want its value. But as a reward, you gain safer code in return.

With this book's help, you'll become so accustomed to optionals that you'll be able to handle them quickly and comfortably. With enough tools under your belt, you may find optionals are pleasant to work with, so let's get started!

4.2   *Clean optional unwrapping*

In this section, you'll see how optionals are represented in code and how to unwrap them in multiple ways.

You'll start by modeling a customer model for the backend of a fictional web store called *The Mayonnaise Depot*, catering to all your mayonnaise needs.

> **JOIN ME!**   It's more educational and fun if you can check out the code and fol-
> low along with the chapter. You can download the source code at http://mng
> .bz/6jO5.

This Customer struct holds a customer's ID, email, name, and current balance, which the web store can use to do business with a customer. For demonstration purposes, we left out some other important properties, such as an address and payment information.

The web store is quite lenient and allows for a customer to leave out their first and last name when ordering delicious mayonnaise; this makes it easier for customers to order mayonnaise. You represent these values as optional firstName and lastName inside the struct as shown in the following.

Listing 4.1   The Customer struct

```
struct Customer {                          The id, email, and balance
    let id: String          ⟵             properties are mandatory.
    let email: String
    let balance: Int // amount in cents
    let firstName: String?     ⟵
    let lastName: String?                  Customer has two
}                                          optional properties:
                                           firstName, and lastName.
```

Optionals are variables or constants denoted by a ?. But if you take a closer look, you'll see that an optional is an enum that may or may not contain a value. Let's look at the Optional type inside the Swift source code.

Listing 4.2 Optionals are an enum

```
// Details omitted from Swift source.
public enum Optional<Wrapped> {
  case none
  case some(Wrapped)
}
```

The `Wrapped` type is a *generic type* that represents the value inside an optional. If it has a value, it is wrapped inside the `some` case; if no value is present, the optional has a `none` case for that.

Swift adds some syntactic sugar to the optional syntax because without this sugar you would be writing your `Customer` struct as follows.

Listing 4.3 Optionals without syntactic sugar

```
struct Customer {
    let id: String
    let email: String          An optional notation
    let balance: Int           without syntactic sugar
    let firstName: Optional<String>   ◄────┐
    let lastName: Optional<String>    ◄──┐  Another optional without
}                                         syntactic sugar
```

NOTE Writing an optional explicitly is still legit Swift code and compiles just fine, but it isn't idiomatic Swift (so only use this knowledge to win pub quizzes).

4.2.1 *Matching on optionals*

In general, you unwrap an optional using `if let`, such as unwrapping a customer's `firstName` property.

Listing 4.4 Unwrapping via `if let`

```
let customer = Customer(id: "30", email: "mayolover@gmail.com",
➥ firstName: "Jake", lastName: "Freemason", balance: 300)

print(customer.firstName) // Optional("Jake")   ◄──────  The optional string
if let firstName = customer.firstName {
    print(firstName) // "Jake"          ◄──┐  The unwrapped
}                                           string
```

But again, without Swift's syntactic sugar you'd be matching on optionals everywhere with switch statements. Matching on an optional is demonstrated in figure 4.1, and it comes in handy later in this chapter—for example, when you want to combine unwrapping with pattern matching.

Swift agrees that you can pattern match on optionals; it even offers a little syntactic sugar for that.

You can omit the `.some` and `.none` cases from the previous example and replace them with `let name?` and `nil`, as shown in listing 4.5.

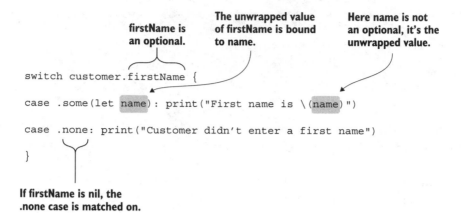

Figure 4.1   **Matching on an optional**

Listing 4.5   Matching on optional with syntactic sugar

```
switch customer.firstName {
  case let name?: print("First name is \(name)")
  case nil: print("Customer didn't enter a first name")
}
```

When firstName has a value,
bind it to name and print it.

You can explicitly match
when firstName is nil.

This code does the same as before, just written a bit differently.

Luckily, Swift offers plenty of syntactic sugar to save us all some typing. Still, it's good to know that optionals are enums at heart once you stumble upon more complicated or esoteric unwrapping techniques.

4.2.2   *Unwrapping techniques*

You can combine the unwrapping of multiple optionals. Combining them instead of indenting helps keep indentation lower. For instance, you can handle two optionals at once by unwrapping both the firstName and the lastName of a Customer, as shown here.

Listing 4.6   Combining optional unwrapping

```
if let firstName = customer.firstName, let lastName = customer.lastName {
    print("Customer's full name is \(firstName) \(lastName)")
}
```

Unwrapping optionals doesn't have to be the only action inside an if statement; you can combine if let statements with Booleans.

For example, you can unwrap a customer's firstName and combine it with a Boolean, such as the balance property, to write a customized message.

Listing 4.7 Combining a Boolean with an optional

```
if let firstName = customer.firstName, customer.balance > 0 {
    let welcomeMessage = "Dear \(firstName), you have money on your account,
    want to spend it on mayonnaise?"
}
```

But it doesn't have to stop at Booleans. You can also pattern match while you unwrap an optional. For example, you can pattern match on balance as well.

In the following example, you'll create a notification for the customer when their balance (indicated by cents) has a value that falls inside a range between 4,500 and 5,000 cents, which would be 45 to 50 dollars.

Listing 4.8 Combining pattern matching with optional unwrapping

```
if let firstName = customer.firstName, 4500..<5000 ~= customer.balance {
    let notification = "Dear \(firstName), you are getting close to afford
    our $50 tub!"
}
```

Embellishing if statements with other actions can clean up your code. You can separate Boolean checks and pattern matching from optional unwrapping, but then you'd usually end up with nested if statements and sometimes multiple else blocks.

4.2.3 *When you're not interested in a value*

Using if let to unwrap optionals is great for when you're interested in a value. But if you want to perform actions when a value is nil or not relevant, you can use a traditional nil check as other languages do.

In the next example, you'd like to know whether a customer has a full name filled in, but you aren't interested in what this name may be. You can again use the "don't care" wildcard operator to bind the unwrapped values to nothing.

Listing 4.9 Underscore use

```
if
  let _ = customer.firstName,
  let _ = customer.lastName {
  print("The customer entered his full name")
}
```

Alternatively, you can use nil checks for the same effect.

Listing 4.10 Nil checking optionals

```
if
  customer.firstName != nil,
  customer.lastName != nil {
  print("The customer entered his full name")
}
```

You can also perform actions when a value is empty.

Next, you check if a customer has a name set, without being interested in what this name may be.

Listing 4.11   When an optional is nil

```
if customer.firstName == nil,
    customer.lastName == nil {
    print("The customer has not supplied a name.")
}
```

Some may argue that nil checking isn't "Swifty." But you can find nil checks inside the Swift source code. Feel free to use nil checks if you think it helps readability. Clarity is more important than style.

4.3   *Variable shadowing*

At first, you may be tempted to come up with unique names when unwrapped (for instance, having a constant firstName and naming the unwrapped constant unwrappedFirstName), but this is not necessary.

You can give the unwrapped value the same name as the optional in a different scope; this is a technique called *variable shadowing*. Let's see how this looks.

4.3.1   *Implementing CustomStringConvertible*

To demonstrate variable shadowing, you'll create a method that uses the optional properties of Customer. Let's make Customer conform to the CustomStringConvertible protocol so that you can demonstrate this.

By making Customer adhere to the CustomStringConvertible protocol, you indicate that it prints a custom representation in print statements. Conforming to this protocol forces you to implement the description property.

Listing 4.12   Conforming to the CustomStringConvertible protocol

```
extension Customer: CustomStringConvertible {          ◁── Customer implements the
    var description: String {                               CustomStringConvertible
        var customDescription: String = "\(id), \(email)"   protocol.

        if let firstName = firstName {                  ◁── Inside the unwrapped if let
            customDescription += ", \(firstName)"   ◁──     scope, firstName is unwrapped
        }                                                   and not optional.

        if let lastName = lastName {                    ◁── Unwrap the lastName optional
            customDescription += " \(lastName)"   ◁──       property, binding it to a
        }                                                   constant with the same name.

        return customDescription                            The lastName constant is
    }                                                       unwrapped in the if let scope.
}
```

Unwrap the firstName optional property, binding it to a constant with the same name.

```
let customer = Customer(id: "30", email: "mayolover@gmail.com",
➡ firstName: "Jake", lastName: "Freemason", balance: 300)

print(customer) // 30, mayolover@gmail.com, Jake Freemason   ◁─┐
```
A custom description is now shown when you print a customer.

This example shows how both `firstName` and `lastName` were unwrapped using variable shadowing, preventing you from coming up with special names. At first, variable shadowing may look confusing, but once you've been handling optionals for a while, you can be assured that it is nice to read.

4.4　When optionals are prohibited

Let's see how you handle multiple optionals when nil values aren't usable. When The Mayonnaise Depot web store receives an order, customers get a confirmation message sent by email, which needs to be created by the backend. This message looks as follows.

Listing 4.13　Confirmation message

```
Dear Jeff,
Thank you for ordering the economy size party tub!
Your order will be delivered tomorrow.

Kind regards,
The Mayonnaise Depot
```

The function helps create a confirmation message by accepting a customer's name and the product that the customer ordered.

Listing 4.14　An order confirmation message

```
func createConfirmationMessage(name: String, product: String) -> String {
    return """                                                ◁─
    Dear \(name),                                             ◁─┐
    Thank you for ordering the \(product)!
    Your order will be delivered tomorrow.

    Kind regards,
    The Mayonnaise Depot
    """
}

let confirmationMessage = createConfirmationMessage(name: "Jeff", product:
    "economy size party tub")   ◁─┐
```
Use Swift's multiline string operator—denoted with """— to create a multiline string.

Replace name and product inside the string with the one you pass into the function.

You can call this function with a name and a product.

To get the customer's name, first decide on the name to display. Because both `firstName` and `lastName` are optional, you want to make sure you have these values to display in an email.

4.4.1 Adding a computed property

You're going to introduce a computed property to supply a valid customer name. You'll call this property displayName. Its goal is to help display a customer's name for use in emails, web pages, and so on.

You can use a guard to make sure that all properties have a value; if not, you return an empty string. But you'll quickly see a better solution than returning an empty string, as shown in this listing.

Listing 4.15 The Customer struct

```
struct Customer {
    let id: String
    let email: String
    let firstName: String?                    The guard clause binds the
    let lastName: String?                     unwrapped values of
                                              firstName and lastName to
                                              equally named constants.
    var displayName: String {
        guard let firstName = firstName, let lastName = lastName else {   ◄─
            return ""                  ◄─
        }                                     If both or either firstName
        return "\(firstName) \(lastName)"  ◄─  or lastName is nil, guard
    }                                         returns an empty name.
}                    Underneath the guard, the   You'll improve this soon.
                     optionals are unwrapped. A
                     full name is returned.
```

Guards are great for a "none shall pass" approach where optionals are not wanted. In a moment you'll see how to get more granular control with multiple optionals.

> **GUARDS AND INDENTATION** Guards keep the indentation low! This makes them a good candidate for unwrapping without increasing indentation.

Now you can use the displayName computed property to use it in any customer communication.

Listing 4.16 displayName in action

```
let customer = Customer(id: "30", email: "mayolover@gmail.com",
    firstName: "Jake", lastName: "Freemason", balance: 300)

customer.displayName // Jake Freemason
```

4.5 Returning optional strings

In real-world applications, you may be tempted to return an empty string because it saves the hassle of unwrapping an optional string. Empty strings often make sense, too, but in this scenario, they aren't beneficial. Let's explore why.

The displayName computed property serves its purpose, but a problem occurs when the firstName and lastName properties are nil: displayName returns an empty string, such as "". Unless you rely on a sharp coworker to add displayName.isEmpty checks throughout the whole application, you may miss one case, and some customers will get an email starting with `"Dear ,"` where the name is missing.

Strings are expected to be empty where they make sense, such as loading a text file that may be empty, but an empty string makes less sense in `displayName` because implementers of this code expect some name to display.

In such a scenario, a better method is to be explicit and tell the implementers of the method that the string can be optional; you do this by making `displayName` return an optional string.

The benefit of returning an optional `String` is that you would know at compile-time that `displayName` may not have a value, whereas with the `isEmpty` check you'd know it at runtime. This compile-time safety comes in handy when you send out a newsletter to 500,000 people, and you don't want it to start with "Dear ,".

Returning an optional string may sound like a strawman argument, but it happens plenty of times inside projects, especially when developers aren't too keen on optionals. By not returning an optional, you are trading compile-time safety for a potential runtime error.

To set the right example, `displayName` would return an optional `String` for `displayName`.

Listing 4.17 Making `displayName` return an optional `String`

```
struct Customer {
    // ... snip

    var displayName: String? {          ←  displayName
        guard let firstName = firstName, let lastName = lastName else {   now returns an
            return nil                  ←  optional String.
        }
        return "\(firstName) \(lastName)"    The guard returns
    }                                        nil when the
}                                            names are empty.
```

Now that `displayName` returns an optional `String`, the caller of the method must deal with unwrapping the optional explicitly. Having to unwrap `displayName`, as shown next, may be a hassle, but you get more safety in return.

Listing 4.18 Unwrapping the optional `displayName`

```
if let displayName = customer.displayName {
    createConfirmationMessage(name: displayName, product: "Economy size party
      tub")
} else {
    createConfirmationMessage(name: "customer", product: "Economy size party
      tub")
}
```

For peace of mind, you can add an `isEmpty` check for extra runtime safety to be super-duper safe in critical places in your application—such as sending newsletters—but at least you now get some help from the compiler.

4.6   *Granular control over optionals*

Currently, `displayName` on a customer needs to have both a `firstName` and `lastName` value before it returns a proper string. Let's loosen `displayName` up a little so that it can return whatever name it can find, making the property more lenient. If only a first name or last name is known, the `displayName` function can return either or both of those values, depending on which names are filled in.

You can make `displayName` more flexible by replacing the `guard` with a `switch` statement. Essentially this means that unwrapping the two optionals becomes part of the logic of a `displayName`, whereas with `guard` you would block any nil values before the property's method continues.

As an improvement, you put both optionals inside a tuple, such as `(firstName, lastName)`, and then match on both optionals at once. This way you can return a value depending on which optionals carry a value.

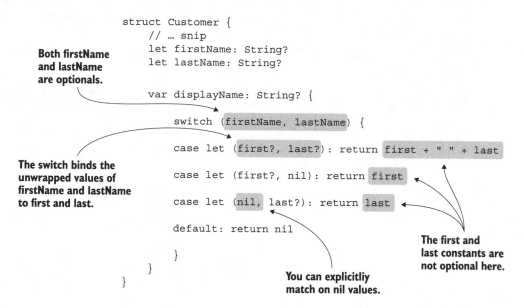

By using the `"?"` operator in the cases, you bind *and* unwrap the optionals. This is why you end up with a non-optional property in the strings inside the case statements.

Now when a customer doesn't have a full name, you can still use part of the name, such as the last name only.

Listing 4.19   `displayName` works with a partially filled-in name

```
let customer = Customer(id: "30", email: "famthompson@gmail.com",
    firstName: nil, lastName: "Thompson", balance: 300)

print(customer.displayName) // "Thompson"
```

Just be wary of adding too many optionals in a tuple. Usually, when you're adding three or more optionals inside a tuple, you may want to use a different abstraction for readability, such as falling back to a combination of if let statements.

4.6.1 Exercises

1 If no optionals in a function are allowed to have a value, what would be a good tactic to make sure that all optionals are filled?
2 If the functions take different paths depending on the optionals inside it, what would be a correct approach to handle all these paths?

4.7 Falling back when an optional is nil

Earlier you saw how you checked empty and optional strings for a customer's displayName property.

When you ended up with an unusable displayName, you fell back to "customer," so that in the communication, The Mayonnaise Depot starts their emails with "Dear customer."

When an optional is nil, it's a typical scenario to resort to a fallback value. Because of this, Swift offers some syntactic sugar in the shape of the ?? operator, called the nil-coalescing operator.

You could use the ?? operator to fall back to "customer" when a customer has no name available.

> **Listing 4.20 Defaulting back on a value with the nil-coalescing operator**

```
let title: String = customer.displayName ?? "customer"
createConfirmationMessage(name: title, product: "Economy size party tub")
```

Just like before, any time the customer's name isn't filled in, the email form starts with "Dear customer." This time, however, you shaved off some explicit if let unwrapping from your code.

Not only does the nil-coalescing operator fall back to a default value, but it also *unwraps* the optional when it does have a value.

Notice how title is a String, yet you feed it the customer.displayName optional. This means that title will either have the customer's unwrapped name *or* fall back to the non-optional "customer" value.

4.8 Simplifying optional enums

You saw before how optionals are enums and that you can pattern match on them, such as when you were creating the displayName value on the Customer struct. Even though optionals are enums, you can run into an enum that is an optional. An optional enum is an enum inside an enum. In this section, you'll see how to handle these optional enums.

Our favorite web store, The Mayonnaise Depot, introduces two memberships, silver and gold, each with respectively five and ten percent discounts on their delicious products. Customers can pay for these memberships to get discounts on all their orders.

A Membership enum, as shown in this example, represents these membership types; it contains the silver and gold cases.

Listing 4.21 The Membership enum

```
enum Membership {
    /// 10% discount
    case gold
    /// 5% discount
    case silver
}
```

Not all customers have upgraded to a membership, resulting in an optional membership property on the Customer struct.

Listing 4.22 Adding a membership property to Customer

```
struct Customer {
    // ... snip
    let membership: Membership?
}
```

When you want to read this value, a first implementation tactic could be to unwrap the enum first and act accordingly.

Listing 4.23 Unwrapping an optional before pattern matching

```
if let membership = customer.membership {
    switch membership {
      case .gold: print("Customer gets 10% discount")
      case .silver: print("Customer gets 5% discount")
    }
} else {
    print("Customer pays regular price")
}
```

Even better, you can take a shorter route and match on the optional enum by using the ? operator. The ? operator indicates that you are unwrapping and reading the optional membership at the same time.

Listing 4.24 Pattern matching on an optional

```
switch customer.membership {
case .gold?: print("Customer gets 10% discount")
case .silver?: print("Customer gets 5% discount")
case nil: print("Customer pays regular price")
}
```

NOTE If you match on `nil`, the compiler tells you once you add a new case to the enum. With `default` you don't get this luxury.

In one fell swoop, you both pattern matched on the enum and unwrapped it in the process, helping you eliminate an extra `if let` unwrapping step from your code.

4.8.1 Exercise

3 You have two enums. One enum represents the contents of a pasteboard (some data that a user cut or copied to the pasteboard):

```
enum PasteBoardContents {
    case url(url: String)
    case emailAddress(emailAddress: String)
    case other(contents: String)
}
```

The `PasteBoardEvent` represents the event related to `PasteBoardContents`. Perhaps the contents were added to the pasteboard, erased from the pasteboard, or pasted from the pasteboard:

```
enum PasteBoardEvent {
    case added
    case erased
    case pasted
}
```

The `describeAction` function takes on the two enums, and it returns a `String` describing the event, such as "The user added an email address to pasteboard." The goal of this exercise is to fill the body of a function:

```
func describeAction(event: PasteBoardEvent?, contents:
  PasteBoardContents?) -> String {
    // What goes here?
}
```

Given this input

```
describeAction(event: .added, contents: .url(url: "www.manning.com"))
describeAction(event: .added, contents: .emailAddress(emailAddress:
    "info@manning.com"))
describeAction(event: .erased, contents: .emailAddress(emailAddress:
    "info@manning.com"))
describeAction(event: .erased, contents: nil)
describeAction(event: nil, contents: .other(contents: "Swift in Depth"))
```

make sure that the output is as follows:

```
"User added an url to pasteboard: www.manning.com."
"User added something to pasteboard."
"User erased an email address from the pasteboard."
"The pasteboard is updated."
"The pasteboard is updated."
```

4.9   *Chaining optionals*

Sometimes you need a value from an optional property that can also contain another optional property.

Let's demonstrate by creating a product type that The Mayonnaise Depot offers in their store, such as a giant tub of mayonnaise. The following struct represents a product.

Listing 4.25   Introducing `Product`

```
struct Product {
    let id: String
    let name: String
    let image: UIImage?
}
```

A customer can have a favorite product for special quick orders. Add it to the `Customer` struct.

Listing 4.26   Adding an optional `favoriteProduct` to `Customer`

```
struct Customer {
    // ... snip
    let favoriteProduct: Product?
}
```

If you were to get the image from a `favoriteProduct`, you'd have to dig a bit to reach it from a customer. You can dig inside optionals by using the ? operator to perform *optional chaining.*

Additionally, if you were to set an image to UIKit's `UIImageView`, you could give it a customer's product's image with the help of chaining.

Listing 4.27   Applying optional chaining

```
let imageView = UIImageView()
imageView.image = customer.favoriteProduct?.image
```

Notice how you used the ? to reach for the `image` inside `favoriteProduct`, which is an optional.

You can still perform regular unwraps on chained optionals by using `if let`, which is especially handy when you want to perform some action when a chained optional is nil.

The following listing tries to display the image from a product and fall back on a missing default image if either `favoriteProduct` or its `image` property is nil.

Listing 4.28   Unwrapping a chained optional

```
if let image = customer.favoriteProduct?.image {
  imageView.image = image
} else {
  imageView.image = UIImage(named: "missing_image")
}
```

For the same effect, you can also use a combination of optional chaining and nil coalescing.

Listing 4.29 Combining nil coalescing with optional chaining

```
imageView.image = customer.favoriteProduct?.image ?? UIImage(named: "missing_
    image")
```

Optional chaining isn't a mandatory technique, but it helps with concise optional unwrapping.

4.10 *Constraining optional Booleans*

Booleans are a value that can either be true or false, making your code nice and predictable. Now Swift comes around and says "Here's a Boolean with three states: true, false, and nil."

Ending up with some sort of quantum Boolean that can contain three states can make things awkward. Is a nil Boolean the same as false? It depends on the context. You can deal with Booleans in three scenarios: one where a nil Boolean represents false, one where it represents a true value, and one where you explicitly want three states.

Whichever approach you pick, these methods are here to make sure that nil Booleans don't propagate too far into your code and cause mass confusion.

4.10.1 *Reducing a Boolean to two states*

You can end up with an optional Boolean, for example, when you're parsing data from an API in which you try to read a Boolean, or when retrieving a key from a dictionary.

For instance, a server can return some preferences a user has set for an app, such as wanting to log in automatically, or whether or not to use Apple's Face ID to log in, as shown in the following example.

Listing 4.30 Receiving an optional Boolean

```
let preferences = ["autoLogin": true, "faceIdEnabled": true]    ◁─┐ Received this
                                                                     dictionary
let isFaceIdEnabled = preferences["faceIdEnabled"]    ◁─┐ Find out if  from a server
print(isFaceIdEnabled) // Optional(true)                  Face ID is
                                                          enabled.
```

When you want to treat a nil as `false`, making it a regular Boolean straight away can be beneficial, so dealing with an optional Boolean doesn't propagate far into your code.

You can do this by using a fallback value, with help from the nil-coalescing operator `??`.

Listing 4.31   Falling back with the nil-coalescing operator

```
let preferences = ["autoLogin": true, "faceIdEnabled": true]

let isFaceIdEnabled = preferences["faceIdEnabled"] ?? false
print(isFaceIdEnabled) // true, not optional any more.
```

Via the use of the nil-coalescing operator, the Boolean went from three states to a regular Boolean again.

4.10.2   *Falling back on true*

Here's a counterpoint: blindly falling back to `false` is not recommended. Depending on the scenario, you may want to fall back on a `true` value instead.

Consider a scenario where you want to see whether a customer has Face ID enabled so that you can direct the user to a Face ID settings screen. In that case, you can fall back on `true` instead.

Listing 4.32   Falling back on `true`

```
if preferences["faceIdEnabled"] ?? true {
    // go to Face ID settings screen.
} else {
    // customer has disabled Face ID
}
```

It's a small point, but it shows that seeing an optional Boolean and thinking "Let's make it false" isn't always a good idea.

4.10.3   *A Boolean with three states*

You can give an optional Boolean more context when you *do* want to have three states. Consider an enum instead to make these states explicit.

Following the user preference example from earlier, you're going to convert the Boolean to an enum called `UserPreference` with three cases: `.enabled`, `.disabled`, and `.notSet`. You do this to be more explicit in your code and gain compile-time benefits.

Listing 4.33   Converting a Boolean to an enum

```
let isFaceIdEnabled = preferences["faceIdEnabled"]
print(isFaceIdEnabled) // Optional(true)

// We convert the optional Boolean to an enum here.
let faceIdPreference = UserPreference(rawValue: isFaceIdEnabled)

// Now we can pass around the enum.
// Implementers can match on the UserPreference enum.
switch faceIdPreference {
 case .enabled: print("Face ID is enabled")
 case .disabled: print("Face ID is disabled")
 case .notSet: print("Face ID preference is not set")
}
```

A Boolean is passed to create a UserPreference.

The enum can be matched on with three explicit cases: .enabled, .disabled, or .notSet.

A nice benefit is that now receivers of this enum have to explicitly handle all three cases, unlike with the optional Boolean.

4.10.4 *Implementing RawRepresentable*

You can add a regular initializer to an enum to convert it from a Boolean. Still, you can be "Swiftier" and implement the `RawRepresentable` protocol (https://developer .apple.com/documentation/swift/rawrepresentable) as a convention.

Conforming to `RawRepresentable` is the idiomatic way of turning a type to a raw value and back again. Adhering to this protocol makes streamlining to Objective-C easier and simplifies conformance to other protocols, such as `Equatable`, `Hashable`, and `Comparable`—more on that in chapter 7.

Once you implement the `RawRepresentable` protocol, a type has to implement a `rawValue` initializer as well as a `rawValue` property to convert a type to the enum and back again.

The `UserPreference` enum looks as follows.

Listing 4.34 The `UserPreference` enum

```
enum UserPreference: RawRepresentable {        ◁── The enum conforms to
    case enabled                                    RawRepresentable.
    case disabled
    case notSet

                                           The reason you can use a switch on
                                           rawValue is that it's an optional, and
                                           optionals are enums.
    init(rawValue: Bool?) {
        switch rawValue {              ◁──
            case true?: self = .enabled
            case false?: self = .disabled       You use the question
            default: self = .notSet             mark to match on an
        }                                       optional value.
    }

    var rawValue: Bool? {          ◁──    To conform to RawRepresentable,
        switch self {                     UserPreference also has to return
            case .enabled: return true    the original rawValue.
            case .disabled: return false
            case .notSet: return nil
        }
    }

}
```

You can initialize UserPreference with an optional Boolean.

Inside the initializer, you pattern match on the optional Boolean. By using the question mark, you pattern match directly on the value inside the optional; then you set the enum to the proper case.

As a final step, you default to setting the enum to `.notSet`, which happens if the preference is nil.

Now you constrained a Boolean to an enum and gave it more context. But it comes at a cost: you are introducing a new type, which may muddy up the codebase. When you want to be explicit and gain compile-time benefits, an enum might be worth that cost.

4.10.5 Exercise

4 Given this optional Boolean

```
let configuration = ["audioEnabled": true]
```

create an enum called `AudioSetting` that can handle all three cases:

```
let audioSetting = AudioSetting(rawValue: configuration["audioEnabled"])

switch audioSetting {
case .enabled: print("Turn up the jam!")
case .disabled: print("sshh")
case .unknown: print("Ask the user for the audio setting")
}
```

Also, make sure you can get the value out of the enum again:

```
let isEnabled = audioSetting.rawValue
```

4.11 Force unwrapping guidelines

Force unwrapping means you unwrap an optional without checking to see if a value exists. By force unwrapping an optional, you reach for its wrapped value to use it. If the optional has a value, that's great. If the optional is empty, however, the application crashes, which is not so great.

Take Foundation's `URL` type, for example. It accepts a `String` parameter in its initializer. Then a `URL` is either created or not, depending on whether the passed string is a proper path—hence `URL`'s initializer can return nil.

Listing 4.35   Creating an optional `URL`

```
let optionalUrl = URL(string: "https://www.themayonnaisedepot.com")
// Optional(http://www.themayonnaisedepot.com)
```

You can force unwrap the optional by using an exclamation mark, bypassing any safe techniques.

Listing 4.36   Force unwrapping an optional `URL`

```
let forceUnwrappedUrl = URL(string: "https://www.themayonnaisedepot.com")!
// http://www.themayonnaisedepot.com. Notice how we use the ! to force
   unwrap.
```

Now you don't need to unwrap the optional anymore. But force unwrapping causes your app to crash on an invalid path.

Listing 4.37   A crashing optional `URL`

```
let faultyUrl = URL(string: "mmm mayonnaise")!   ⟵⎯ Crash—URL can't be instantiated
                                                     and is force unwrapped.
```

4.11.1   When force unwrapping is "acceptable"

Ideally, you would never use force unwrapping. But sometimes you can't avoid force unwrapping because your application can end up in a bad state. Still, think about it: Is there truly no other way you can prevent a force unwrap? Perhaps you can return a nil instead, or throw an error.

As a heuristic, only use a force unwrap as a last resort and consider the following exceptions.

POSTPONING ERROR HANDLING

Having error handling in place at the start can slow you down. When your functions can throw an error, the caller of the function must now deal with the error, which is extra work and logic that takes time to implement.

One reason to apply a force unwrap is to produce some working piece of code quickly, such as creating a prototype or a quick and dirty Swift script. Then you can worry about error handling later.

You could use force unwraps to get your application started, then consider them as markers to replace the force unwraps with proper error handling. But you and I both know that in programming "I'll do it later" means "I'm never going to do it," so take this advice with a grain of salt.

WHEN YOU KNOW BETTER THAN THE COMPILER

If you're dealing with a value that's fixed at compile-time, force unwrapping an optional can make sense.

In the following listing, you know that the passed URL will parse, even though the compiler doesn't know it yet. It's safe to force unwrap here.

Listing 4.38   Force unwrapping a valid URL

```
let url = URL(string: "http://www.themayonnaisedepot.com")! //
    http://www.themayonnaisedepot.com
```

But if this URL is a runtime-loaded variable—such as user input—you can't guarantee a safe value, in which case you would risk a crash if you were to force unwrap it.

4.11.2 Crashing with style

Sometimes you may not be able to avoid a crash. But then you may want to supply more information instead of performing a force unwrap.

For example, imagine you're creating a URL from a path you get at runtime—meaning that the passed path isn't guaranteed to be usable—and the application for some reason cannot continue when this URL is invalid, which means that the URL type returns nil.

Instead of force unwrapping the URL type, you can choose to crash manually and add some more information, which helps you with debugging in the logs.

You can do this by manually crashing your application with the fatalError function. You can then supply extra information such as #line and #function, which supplies the precise information where an application crashed.

In the following listing you try to unwrap the URL first using a guard. But if the unwrapping fails, you manually cause a fatalError with some extra information that can help you during debugging.

Listing 4.39   Crashing manually

```
guard let url = URL(string: path) else {
  fatalError("Could not create url on \(#line) in \(#function)")
}
```

One big caveat though: if you're building an iOS app, for example, your users may see sensitive information that you supply in the crash log. What you put in the fatalError message is something you'll have to decide on a case-by-case basis.

4.12 Taming implicitly unwrapped optionals

Implicitly unwrapped optionals, or IUOs, are tricky because they are unique optionals that are automatically unwrapped depending on their context. But if you aren't careful, they can crash your application!

This section is about bending IUOs to your will while making sure they won't hurt you.

4.12.1 Recognizing IUOs

An IUO force unwraps a type, instead of an instance.

Listing 4.40 Introducing an IUO

```
let lastName: String! = "Smith"          Implicitly unwrapped
                                         optional
let name: String? = 3
let firstName = name!          Force unwrapped
                               instance
```

You can recognize IUOs by the bang (!) after the type, such as `String!`. You can think of them as *pre-unwrapped* optionals.

Like force unwrapping, the ! indicates a danger sign in Swift. IUOs also can crash your application, which you'll see shortly.

4.12.2 IUOs in practice

IUOs are like a power drill. You may not use them often, but they come in handy when you need them. But if you make a mistake, they can mess up your foundation.

When you create an IUO, you promise that a variable or constant is populated shortly *after* initialization, but *before* you need it. When that promise is broken, people get hurt (well, technically, the application can crash). But disaster happens if your application controls nuclear power plants or helps dentists administer laughing gas to patients.

Going back to The Mayonnaise Depot, they have decided to add a chat service to their backend so that customers can ask for help ordering products.

When the backend server starts, the server initiates a process monitor before anything else. This process monitor makes sure that the system is ready before other services are initialized and started, which means that you'll have to start the chat server after the process monitor. After the process monitor is ready, the chat server is passed to the process monitor (see figure 4.2).

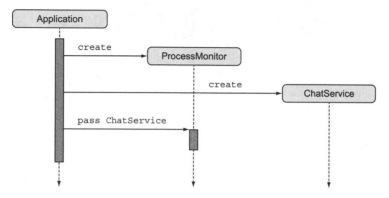

Figure 4.2 Starting the process monitor

Since the server initiates `ProcessMonitor` before anything else, `ProcessMonitor` could have an optional reference to the chat service. As a result, the `ChatService` can be given to `ProcessMonitor` at a later time. But making the chat server optional on the process monitor is cumbersome because to access the chat server, you'd have to unwrap the chat service every time while knowing that the process monitor has a valid reference.

You could also make the chat service a lazy property on `ProcessMonitor`, but then `ProcessMonitor` is in charge of initializing `ChatService`. In this case, `ProcessMonitor` doesn't want to handle the possible dependencies of `ChatService`.

This is a good scenario for an IUO. By making the chat service an IUO, you don't have to pass the chat service to the process monitor's initializer, but you don't need to make chat service an optional, either.

CREATING AN IUO

The following listing shows the code for `ChatService` and `ProcessMonitor`. The `ProcessMonitor` has a `start()` method to create the monitor. It has a `status()` method to check if everything is still up and running.

Listing 4.41   Introducing `ChatService` and `ProcessMonitor`

```
class ChatService {
    var isHealthy = true
    // Left empty for demonstration purposes.
}

class ProcessMonitor {

    var chatService: ChatService!

    class func start() -> ProcessMonitor {
        // In a real-world application: run elaborate diagnostics.
        return ProcessMonitor()
    }

    func status() -> String {
        if chatService.isHealthy {
            return "Everything is up and running"
        } else {
            return "Chatservice is down!"
        }
    }
}
```

> **chatService is an IUO, recognizable by the bang !.**

The initialization process starts the monitor, then the chat service, and then finally passes the service to the monitor.

Listing 4.42   The initialization process

```
let processMonitor = ProcessMonitor.start()
// processMonitor runs important diagnostics here.
// processMonitor is ready.

let chat = ChatService() // Start Chatservice.

processMonitor.chatService = chat
processMonitor.status() // "Everything is up and running"
```

This way you can kick off the `processMonitor` first, but you have the benefit of having `chatService` available to `processMonitor` right before you need it.

But `chatService` is an IUO, and IUOs can be dangerous. If you for some reason accessed the `chatService` property before it passed to `processMonitor`, you'd end up with a crash.

Listing 4.43   A crash from an IUO

```
let processMonitor = ProcessMonitor.start()
processMonitor.status() // fatal error: unexpectedly found nil
```

By making `chatService` an IUO, you don't have to initialize it via an initializer, but you also don't have to unwrap it every time you want to read a value. It's a win-win with some danger added. As you work more with Swift, you'll find other ways to get rid of IUOs because they are a double-edged sword. For instance, you could pass a `Chat-ServiceFactory` to `ProcessMonitor` that can produce a chat server for `Process-Monitor` without `ProcessMonitor` needing to know about dependencies.

4.12.3 Exercise

5 What are good alternatives to IUOs?

4.13 Closing thoughts

This chapter covered many scenarios involving optionals. Going over all these techniques was no easy feat—feel free to be proud!

Being comfortable with optionals is powerful and an essential foundation as a Swift programmer. Mastering optionals helps you make the right choices in a plethora of situations in daily Swift programming.

Later chapters expand on the topic of optionals when you start looking at applying `map`, `flatMap`, and `compactMap` on optionals. After you've worked through these advanced topics, you'll be optionally zen and handle every optional curveball Swift throws at you.

Summary

- Optionals are enums with syntactic sugar sprinkled over them.
- You can pattern match on optionals.
- Pattern match on multiple optionals at once by putting them inside a tuple.
- You can use nil-coalescing to fall back to default values.
- Use optional chaining to dig deep into optional values.
- You can use nil-coalescing to transform an optional Boolean into a regular Boolean.
- You can transform an optional Boolean into an enum for three explicit states.
- Return optional strings instead of empty strings when a value is expected.
- Use force unwrapping only if your program can't recover from a nil value.
- Use force unwrapping when you want to delay error handling, such as when prototyping.
- It's safer to force unwrap optionals if you know better than the compiler.
- Use implicitly unwrapped optionals for properties that are instantiated right after initialization.

Answers

1 If no optionals in a function are allowed to have a value, what would be a good tactic to make sure that all optionals are filled?

   Use a guard—this can block optionals at the top of a function.

2 If the functions take different paths depending on the optionals inside it, what would be a correct approach to handle all these paths?

Putting multiple optionals inside a tuple allows you to pattern match on them and take different paths in a function.

3 The code looks like this:

```
// Use a single switch statement inside describeAction.
func describeAction(event: PasteBoardEvent?, contents:
  PasteBoardContents?) -> String {
    switch (event, contents) {
    case let (.added?, .url(url)?): return "User added a url to
pasteboard: \(url)"
    case (.added?, _): return "User added something to pasteboard"
    case (.erased?, .emailAddress?): return "User erased an email
address from the pasteboard"
    default: return "The pasteboard is updated"
    }
}
```

4 The code looks like this:

```
enum AudioSetting: RawRepresentable {
    case enabled
    case disabled
    case unknown

    init(rawValue: Bool?) {
        switch rawValue {
        case let isEnabled? where isEnabled: self = .enabled
        case let isEnabled? where !isEnabled: self = .disabled
        default: self = .unknown
        }
    }

    var rawValue: Bool? {
        switch self {
        case .enabled: return true
        case .disabled: return false
        case .unknown: return nil
        }
    }

}
```

5 What are good alternatives to IUOs?

Lazy properties or factories that are passed via an initializer

Demystifying initializers

This chapter covers

- Demystifying Swift's initializer rules
- Understanding quirks of struct initializers
- Understanding complex initializer rules when subclassing
- How to keep the number of initializers low when subclassing
- When and how to work with required initializers

As a Swift developer, initializing your classes and structs are one of the core fundamentals that you have been using.

But initializers in Swift are not intuitive. Swift offers memberwise initializers, custom initializers, designated initializers, convenience initializers, required initializers, and I didn't even mention the optional initializers, failable initializers, and throwing initializers. Frankly, it can get bewildering sometimes.

This chapter sheds some light on the situation so that instead of having a boxing match with the compiler, you can make the most out of initializing structs, classes, and subclasses.

In this chapter, we model a boardgame hierarchy that you'll compose out of structs and classes. While building this hierarchy, you'll experience the joy of Swift's strange initializer rules and how you can deal with them. Since creating game mechanics is a topic for a book itself, we only focus on the initializer fundamentals in this chapter.

First, you'll tinker with struct initializers and learn about the quirks that come with them. After that, you'll move on to class initializers and the subclassing rules that accompany them; this is usually where the complexity kicks in with Swift. Then you'll see how you can reduce the number of initializers while you're subclassing, to keep the number of initializers to a minimum. Finally, you'll see the role that required initializers play, and when and how to use them.

The goal of this chapter is for you to be able to write initializers in one go, versus doing an awkward dance of trial and error to please the compiler gods.

5.1 *Struct initializer rules*

Structs can be initialized in a relatively straightforward way because you can't subclass them. Nevertheless, there are still some special rules that apply to structs, which we explore in this section. In the next section, we model a board game, but first we model the players that can play the board game. You'll create a Player struct containing the name and type of each player's pawn. You're choosing to model a Player as a struct because structs are well suited for small data models (amongst other things). Also, a struct can't be subclassed, which is fine for modeling Player.

> **JOIN ME!** It's more educational and fun if you can check out the code and follow along with the chapter. You can download the source code at http://mng .bz/nQE5.

The Player that you'll model resembles a pawn on a board game. You can instantiate a Player by passing it a name and a type of pawn, such as a car, shoe, or hat.

Listing 5.1 Creating a `player`

```
let player = Player(name: "SuperJeff", pawn: .shoe)
```

You see that a Player has two properties: name and pawn. Notice how the struct has no initializer defined. Under the hood, you get a so-called *memberwise initializer*, which is a free initializer the compiler generates for you, as shown here.

Listing 5.2 Introducing the `Player` struct

```
enum Pawn {
    case dog, car, ketchupBottle, iron, shoe, hat
}

struct Player {
  let name: String
```

```
    let pawn: Pawn
}

let player = Player(name: "SuperJeff", pawn: .shoe)
```

Swift offers a
free memberwise
initializer.

5.1.1 Custom initializers

Swift is very strict about wanting all properties populated in structs and classes, which is no secret. If you're coming from languages where this wasn't the case (such as Ruby and Objective-C), fighting the Swift compiler can be quite frustrating at first.

To illustrate, you can't initialize a Player with only a name, omitting a pawn. The following won't compile.

Listing 5.3 Omitting a property

```
let player = Player(name: "SuperJeff")

error: missing argument for parameter 'pawn' in call
let player = Player(name: "SuperJeff")
                                      ^
                                       , pawn: Pawn
```

To make initialization easier, you can omit pawn from the initializer parameters. The struct needs all properties propagated with a value. If the struct initializes its properties, you don't have to pass values. In listing 5.4 you're going to add a custom initializer where you can *only* pass a name of the Player. The pawn can then randomly be picked for players, making your struct easier to initialize. The custom initializer accepts a name and randomly selects the pawn.

First, you make sure that the Pawn enum conforms to the CaseIterable protocol; doing so allows you to obtain an array of all cases via the allCases property. Then in the initializer of Player, you can use the randomElement() method on allCases to pick a random element.

> **NOTE** CaseIterable works only on enums without associated values, because with associated values an enum could theoretically have an infinite number of variations.

Listing 5.4 Creating your initializer

```
enum Pawn: CaseIterable {
    case dog, car, ketchupBottle, iron, shoe, hat
}

struct Player {
    let name: String
    let pawn: Pawn

    init(name: String) {
        self.name = name
```

**Make Pawn conform to
CaseIterable, which gives you
an allCases property on Pawn,
returning an array of all cases.**

**Manually create an
initializer, accepting a
name String.**

```
            self.pawn = Pawn.allCases.randomElement()!  ⟵┐   Randomize a pawn using
        }                                                │   the randomElement()
    }                                                    │   method on Pawn.allCases.
```

```
// The custom initializer in action.
let player = Player(name: "SuperJeff")
print(player.pawn) // shoe
```

NOTE The `randomElement()` method returns an optional that you need to unwrap. You force unwrap it via a `!`. Usually, a force unwrap is considered bad practice. But in this case, you know at compile-time that it's safe to unwrap.

Now indecisive players can have a pawn picked for them.

5.1.2 *Struct initializer quirk*

Here is an interesting quirk. You can't use the memberwise (free) initializer from earlier; it won't work.

Listing 5.5 **Initializing a `player` with a custom initializer**

```
let secondPlayer = Player(name: "Carl", pawn: .dog)
error: extra argument 'pawn' in call
```

The reason that the memberwise initializer doesn't work any more is to make sure that developers can't circumvent the logic in the custom initializer. It's a useful protection mechanism! In your case, offering both the custom and memberwise initializers would be favorable. You can offer both initializers by extending the struct and putting your custom initializer there.

First, you restore the `Player` struct, so it won't contain any custom initializers, giving you the memberwise initializer back. Then you extend the `Player` struct and put your custom initializer in there.

Listing 5.6 **Restoring the `Player` struct**

```
struct Player {
    let name: String              Extend Player,
    let pawn: Pawn                 opening it up for
}                                  more functionality.

extension Player {          ⟵─┐   Add your custom initializer
    init(name: String) {    ⟵─┘   in the extension.
        self.name = name
        self.pawn = Pawn.allCases.randomElement()!
    }
}
```

You can confirm this worked because you now can initialize a `Player` via both initializers.

```
Listing 5.7   Initializing a player with both initializers
```

```
// Both initializers work now.
let player = Player(name: "SuperJeff")
let anotherPlayer = Player(name: "Mary", pawn: .dog)
```

By using an extension, you can keep the best of both worlds. You can offer the free memberwise and a custom initializer with specific logic.

5.1.3 Exercises

1 Given the following struct

```
struct Pancakes {

    enum SyrupType {
        case corn
        case molasses
        case maple
    }

    let syrupType: SyrupType
    let stackSize: Int

    init(syrupType: SyrupType) {
        self.stackSize = 10
        self.syrupType = syrupType
    }
}
```

will the following initializers work?

```
let pancakes = Pancakes(syrupType: .corn, stackSize: 8)
let morePancakes = Pancakes(syrupType: .maple)
```

2 If these initializers didn't work, can you make them work without adding another initializer?

5.2 Initializers and subclassing

Subclassing is a way to achieve polymorphism. With polymorphism, you can offer a single interface, such as a function, that works on multiple types.

But subclassing isn't too popular in the Swift community, especially because Swift often is marketed as a protocol-oriented language, which is one subclassing alternative.

You saw in chapter 2 how subclasses tend to be a rigid data structure. You also saw how enums are a flexible alternative to subclassing, and you'll see more flexible approaches when you start working with protocols and generics.

Nevertheless, subclassing is still a valid tool that Swift offers. You can consider overriding or extending behavior from classes; this includes code from frameworks you don't even own. Apple's UIKit is a recurring example of this, where you can subclass `UIView` to create new elements for the screen.

This section will help you understand how initializers work in regard to classes and subclassing—also known as inheritance—so that when you're not jumping on the protocol-oriented programming bandwagon, you can offer clean subclassing constructions.

5.2.1 Creating a board game superclass

The `Player` model is all set up; now it's time to start modeling the board game hierarchy.

First, you're going to create a class called `BoardGame` that serves as a superclass. Then you'll subclass `BoardGame` to create your own board game called Mutability Land: an exciting game that teaches Swift developers to write immutable code.

After the hierarchy is set up, you'll discover Swift's quirks that come with subclassing and approaches on how to deal with them.

5.2.2 The initializers of BoardGame

The `BoardGame` superclass has three initializers: one designated initializer and two convenience initializers to make initialization easier (see figure 5.1).

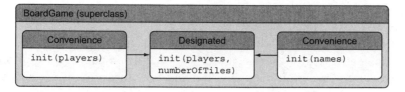

Figure 5.1   `BoardGame` **initializers**

Before continuing, get acquainted with the two types of initializers for classes.

First is the *designated initializer*, which is the run-of-the-mill variety. Designated initializers are there to make sure all properties get initialized. Classes tend to have very few designated initializers, usually just one, but more are possible. Designated initializers point to a superclass if there is one.

Second is the *convenience initializer*, which can help make initialization easier by supplying default values or create a simpler initialization syntax. Convenience initializers can call other convenience initializers, but they ultimately call a designated initializer from the same class.

If you look inside `BoardGame`, you can confirm the use of one designated initializer and two convenience initializers, as shown here.

Listing 5.8   The `BoardGame` superclass

```swift
class BoardGame {
    let players: [Player]
    let numberOfTiles: Int

    init(players: [Player], numberOfTiles: Int) {        ◁─┐ The designated
        self.players = players                                initializer
        self.numberOfTiles = numberOfTiles
    }
                                                          ┌─ A convenience
    convenience init(players: [Player]) {             ◁──┤   initializer accepting
        self.init(players: players, numberOfTiles: 32)     players
    }

    convenience init(names: [String]) {          ◁──┐ A convenience
        var players = [Player]()                        initializer converting
        for name in names {                             strings to players
            players.append(Player(name: name))
        }
        self.init(players: players, numberOfTiles: 32)
    }
}
```

NOTE Alternatively, you could also add a default numberOfTiles value to the designated initializer, such as init(players: [Player], numberOfTiles: Int = 32). By doing so, you can get rid of one convenience initializer. For example purposes, you continue with two separate convenience initializers.

The BoardGame contains two properties: a players array containing all players in the board game, and a numberOfTiles integer indicating the size of the board game.

Here are the different ways you can initialize the BoardGame superclass.

> **Listing 5.9 Initializing BoardGame**

```
//Convenience initializer
let boardGame = BoardGame(names: ["Melissa", "SuperJeff", "Dave"])

let players = [
    Player(name: "Melissa"),
    Player(name: "SuperJeff"),
    Player(name: "Dave")
]

//Convenience initializer
let boardGame = BoardGame(players: players)

//Designated initializer
let boardGame = BoardGame(players: players, numberOfTiles: 32)
```

The convenience initializers accept only an array of players or an array of names, which BoardGame turns into players. These convenience initializers point at the designated initializer.

LACK OF MEMBERWISE INITIALIZERS Unfortunately, classes don't get free memberwise initializers like structs do. With classes you'll have to manually type them out. So much for being lazy!

5.2.3 Creating a subclass

Now that you created BoardGame, you can start subclassing it to build board games. In this chapter, you're creating only one game, which doesn't exactly warrant a superclass setup. Theoretically, you can create lots of board games that subclass BoardGame.

The subclass is called MutabilityLand, which subclasses BoardGame (see figure 5.2). MutabilityLand inherits all the initializers from BoardGame.

As shown in listing 5.10, you can initialize MutabilityLand the same way as BoardGame because it inherits all the initializers that BoardGame has to offer.

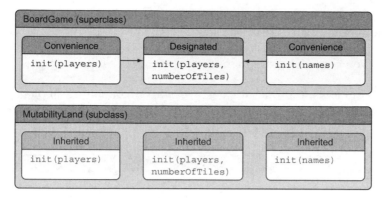

Figure 5.2   Subclassing BoardGame

Listing 5.10   MutabilityLand inherits all the BoardGame initializers

```
// Convenience initializer
let mutabilityLand = MutabilityLand(names: ["Melissa", "SuperJeff", "Dave"])
// Convenience initializer
let mutabilityLand = MutabilityLand(players: players)
// Designated initializer
let mutabilityLand = MutabilityLand(players: players, numberOfTiles: 32)
```

Looking inside MutabilityLand, you see that it has two properties of its own, score-
Board and winner. The scoreboard keeps track of each player's name and their score.
The winner property remembers the latest winner of the game.

Listing 5.11   The MutabilityLand class

```
class MutabilityLand: BoardGame {
    // ScoreBoard is initialized with an empty dictionary
    var scoreBoard = [String: Int]()
    var winner: Player?
}
```

Perhaps surprisingly these properties don't need an initializer; this is because score-
Board is already initialized outside of an initializer, and winner is an optional, which is
allowed to be nil.

5.2.4   *Losing convenience initializers*

Here is where the process gets tricky: *once a subclass adds unpopulated properties, consumers of the subclass lose ALL the superclass's initializers.*

Let's see how this works. First, you'll add an instructions property to Mutability-
Land, which tells players the rules of the game.

Figure 5.3 shows your current hierarchy with your new setup. Notice how the inherited initializers are gone now that you've added a new property (instructions) to MutabilityLand.

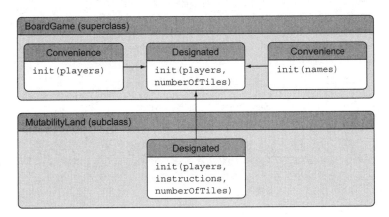

Figure 5.3 Disappearing initializers

To populate the new instructions property, you'll create the designated initializer to populate it.

Let's see how this looks in code.

Listing 5.12 Creating a designated initializer for MutabilityLand

```
class MutabilityLand: BoardGame {
    var scoreBoard = [String: Int]()                      A new designated
    var winner: Player?              The new               initializer to
                                     instructions         instantiate
    let instructions: String         property             instructions

    init(players: [Player], instructions: String, numberOfTiles: Int) {
        self.instructions = instructions
        super.init(players: players, numberOfTiles: numberOfTiles)
    }                                The designated initializer calls the
}                                    boardgame's initializer.
```

At this stage, MutabilityLand has lost the three inherited initializers from its superclass Boardgame.

You can't initialize MutabilityLand anymore with the inherited initializers.

Listing 5.13 Inherited initializers don't work any more

```
// These don't work any more.
let mutabilityLand = MutabilityLand(names: ["Melissa", "SuperJeff", "Dave"])
let mutabilityLand = MutabilityLand(players: players)
let mutabilityLand = MutabilityLand(players: players, numberOfTiles: 32)
```

To prove that you've lost the inherited initializers, try to create a `MutabilityLand` instance with an initializer from `BoardGame`—only this time, you get an error.

Listing 5.14   Losing superclass initializers

```
error: missing argument for parameter 'instructions' in call
let mutabilityLand = MutabilityLand(names: ["Melissa", "SuperJeff", "Dave"])
                                                                          ^
                                                                            ,
```

Losing inherited initializers may seem strange, but there is a legitimate reason why `MutabilityLand` loses them. The inherited initializers are gone because `BoardGame` can't populate the new `instructions` property of its subclass. Moreover, since Swift wants all properties populated, it can now *only* rely on the newly designated initializer on `MutabilityLand`.

5.2.5   *Getting the superclass initializers back*

There is a way to get all the superclass' initializers back so that `MutabilityLand` can enjoy the free initializers from `BoardGame`.

By overriding the *designated* initializer from a superclass, a subclass gets the superclass's initializers back. In other words, `MutabilityLand` overrides the designated initializer from `BoardGame` to get the convenience initializers back. The designated initializer from `MutabilityLand` still points to the designated initializer from `BoardGame` (see figure 5.4).

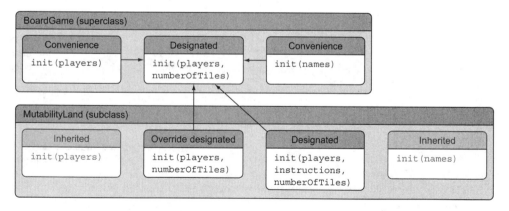

Figure 5.4 `MutabilityLand` **regains the free initializers from** `BoardGame`.

By overriding the superclass' designated initializer, `MutabilityLand` gets all the convenience initializers back from `BoardGame`. Overriding an initializer is achieved by adding the `override` keyword on a designated initializer in `MutabilityLand`. The code can be found in listing 5.15.

DESIGNATED INITIALIZER FUNNELS You can see how designated initializers are like *funnels*. In a class hierarchy, convenience initializers go horizontal, and designated initializers go vertical.

Listing 5.15 `MutabilityLand` **overrides the designated initializer**

> You need to initialize the properties of MutabilityLand before you call super.init. Notice how you give instructions a default value here.

```
class MutabilityLand: BoardGame {
    // ... snip
    override init(players: [Player], numberOfTiles: Int) {
        self.instructions = "Read the manual"          ◄──
        super.init(players: players, numberOfTiles: numberOfTiles)
    }
}
```

Since you override the superclass initializer, `MutabilityLand` needs to come up with its instructions there. Now that the designated initializer from `BoardGame` is overridden, you have a lot to choose from when initializing `MutabilityLand`.

Listing 5.16 **All available initializers for** `MutabilityLand`

```
// MutabilityLand's initializer
let mutabilityLand = MutabilityLand(players: players, instructions: "Just
➡ read the manual", numberOfTiles: 40)

// BoardGame initializers all work again.
let mutabilityLand = MutabilityLand(names: ["Melissa", "SuperJeff", "Dave"])
let mutabilityLand = MutabilityLand(players: players)
let mutabilityLand = MutabilityLand(players: players, numberOfTiles: 32)
```

Thanks to a single override, you get all initializers back that the superclass has to offer.

5.2.6 Exercise

3 The following superclass, called `Device`, registers devices in an office and keeps track of the rooms where these devices can be found. Its subclass `Television` is one of such devices that subclasses `Device`.

   The challenge is to initialize the `Television` subclass with a `Device` initializer. In other words, make the following line of code work by adding a single initializer somewhere:

```
let firstTelevision = Television(room: "Lobby")
let secondTelevision = Television(serialNumber: "abc")
```

The classes are as follows:

```
class Device {

    var serialNumber: String
    var room: String
```

```
        init(serialNumber: String, room: String) {
            self.serialNumber = serialNumber
            self.room = room
        }

        convenience init() {
            self.init(serialNumber: "Unknown", room: "Unknown")
        }

        convenience init(serialNumber: String) {
            self.init(serialNumber: serialNumber, room: "Unknown")
        }

        convenience init(room: String) {
            self.init(serialNumber: "Unknown", room: room)
        }

    }

    class Television: Device {
        enum ScreenType {
            case led
            case oled
            case lcd
            case unknown
        }

        enum Resolution {
            case ultraHd
            case fullHd
            case hd
            case sd
            case unknown
        }

        let resolution: Resolution
        let screenType: ScreenType

        init(resolution: Resolution, screenType: ScreenType, serialNumber:
    String, room: String) {
            self.resolution = resolution
            self.screenType = screenType
            super.init(serialNumber: serialNumber, room: room)
        }

    }
```

5.3   *Minimizing class initializers*

You saw that BoardGame has one designated initializer; its subclass MutabilityLand has
two designated initializers. If you were to subclass MutabilityLand again and add a
stored property, that subclass would have three initializers, and so on. At this rate,
you'd have to override more initializers the more you subclass, making your hierarchy

complicated. Luckily there is a solution to keep the number of designated initializers low so that each subclass holds only a single designated initializer.

5.3.1 Convenience overrides

In the previous section, MutabilityLand was overriding the designated initializer from the BoardGame class. But a neat trick is to make the overridden initializer in MutabilityLand into a *convenience override* initializer (see figure 5.5).

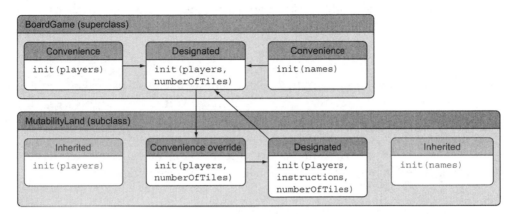

Figure 5.5 MutabilityLand **performs a convenience override on a designated initializer.**

Now the overriding initializer in MutabilityLand is a convenience override initializer that points sideways to the designated initializer inside MutabilityLand. This designated initializer from MutabilityLand still points upwards to the designated initializer inside BoardGame.

In your class you make this happen using the convenience override keywords.

Listing 5.17 A convenience override

```
class MutabilityLand: BoardGame {
    var scoreBoard = [String: Int]()
    var winner: Player?

    let instructions: String

    convenience override init(players: [Player], numberOfTiles: Int) {
        self.init(players: players, instructions: "Read the manual",
    numberOfTiles: numberOfTiles)
    }

    init(players: [Player], instructions: String, numberOfTiles: Int) {
        self.instructions = instructions
        super.init(players: players, numberOfTiles: numberOfTiles)
    }
}
```

The overriding initializer is now an overriding convenience initializer.

The initializer now points sideways (self.init) versus upwards (super.init).

Leave the designated initializer as is.

Since the overriding initializer is now a convenience initializer, it points horizontally to the designated initializer in the same class. This way, MutabilityLand goes from having two designated initializers to one convenience initializer and a single designated initializer. Any subclass now only has to override a single designated initializer to get all initializers from the superclass.

The downside is that this approach is not as flexible. For example, the convenience initializer now has to figure out how to fill the instructions property. But if a convenience override works in your code, it reduces the number of designated initializers.

5.3.2 Subclassing a subclass

To prove that you can keep the number of designated initializers low, you'll introduce a subclass from MutabilityLand called MutabilityLandJunior, for kids. This game is a bit easier and has the option to play sounds, indicated by a new soundsEnabled property.

Because of your convenience override trick, this new subclass only has to override a single designated initializer. The hierarchy is shown in figure 5.6.

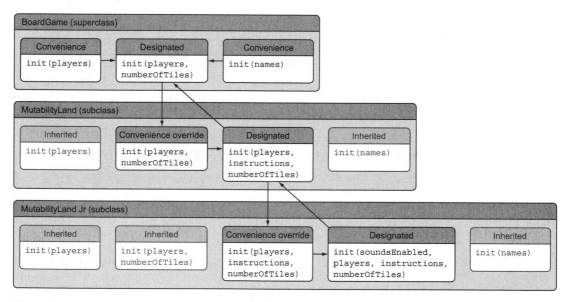

Figure 5.6 MutabilityLandJunior **only needs to override one initializer.**

You can see how this sub-subclass only needs to override a single initializer to inherit all initializers. Out of good habit, this initializer is a convenience override as well, in case MutabilityLandJunior gets subclassed again, as shown in the following listing.

Listing 5.18 `MutabilityLandJunior`

```
class MutabilityLandJunior: MutabilityLand {
    let soundsEnabled: Bool

    init(soundsEnabled: Bool, players: [Player], instructions: String,
     numberOfTiles: Int) {
        self.soundsEnabled = soundsEnabled
        super.init(players: players, instructions: instructions,
        numberOfTiles: numberOfTiles)
    }

    convenience override init(players: [Player], instructions: String,
     numberOfTiles: Int) {
        self.init(soundsEnabled: false, players: players, instructions:
    instructions, numberOfTiles: numberOfTiles)
    }
}
```

MutabilityLandJunior gets its own designated initializer.

A single overriding init is added.

You can now initialize this game in five ways.

Listing 5.19 Initializing `MutabilityLandJunior` with all initializers

```
let mutabilityLandJr =
MutabilityLandJunior(players: players, instructions: "Kids don't read
manuals", numberOfTiles: 8)

let mutabilityLandJr = MutabilityLandJunior(soundsEnabled: true, players:
players, instructions: "Kids don't read manuals", numberOfTiles: 8)

let mutabilityLandJr = MutabilityLandJunior(names: ["Philippe", "Alex"])

let mutabilityLandJr = MutabilityLandJunior(players: players)

let mutabilityLandJr = MutabilityLandJunior(players: players, numberOfTiles: 8)
```

Thanks to convenience overrides, this subclass gets many initializers for free.

Also, no matter how many subclasses you have (hopefully not too many), subclasses only have to override a single initializer!

5.3.3 *Exercise*

4　Given the following class, which subclasses `Television` from the previous exercise

```
class HandHeldTelevision: Television {
    let weight: Int

    init(weight: Int, resolution: Resolution, screenType: ScreenType,
    serialNumber: String, room: String) {
        self.weight = weight
        super.init(resolution: resolution, screenType: screenType,
    serialNumber: serialNumber, room: room)
    }

}
```

add two convenience override initializers in the subclassing hierarchy to make this initializer work from the top-most superclass:

```
let handheldTelevision = HandHeldTelevision(serialNumber: "293nr30znNdjW")
```

5.4   *Required initializers*

You may have seen *required* initializers pop up in the wild sometimes, such as when working with UIKit's `UIViewController`. Required initializers play a crucial role when subclassing classes. You can decorate initializers with a `required` keyword. Adding the `required` keyword assures that subclasses implement the required initializer. You need the `required` keyword for two reasons—factory methods and protocols—which you'll explore in this section.

5.4.1   *Factory methods*

Factory methods are the first reason why you need the `required` keyword. Factory methods are a typical design pattern that facilitates creating instances of a class. You can call these methods on a type, such as a class or a struct (as opposed to an instance), for easy instantiating of preconfigured instances. Here's an example where you create a `BoardGame` instance or `MutabilityLand` instance via the `makeGame` factory method.

Listing 5.20   Factory methods in action

```
let boardGame = BoardGame.makeGame(players: players)
let mutabilityLand = MutabilityLand.makeGame(players: players)
```

Now return to the `BoardGame` superclass where you add the `makeGame` class function.

The `makeGame` method accepts only players and returns an instance of `Self`. `Self` refers to the current type that `makeGame` is called on; this could be `BoardGame` or one of its subclasses.

In a real-world scenario, the board game could be set up with all kinds of settings, such as a time limit and locale, as shown in the following example, adding more benefits to creating a factory method.

Listing 5.21   Introducing the `makeGame` factory method

```
class BoardGame {
    // ... snip

    class func makeGame(players: [Player]) -> Self {
        let boardGame = self.init(players: players, numberOfTiles: 32)
        // Configuration goes here.
        // E.g.
        // boardGame.locale = Locale.current
        // boardGame.timeLimit = 900
        return boardGame
    }
}
```

The reason that makeGame returns Self is that Self is different for each subclass. If the method were to return a BoardGame instance, makeGame wouldn't be able to return an instance of MutabilityLand for example. But you're not there yet; this gives the following error.

Listing 5.22 required error

```
constructing an object of class type 'Self' with a metatype value must use a
    'required' initializer
return self.init(players: players, numberOfTiles: 32)
                 ~~~~ ^
```

The initializer throws an error because makeGame can return BoardGame or any subclass instance. Because makeGame refers to self.init, it needs a guarantee that subclasses implement this method. Adding a required keyword to the designated initializer enforces subclasses to implement the initializer, which satisfies this requirement.

First, you add the required keyword to the initializer referred to in makeGame.

Listing 5.23 Adding the required keyword to initializers

```
class BoardGame {
    // ... snip

    required init(players: [Player], numberOfTiles: Int) {
        self.players = players
        self.numberOfTiles = numberOfTiles
    }
}
```

Subclasses can now replace override with required in the related initializer.

Listing 5.24 Subclass required

```
class MutabilityLand: BoardGame {

    // ... snip

    convenience required init(players: [Player], numberOfTiles: Int) {
        self.init(players: players, instructions: "Read the manual",
    numberOfTiles: numberOfTiles)
    }
}
```

Now the compiler is happy, and you can reap the benefits of factory methods on superclasses and subclasses.

5.4.2 Protocols

Protocols are the second reason the required keyword exists.

PROTOCOLS We'll handle protocols in depth in chapters 7, 8, 12, and 13.

When a protocol has an initializer, a class adopting that protocol *must* decorate that initializer with the `required` keyword. Let's see why and how this works.

First, you introduce a protocol called `BoardGameType`, which contains an initializer.

Listing 5.25   Introducing the `BoardGameType` protocol

```
protocol BoardGameType {
    init(players: [Player], numberOfTiles: Int)
}
```

Then you'll implement this protocol on the `BoardGame` class so that `BoardGame` implements the `init` method from the protocol.

Listing 5.26   Implementing the `BoardGameType` protocol

```
class BoardGame: BoardGameType {
// ... snip
```

At this point, the compiler still isn't happy. Because `BoardGame` conforms to the `BoardGameType` protocol, its subclasses also have to conform to this protocol and implement `init(players: [Player], numberOfTiles: Int)`.

You can again use `required` to force your subclasses to implement this initializer, in precisely the same way as in the previous example.

5.4.3   *When classes are final*

One way to avoid needing the `required` keyword is by adding the `final` keyword to a class. Making a class final indicates that you can't subclass it. Making classes final until you explicitly need subclassing behavior can be a good start because adding a `final` keyword helps performance.[1]

If a class is final, you can drop any `required` keywords from the initializers. For example, let's say nobody likes playing the games that are subclassed, except for the `BoardGame` itself. Now you can make `BoardGame` final and delete any subclasses. Note that you're omitting the `required` keyword from the designated initializer.

Listing 5.27   `BoardGame` is now a final class

```
protocol BoardGameType {
    init(players: [Player], numberOfTiles: Int)
}

final class BoardGame: BoardGameType {          ◁──┐ The class is now
    let players: [Player]                            a final class.
    let numberOfTiles: Int

    // No need to make this required                ┌─ The designated
    init(players: [Player], numberOfTiles: Int) {  ◁──┘ initializer isn't
                                                          required any more.
```

---

[1] "Increasing Performance by Reducing Dynamic Dispatch" https://developer.apple.com/swift/blog/?id=27

```
        self.players = players
        self.numberOfTiles = numberOfTiles
    }

    class func makeGame(players: [Player]) -> Self {
        return self.init(players: players, numberOfTiles: 32)
    }

    // ... snip
}
```

Despite implementing the `BoardGameType` protocol and having a `makeGame` factory method, `BoardGame` won't need any required initializers because it's a *final* class.

5.4.4 Exercises

5 Would required initializers make sense on structs? Why or why not?

6 Can you name two use cases for needing required initializers?

5.5 Closing thoughts

You witnessed how Swift has many types of initializers, each one paired with its own rules and oddities. You noticed how initializers are even more complicated when you're subclassing. Subclassing may not be popular, yet it can be a viable alternative depending on your background, coding style, and the code that you may inherit when joining an exciting company.

After this chapter, I hope that you feel confident enough to write your initializers without problems and that you'll be able to offer clean interfaces to get your types initialized.

Summary

- Structs and classes want all their non-optional properties initialized.
- Structs generate "free" memberwise initializers.
- Structs lose memberwise initializers if you add a custom initializer.
- If you extend structs with your custom initializers, you can have both memberwise and custom initializers.
- Classes must have one or more designated initializers.
- Convenience initializers point to designated initializers.
- If a subclass has its own stored properties, it won't directly inherit its superclass initializers.
- If a subclass overrides designated initializers, it gets the convenience initializers from the superclass.
- When overriding a superclass initializer with a convenience initializer, a subclass keeps the number of designated initializers down.
- The required keyword makes sure that subclasses implement an initializer and that factory methods work on subclasses.

- Once a protocol has an initializer, the required keyword makes sure that sub-classes conform to the protocol.
- By making a class final, initializers can drop the required keyword.

Answers

1 Will the following initializers work?

```
let pancakes = Pancakes(syrupType: .corn, stackSize: 8)
let morePancakes = Pancakes(syrupType: .maple)
```

No. When you use a custom initializer, a memberwise initializer won't be available.

2 If these initializers didn't work, can you make them work without adding another initializer?

```
struct Pancakes {

    enum SyrupType {
        case corn
        case molasses
        case maple
    }

    let syrupType: SyrupType
    let stackSize: Int

}

extension Pancakes {          ◁——  Extend
                                    Pancakes.

    init(syrupType: SyrupType) {          ◁——  Put the custom
        self.stackSize = 10                     initializer inside
        self.syrupType = syrupType              the extension.
    }

}

let pancakes = Pancakes(syrupType: .corn, stackSize: 8)
let morePancakes = Pancakes(syrupType: .maple)
```

3 The following superclass called `Device` registers devices in an office and keeps track of the rooms where these devices can be found. `Television` is one such device that subclasses `Device`.

The challenge is to initialize the `Television` subclass with a `Device` initializer. In other words, make the following line of code work by adding a single initializer somewhere:

```
class Television: Device {

    override init(serialNumber: String, room: String) {          ◁——  Override a
        self.resolution = .unknown                                     designated
        self.screenType = .unknown                                     initializer
                                                                       from Device.
```

```
        super.init(serialNumber: serialNumber, room: room)
    }

    // ... snip
}
```

4 Given the following class, which subclasses `Television` from the previous exercise, add two convenience override initializers in the subclassing hierarchy to make this initializer work from the top-most superclass:

```
class Television {

    convenience override init(serialNumber: String, room: String) {
        self.init(resolution: .unknown, screenType: .unknown,
    serialNumber: serialNumber, room: room)
    }

    // ... snip

}
```

Add a convenience initializer to Television which overrides a designated initializer from Device.

```
class HandHeldTelevision: Television {

    convenience override init(resolution: Resolution, screenType:
    ScreenType, serialNumber: String, room: String) {
        self.init(weight: 0, resolution: resolution, screenType:
    screenType, serialNumber: "Unknown", room: "UnKnown")
    }

    // ... snip

}
```

Add a convenience initializer to HandHeldTelevision which overrides a designated initializer from Television.

5 Would required initializers make sense on structs? Why or why not?

No, required initializers enforce initializers on subclasses, and structs can't be subclassed.

6 Can you name two use cases for required initializers?

To enforce factory methods on subclasses and to conform to a protocol defining an initializer.

Effortless error handling

6

This chapter covers

- Error-handling best practices (and downsides)
- Keeping your application in a proper state when throwing
- How errors are propagated
- Adding information for customer-facing applications (and for troubleshooting)
- Bridging to `NSError`
- Making APIs easier to use without harming the integrity of an application

Error handling is an integral part of any software development and not Swift-centric. But how Swift treats error handling does impact the way you deliver code that is pleasant to use and respects problems that can arise in a system. In this chapter, you'll elegantly throw and catch errors while walking the fine line between creating a useful API instead of a tedious one.

Error handling sounds simple in theory: throw some errors and catch them, and your program keeps running. But in reality, doing it correctly can get quite tricky. Swift also adds a unique flavor on top where it imposes rules, offers syntactic sugar, and compile-time checks to make sure you're handling thrown errors.

Even though it's a start to throw an error when something goes wrong, there are many subtleties. Moreover, once you do end up with an error, you need to know where the responsibility lies to handle (or ignore) the error. Do you propagate an error all the way up to the user, or can your program prevent errors altogether? Also, when *exactly* do you throw errors?

This chapter explores how Swift treats errors, but it won't be a dry repeat of Apple's documentation. Included are best practices related to keeping an application in a good state, a closer look at the downsides of error handling, and techniques on how to cleanly handle errors.

The first section goes over Swift errors and how to throw them. It also covers some best practices to keep your code in a predictable state when your functions start throwing errors.

Then, you'll see how functions can propagate errors through an application. You'll learn how you can add technical information for troubleshooting and localized information for end users, how to bridge to `NSError`, and more about centralizing error handling, all while implementing useful protocols.

To finish up the chapter, you'll get a look at the downsides of throwing errors and how to negate them. You'll also see how to make your APIs more pleasant to use while making sure that the system integrity stays intact.

6.1   *Errors in Swift*

Errors can come in all shapes and sizes. If you ask three developers what constitutes an error, you may get three different answers and will most likely hear differences between exceptions, errors, problems at runtime, or even blaming the user for ending up with a problem.

To start this chapter right, let's classify errors into three categories so that we are on the same page:

- *Programming errors*—These errors could have been prevented by a programmer with a good night's sleep—for example, arrays being out of bounds, division by zero, and integer overflows. Essentially, these are problems that you can fix on a code level. This is where unit tests and quality assurance can save you when you drop the ball. Usually, in Swift you can use checks such as `assert` to make sure your code acts as intended, and `precondition` to let others know that your API is called correctly. Assertions and preconditions are not what this chapter covers, however.

- *User errors*—A user error is when a user interacts with a system and fails to complete a task correctly, such as accidentally sending drunk selfies to your boss. User errors can be caused by not completely understanding a system, being distracted, or a clumsy user interface. Even though faulting a customer's intelligence may be a fun pastime, you can blame a user error on the application itself, and you can prevent these issues with good design, clear communication, and shaping your software in such as way that it helps users reach their intent.

- *Errors revealed at runtime*—These errors could be an application being unable to create a file because the hard drive is full, a network request that fails, certificates that expire, JSON parsers that barf up after being fed wrong data, and many other things that can go wrong when an application is running. This last category of errors are recoverable (generally speaking) and are what this chapter focuses on.

In this section, you'll see how Swift defines errors, what its weaknesses are, and how to catch them. Besides throwing errors, functions can do some extra housekeeping to make sure an application stays in a predictable state, which is another topic that you'll explore in this section.

6.1.1   *The Error protocol*

JOIN ME!   It's more educational and fun if you can check out the code and follow along with the chapter. You can download the source code at http://mng.bz/oN4j.

Swift offers an `Error` protocol, which you can use to indicate that something went wrong in your application. Enums are well suited as errors because each case is mutually exclusive. You could, for instance, have a `ParseLocationError` enum with three options of failure.

Listing 6.1   An enum `Error`

```
enum ParseLocationError: Error {
    case invalidData
    case locationDoesNotExist
    case middleOfTheOcean
}
```

The `Error` protocol has no requirements and therefore doesn't enforce any implementations, which also means that you don't need to make every error an enum. As an example, you can also use other types, such as structs, to indicate something went wrong. Structs are less conventional to use but can be useful for when you want to add more rich data to an error.

You could, for instance, have an error struct that contains multiple errors and other properties.

Listing 6.2   A struct `Error`

```
struct MultipleParseLocationErrors: Error {
    let parsingErrors: [ParseLocationError]
    let isShownToUser: Bool
}
```

At first glance, enums are the way to go when composing errors, but know that you're not restricted to using them for specific cases.

6.1.2 *Throwing errors*

Errors exist to be thrown and handled. For instance, when a function fails to save a file, it can throw an error with a reason, such as the hard drive being full or lacking the rights to write to disk. When a function or method can throw an error, Swift requires the throws keyword in the function signature behind the closing parenthesis.

You could, for instance, turn two strings into a Location type containing latitude and longitude constants, as shown in the following code. A parseLocation function can then convert the strings by parsing them. If the parsing fails, the parseLocation function throws a ParseLocationError.invalidData error.

Listing 6.3 Parsing location strings

```
struct Location {                          Define a Location type        The parseLocation function
    let latitude: Double                   that parseLocation            either returns a Location or
    let longitude: Double                  returns.                      throws an error, indicated
}                                                                        by the throws keyword.

func parseLocation(_ latitude: String, _ longitude: String) throws ->
    Location {
    guard let latitude = Double(latitude), let longitude = Double(longitude)
    else {
        throw ParseLocationError.invalidData
    }

    return Location(latitude: latitude, longitude: longitude)
}                                          Catch an error with the       Call a throwing
do {                                       do catch keywords.            function with the
    try parseLocation("I am not a double", "4.899431")                   try keyword.
} catch {
    print(error) // invalidData           Swift automatically gives you
}                                          an error constant to match
                                           on in a catch statement.
```

Because parseLocation is a throwing function, as indicated by the throws keyword, you need to call it with the try keyword. The compiler also forces callers of throwing functions to deal with the error somehow. Later on, you'll get to see some techniques to make your APIs more pleasant for implementers.

6.1.3 *Swift doesn't reveal errors*

Another peculiar aspect of Swift's error handling is that functions don't reveal which errors they can throw. A function that is marked as throws could theoretically throw no errors or five million different errors, and you have no way of knowing this by looking at a function signature. Not having to list and handle each error explicitly gives you flexibility, but a significant shortcoming is that you can't quickly know which errors a function can produce or propagate.

Functions don't reveal their errors, so giving *some* information where possible is recommended. Luckily your friend *Quick Help* can jump in and help you provide more information about the errors you can throw. You can also use it to state when errors can be thrown, as shown in listing 6.4.

You can generate Quick Help documentation in Xcode by placing the cursor on a function and pressing Cmd-Alt-/ to generate a Quick Help template, including possible errors (see figure 6.1).

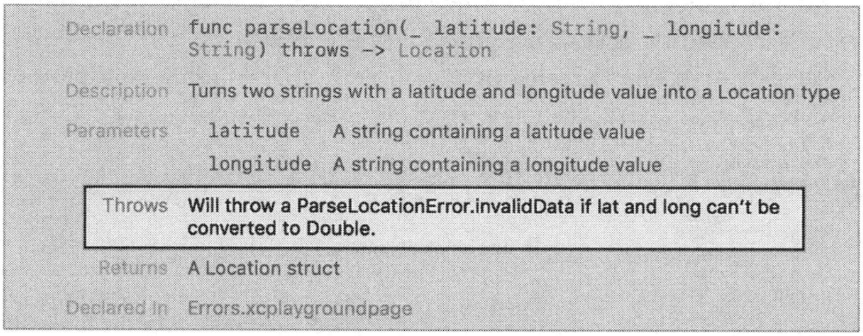

Declaration	`func parseLocation(_ latitude: String, _ longitude: String) throws -> Location`
Description	Turns two strings with a latitude and longitude value into a Location type
Parameters	`latitude` A string containing a latitude value
	`longitude` A string containing a longitude value
Throws	**Will throw a ParseLocationError.invalidData if lat and long can't be converted to Double.**
Returns	A Location struct
Declared In	Errors.xcplaygroundpage

Figure 6.1   A Quick Help informing about errors

Listing 6.4   Adding error information to a function

```
/// Turns two strings with a latitude and longitude value into a Location
    type
///                                                    Add a Throws:
/// - Parameters:                                      comment to the
///   - latitude: A string containing a latitude value     Quick Help
///   - longitude: A string containing a longitude value  documentation.
/// - Returns: A Location struct
/// - Throws: Will throw a ParseLocationError.invalidData if lat and long
   can't be converted to Double.
 func parseLocation(_ latitude: String, _ longitude: String) throws ->
    Location {
    guard let latitude = Double(latitude), let longitude = Double(longitude)
    else {
        throw ParseLocationError.invalidData
    }

    return Location(latitude: latitude, longitude: longitude)
}
```

It's a bandage, but adding this Quick Help gives the developer at least some information regarding the errors to expect.

6.1.4   *Keeping the environment in a predictable state*

You've seen how a caller of a function deals with any possible errors your functions can throw. But throwing an error may not be enough. Sometimes a throwing function can go the extra mile and make sure that an application's state remains the same once an error occurs.

TIP Generally speaking, keeping a throwing function in a predictable state after it throws an error is a good habit to get into.

A predictable state prevents the environment from being in limbo between an error state and a sort-of-okay state. Keeping an application in a predictable state means that when a function or method throws an error, it should prevent, or undo, any changes that it has done to the environment or instance.

Let's say you own a memory cache, and you want to store a value to this cache via a method. If this method throws an error, you probably expect your value *not* to be cached. If the function keeps the value in memory on an error, however, an external retry mechanism may even cause the system to run out of memory. The goal is to get the environment back to normal when throwing errors so the caller can retry or continue in other ways.

The easiest way to prevent throwing functions from mutating the environment is if functions don't even change the environment in the first place. Making a function immutable is one way to achieve this. Immutable functions and methods have benefits in general, but even more so when a function is throwing.

If you look back at the parseLocation function, you see that it touches only the values that it gets passed, and it isn't performing any changes to external values, meaning that there are no hidden side effects. Because parseLocation is immutable, it works predictably.

Let's go over two more techniques to achieve a predictable state.

MUTATING TEMPORARY VALUES

A second way that you can keep your environment in a predictable state is by mutating a copy or temporary value and then saving the new state after the mutation completed without errors.

Consider the following TodoList type, which can store an array of strings. If a string is empty after trimming, however, the append method throws an error.

Listing 6.5 The TodoList that mutates state on errors

```
enum ListError: Error {
    case invalidValue
}

struct TodoList {

    private var values = [String]()

    mutating func append(strings: [String]) throws {
        for string in strings {
            let trimmedString = string.trimmingCharacters(in: .whitespacesAnd
➥ Newlines)

            if trimmedString.isEmpty {        If a string is empty,
                throw ListError.invalidValue  ◁── you throw an error.
            } else {
```

```
                    values.append(trimmedString)
                }                                              If a string is not empty,
            }                                                  you add a value to the
        }                                                      values array.
    }
}
```

The problem is that after append throws an error, the type now has a half-filled state. The caller may assume everything is back to what it was and retry again later. But in the current state, the TodoList leaves some trailing information in its values.

Instead, you can consider mutating a temporary value, and only adding the final result to the actual values property after every iteration was successful. If the append method throws during an iteration, however, the new state is never saved, and the temporary value will be gone, keeping the TodoList in the same state as before an error is thrown.

Listing 6.6   TodoList works with temporary values

```
struct TodoList {

    private var values = [String]()

    mutating func append(strings: [String]) throws {        A temporary
        var trimmedStrings = [String]()                      array is created.
        for string in strings {
            let trimmedString = string.trimmingCharacters(in: .whitespacesAnd
➥   Newlines)

            if trimmedString.isEmpty {
                throw ListError.invalidValue
            } else {                                          The temporary
                trimmedStrings.append(trimmedString)          array is modified.
            }
        }                                                     If no error is thrown,
                                                              the values property
        values.append(contentsOf: trimmedStrings)             is updated.
    }

}
```

RECOVERY CODE WITH DEFER

One way to recover from a throwing function is to *undo* mutations while being in the middle of an operation. Undoing mutating operations halfway tends to be rarer, but can be the only option you may have when you are writing data, such as files to a hard drive.

As an example, consider the following writeToFiles function that can write multiple files to multiple local URLs. The caveat, however, is that this function has an all-or-nothing requirement. If writing to one file fails, don't write any files to disk. To keep the function in a predictable state if an error occurs, you need to write some cleanup code that removes written files after a function starts throwing errors.

You can use `defer` for a cleanup operation. A `defer` closure is executed *after* the function ends, regardless of whether the function is finished normally or via a thrown error. You can keep track of all saved files in the function, and then in the `defer` closure you can delete all saved files, but only if the number of saved files doesn't match the number of paths you give to the function.

Listing 6.7   Recovering writing to files with `defer`

```
import Foundation

func writeToFiles(data: [URL: String]) throws {
    var storedUrls = [URL]()
    defer {
        if storedUrls.count != data.count {
            for url in storedUrls {
                try! FileManager.default.removeItem(at: url)
            }
        }
    }

    for (url, contents) in data {
        try contents.write(to: url, atomically: true, encoding:
        String.Encoding.utf8)
            storedUrls.append(url)
    }
}
```

An array is created to store the successfully stored URLs, in case you need to remove them as a cleanup operation.

Even though it's declared on top, the defer statement is called at the end of the function.

When a file can't be stored, remove all successfully stored files.

Use try! to assert that this operation won't fail (more on this later).

The file is written, but throws if it fails, indicated by the try keyword.

If this writing of a file doesn't throw, you append the URL to the storedUrls array.

Cleaning up after mutation has occurred can be tricky because you're basically rewinding time. The `writeToFiles` function, for instance, removes all files on an error, but what if there were files before the new files were written? The `defer` block in `writeToFiles` would have to be more advanced to keep a more thorough record of what the *exact* state was before an error is thrown. When writing recovery code, be aware that keeping track of multiple scenarios can become increasingly complicated.

6.1.5   Exercises

1   Can you name one or more downsides of how Swift handles errors, and how to compensate for them?
2   Can you name three ways to make sure throwing functions return to their original state after throwing errors?

6.2   *Error propagation and catching*

Swift offers four ways to handle an error: you can catch them, you can throw them higher up the stack (called *propagation*, or informally called "bubbling up"), you can turn them into optionals via the `try?` keyword, and you can assert that an error doesn't happen via the `try!` keyword.

In this section, you'll explore propagation and some techniques for clean catching. Shortly after, you'll dive deeper into the try? and try! keywords.

6.2.1 *Propagating errors*

My favorite way of dealing with problems is to give them to somebody else. Luckily you can do the same in Swift with errors that you receive: you propagate them by throwing them higher in the stack, like a one-sided game of hot potato.

Let's use this section to create a sequence of functions calling each other to see how a lower-level function can propagate an error all the way to a higher-level function.

A trend when looking up cooking recipes is that you have to sift through someone's personal story merely to get to the recipe and start cooking. A long intro helps search engines for the writer, but stripping all the fluff would be nice so you could extract a recipe straight away and get to cooking before stomachs start to growl.

As an example, you'll create a RecipeExtractor struct (see listing 6.8), which extracts a recipe from an HTML web page that it gets passed. RecipeExtractor uses smaller functions to perform this task. You'll focus on the error propagation and not the implementation (see figure 6.2).

RecipeExtractor

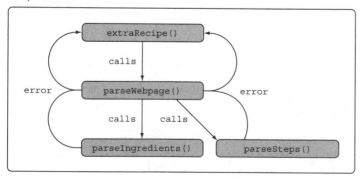

Figure 6.2   Propagating an error

Propagation works via a method that can call a lower-level method, which in turn can also call lower-level methods. But an error can propagate all the way up again to the highest level if you allow it.

When the `extractRecipe` function is called on `RecipeExtractor`, it will call a lower-level function called `parseWebpage`, which in turn will call `parseIngredients` and `parseSteps`. Both `parseIngredients` and `parseSteps` can throw an error, which `parseWebpage` will receive and propagate back up to the `extractRecipe` function as shown in the following code.

Listing 6.8 The `RecipeExtractor`

```swift
struct Recipe {                              ◁──  The Recipe struct that
    let ingredients: [String]                     RecipeExtractor returns
    let steps: [String]
}

enum ParseRecipeError: Error {               ◁──  The error that can
    case parseError                               be thrown inside
    case noRecipeDetected                         RecipeExtractor
    case noIngredientsDetected
}

struct RecipeExtractor {

    let html: String
                                             The extractRecipe
                                             function kickstarts
                                             the extracting.
    func extractRecipe() -> Recipe? {   ◁──┘
        do {                                 ◁──  The propagation of errors
            return try parseWebpage(html)         stops here because of the
        } catch {                                 do catch statement.
            print("Could not parse recipe")
            return nil                       Both parseIngredients and parseSteps
        }                                    are called with the try keyword; any
    }                                        errors that arise will be propagated up.

    private func parseWebpage(_ html: String) throws -> Recipe {
        let ingredients = try parseIngredients(html)
        let steps = try parseSteps(html)
        return Recipe(ingredients: ingredients, steps: steps)
    }

    private func parseIngredients(_ html: String) throws -> [String] {
        // ... Parsing happens here

        // .. Unless an error is thrown
        throw ParseRecipeError.noIngredientsDetected
    }

    private func parseSteps(_ html: String) throws -> [String] {
        // ... Parsing happens here
```

```
        // .. Unless an error is thrown
        throw ParseRecipeError.noRecipeDetected
    }

}
```

Getting a recipe may fail for multiple reasons; perhaps the HTML file doesn't contain a recipe at all, or the extractor fails to obtain the ingredients. The lower-level functions `parseIngredients` and `parseSteps` can, therefore, throw an error. Since their parent function `parseWebpage` doesn't know how to handle the errors, it propagates the error back up again to the `extractRecipe` function of the struct by using the `try` keyword. Since `parseWebpage` propagates an error up again, it also contains the `throws` keyword in its function signature.

Notice how the `extractRecipe` method has a `catch` clause without specifically matching on an error; this way the `extractRecipe` catches all possibly thrown errors. If the `catch` clause were matching on specific errors, theoretically some errors would not be caught and would have to propagate up even higher, making the `extractRecipe` function throwing as well.

6.2.2   *Adding technical details for troubleshooting*

Near where the error occurs, plenty of context surrounds it. You have the environment at your hands at the exact point in time; you know precisely which action failed and what the state is of each variable in the proximity of the error. When an error gets propagated up, this exact state may get lost, losing some useful information to handle the error.

When logging an error to help the troubleshooting process, adding some useful information for developers can be beneficial, such as where the parsing of recipes failed, for instance. After you've added this extra information, you can pattern match on an error and extract the information when troubleshooting.

For instance, as shown in the following, you can add a `symbol` and `line` property on the `parseError` case of `ParseRecipeError`, to give a little more info about where the parsing went wrong.

> **Listing 6.9   Adding more information to the `ParseRecipeError`**

```
enum ParseRecipeError: Error {
    case parseError(line: Int, symbol: String)    ◁──┐  Adding more
    case noRecipeDetected                            │  information
    case noIngredientsDetected                       │  to the error
}
```

This way, you can pattern match against the cases more explicitly when troubleshooting. Notice how you still keep a `catch` clause in there, to prevent `extractRecipes` from becoming a throwing function.

Listing 6.10   Matching on a specific error

```
struct RecipeExtractor {

    let html: String                                      Pattern match and
                                                          extract specific
    func extractRecipe() -> Recipe? {                        information
        do {
            return try parseWebpage(html)
        } catch let ParseRecipeError.parseError(line, symbol) {       ⟵
            print("Parsing failed at line: \(line) and symbol: \(symbol)")
            return nil
        } catch {
            print("Could not parse recipe")
            return nil
        }
    }

    // ... snip
}
```

ADDING USER-READABLE INFORMATION

Now that the technical information is there, you can use it to translate the data to a user-readable error. The reason you don't pass a human-readable string to an error is that with technical details you can make a distinction between a human-readable error and detailed technical information for a developer.

One approach to get human-readable information is to incorporate the Localized-Error protocol. When adhering to this protocol, you indicate that the error follows certain conventions and contains user-readable information. Conforming to Localized-Error tells an error handler that information is present that it can confidently show the user without needing to do some conversion.

To incorporate the LocalizedError protocol, you can implement a few properties, but they all have a default value of nil so you can tailor the error to which properties you would like to implement. An example is given in listing 6.11. In this scenario, you are choosing to incorporate the errorDescription property, which can give more information about the error itself. You are also adding the failureReason property, which helps explain why an error failed. You are also incorporating a recovery-Suggestion to help users with an action of what they should do, which in this case is to try a different recipe page. On OS X, you could also include the helpAnchor property, which you can use to link to Apple's Help Viewer, but this property isn't necessary in this example.

Since the strings are user-facing, consider returning localized strings instead of regular strings, so that the messages may fit the user's locale.

Listing 6.11   Implementing `LocalizedError`

The error-
Description
property helps
explain what
went wrong.

You can separately adhere to
a protocol via an extension
to separate code.

```
extension ParseRecipeError: LocalizedError {
    var errorDescription: String? {
        switch self {
        case .parseError:
            return NSLocalizedString("The HTML file had unexpected symbols.",
                               comment: "Parsing error reason
    unexpected symbols")
        case .noIngredientsDetected:
            return NSLocalizedString("No ingredients were detected.",
                                comment: "Parsing error no ingredients.")
        case .noRecipeDetected:
            return NSLocalizedString("No recipe was detected.",
                                comment: "Parsing error no recipe.")
        }
    }

    var failureReason: String? {
        switch self {
        case let .parseError(line: line, symbol: symbol):
            return String(format: NSLocalizedString("Parsing data failed at
    line: %i and symbol: %@",

                                                comment: "Parsing error
    line symbol"), line, symbol)
        case .noIngredientsDetected:
            return NSLocalizedString("The recipe seems to be missing its
    ingredients.",

                                                comment: "Parsing error reason missing
    ingredients.")
        case .noRecipeDetected:
            return NSLocalizedString("The recipe seems to be missing a
    recipe.",

                                                comment: "Parsing error reason missing
    recipe.")
        }
    }

    var recoverySuggestion: String? {
        return "Please try a different recipe."
    }

}
```

Rarer, but you can
implement a failure-
Reason property.

Via the recoverySuggestion
you can suggest how to
recover from an error.

All the properties are optional. Generally speaking, implementing `errorDescription` and `recoverySuggestion` should be enough.

Once a human-readable error is in place, you can pass it safely to anything user-facing, such as a `UIAlert` on iOS, printing to the command line, or a notification on OS X.

BRIDGING TO NSERROR

With a little effort, you can implement the `CustomNSError` protocol, which helps to bridge a `Swift.Error` to `NSError` in case you're calling Objective-C from Swift. The

CustomNSError expects three properties: a static errorDomain, an errorCode integer, and an errorUserInfo dictionary.

The errorDomain and errorCode are something you need to decide. For convenience, you can fill up the errorUserInfo with values you predefined (and fall back on empty values if they are nil).

Listing 6.12 Implementing NSError

For the errorUserInfo, you use three default keys, but you can reuse the properties you had before. Also notice how you fall back to empty strings (nil will give you warnings).

Come up with the domain that relates to the error.

```
extension ParseRecipeError: CustomNSError {
    static var errorDomain: String { return "com.recipeextractor" }   ⟵

    var errorCode: Int { return 300 }   ⟵  Create some kind of code
                                            unique to this error.

    var errorUserInfo: [String: Any] {
        return [
            NSLocalizedDescriptionKey: errorDescription ?? "",
            NSLocalizedFailureReasonErrorKey: failureReason ?? "",
            NSLocalizedRecoverySuggestionErrorKey: recoverySuggestion ?? ""
        ]
    }
}
```

Easily convert an error to NSError via the as NSError action.

```
let nsError: NSError = ParseRecipeError.parseError(line: 3, symbol: "#") as
    NSError                                                               ⟵
 print(nsError) // Error Domain=com.recipeextractor Code=300 "Parsing data
⇒ failed at line: 3 and symbol: #" UserInfo={NSLocalizedFailureReason=The
⇒ HTML file had unexpected symbols., NSLocalizedRecoverySuggestion=Please
⇒ try a different recipe., NSLocalizedDescription=Parsing data failed at
⇒ line: 3 and symbol: #}
```

Without supplying this information, converting an Error to an NSError means that the error doesn't have the proper code and domain information. Adopting the Custom-NSError gives you tight control over this conversion.

6.2.3 *Centralizing error handling*

A lower-level function can sometimes solve an error itself—such as a retry mechanism when passing data—but usually, a lower-level function would propagate an error up the stack back to the call-site because the lower-level function is missing the context on how to handle an error. For example, if an embedded framework fails to save a file and throws an error, it wouldn't know that an iOS application implementing this framework would want to show a UIAlertController dialog box, or that a Linux command-line tool would want to log to stderr.

A useful practice when handling propagated errors is to centralize the error-handling. Imagine that when you catch an error, you want to show an error dialog in an iOS or OS X application. If you have error-handling code in dozens of places in your application, making changes is tough, which makes your application resistant to change. To remedy a rigid error-handling setup, you can opt to use a central place to present the errors. When catching code, you can pass the error to an error handler that knows what to do with it, such as presenting a dialog to the user, submitting the error to a diagnostics systems, logging the error to stderr, you name it.

As an example, you can have one error handler that has the same `handleError` function multiple times via function overloads. Thanks to the function overloads, the `ErrorHandler` can get granular control over which error is ready to be presented to the user, and which errors need to fall back on a generic message.

Listing 6.13   An `ErrorHandler` with function overloads

```
struct ErrorHandler {

    static let `default` = ErrorHandler()    ◁─┐    Offer a singleton so that any code can
                                                   reach the error handler (singletons
                                                   are often not a good practice but
                                                   fitting for this example).

    let genericMessage = "Sorry! Something went wrong"    ◁─    You have a generic
                                                                message if you don't
    func handleError(_ error: Error) {    ◁─                    have more information
        presentToUser(message: genericMessage)                 to show to the user.
    }

    func handleError(_ error: LocalizedError) {           The ErrorHandler shows
        if let errorDescription = error.errorDescription {    errors without user-
            presentToUser(message: errorDescription)          specific information
        } else {                                              as a generic message.
            presentToUser(message: genericMessage)
        }
    }                                           Not depicted: you can show an
                                                alert on iOS or OS X. You also
    func presentToUser(message: String) {    ◁─    log to the console or a file.
        // Not depicted: Show alert dialog in iOS or OS X, or print to
        stderror.
        print(message) // Now you log the error to console.
    }

}
```

The ErrorHandler passed an error straight to the user, if it conforms to LocalizedErrors.

IMPLEMENTING THE CENTRALIZED ERROR HANDLER

Let's see how you can best call the centralized error handler. Since you are centralizing error handling, the `RecipeExtractor` doesn't have to both return an optional and handle errors. If the caller also treats the optional as an error, you may end up with double the error handling. Instead, the `RecipeExtractor` can return a regular `Recipe` (non-optional) and pass the error to the caller as shown in the following code. Then the caller can pass any error to the central error handler.

Listing 6.14 `RecipeExtractor` **becomes throwing**

```
struct RecipeExtractor {

    let html: String

    func extractRecipe() throws -> Recipe {
        return try parseHTML(html)
    }

    private func parseHTML(_ html: String) throws -> Recipe {
        let ingredients = try extractIngredients(html)
        let steps = try extractSteps(html)
        return Recipe(ingredients: ingredients, steps: steps)
    }

    // ... snip

}

let html = ... // You can obtain html from a source
let recipeExtractor = RecipeExtractor(html: html)

do {
    let recipe = try recipeExtractor.extractRecipe()
} catch {
    ErrorHandler.default.handleError(error)
}
```

Now, extractRecipe doesn't handle errors and becomes throwing, letting the caller deal with any errors. It can stop returning an optional Recipe. Instead, it can return a regular Recipe.

Any error is propagated to the caller.

The caller can now catch an error and pass it on to a central error handler, which knows how to deal with the error. Note that you don't have to define the error at the catch statement.

If you centralize error handling, you separate error handling from code that focuses on the happy path, and you keep an application in a good state. You not only prevent duplication, but changing the way you treat errors is also easier. You could, for instance, decide to show errors in a different way—such as a notification instead of a dialog box—and only need to change this in a single location.

The tricky part is that you can now have one large error-handling type with the risk of it being giant and complicated. Depending on the needs and size of your application, you can choose to split up this type into smaller handlers that hook into the large error handler. Each smaller handler can then specialize in handling specific errors.

6.2.4 Exercises

3 What's the downside of passing messages for the user inside an error?

4 The following code does not compile. What two changes to `loadFile` can you make to make the code compile (without resorting to `try?` and `try!`)?

```
enum LoadError {
    case couldntLoadFile
}

func loadFile(name: String) -> Data? {
    let url = playgroundSharedDataDirectory.appendingPathComponent(name)
```

```
        do {
            return try Data(contentsOf: url)
        } catch let error as LoadError {
            print("Can't load file named \(name)")
            return nil
        }
    }
```

6.3   *Delivering pleasant APIs*

APIs that throw more often than a major league baseball pitcher are not fun to work with in an application. When APIs are trigger-happy about throwing errors, implementing them can become a nuisance. The burden is placed on the developer to handle these errors. Developers may start to catch all errors in one big net and treat them all the same or let low-level errors propagate down to a customer who doesn't always know what to do with them. Sometimes errors are a nuisance because it may not be apparent to the developer what to do with each error. Alternatively, developers may catch errors with a // TODO: Implement comment that lives forever, swallowing both small and severe errors at the same time, leaving critical issues unnoticed.

Ideally speaking, each error gets the utmost care. But in the real world, deadlines need to be met, features need to be launched, and project managers need to be reassured. Error handling can feel like an obstacle that slows you down, which sometimes results in developers taking the easy road.

On top of that, the way Swift treats errors is that you can't know for sure what errors a function throws. Sure, with some documentation you can communicate which errors to expect from a function or method. But in my experience, having 100% up-to-date documentation can be as common as spotting the Loch Ness monster. Functions start throwing new errors or stop throwing several errors altogether, and chances are you may miss an error or two over time.

APIs are quicker and easier to implement if they don't throw often. But you have to make sure that you don't compromise the quality of an application. With the downsides of error handling in mind, let's go over some techniques to make your APIs friendlier and easier to implement, while still paying attention to problems that may arise in your code.

6.3.1   *Capturing validity within a type*

You can diminish the amount of error handling you need to do by capturing validity within a type.

For instance, a first attempt to validate a phone number is to use a validate-PhoneNumber function, and then continuously use it whenever it's needed. Although having a validatePhoneNumber function isn't wrong, you'll quickly discover how to improve it in the next listing.

Listing 6.15   Validating a phone number

```
enum ValidationError: Error {
    case noEmptyValueAllowed
    case invalidPhoneNumber
}

func validatePhoneNumber(_ text: String) throws {
    guard !text.isEmpty else {
        throw ValidationError.noEmptyValueAllowed
    }

    let pattern = "^(\\([0-9]{3}\\) |[0-9]{3}-)[0-9]{3}-[0-9]{4}$"
    if text.range(of: pattern, options: .regularExpression, range:
    nil, locale: nil) == nil {
        throw ValidationError.invalidPhoneNumber
    }
}

do {
    try validatePhoneNumber("(123) 123-1234")
    print("Phonenumber is valid")
} catch {
    print(error)
}
```

The validate-PhoneNumber function throws an error if it's invalid.

The error has to be caught; for instance, via a do catch statement. But this has to happen every time for the same phone number.

With this approach you may end up validating the same string multiple times: for example, once when entering a form, once more before making an API call, and again when updating a profile. In these recurring places, you put the burden on a developer to handle an error.

Instead, you can capture the validity of a phone number within a type by creating a new type, even though the phone number is only a single string, as shown in the following. You create a PhoneNumber type and give it a throwable initializer that validates the phone number for you. This initializer either throws an error or returns a proper PhoneNumber type, so you can catch any errors right when you create the type.

Listing 6.16   The PhoneNumber type

```
struct PhoneNumber {

    let contents: String

    init(_ text: String) throws {
        guard !text.isEmpty else {
            throw ValidationError.noEmptyValueAllowed
        }

        let pattern = "^(\\([0-9]{3}\\) |[0-9]{3}-)[0-9]{3}-[0-9]{4}$"
        if text.range(of: pattern, options: .regularExpression, range: nil,
        locale: nil) == nil {
            throw ValidationError.invalidPhoneNumber
        }
```

Create a failable initializer.

```
            self.contents = text      ◁─────  If the phone number
    }                                          is validated, the value
}                                              is stored.

do {
    let phoneNumber = try PhoneNumber("(123) 123-1234")  ◁───
    print(phoneNumber.contents) // (123) 123-1234         ◁───
} catch {
    print(error)
}
```

Create the PhoneNumber type. You have to use the try keyword because PhoneNumber has a throwing initializer.

You can read the contents of the phone number throughout your application.

After you obtain a `PhoneNumber`, you can safely pass it around your application with the confidence that a specific phone number is valid and without having to catch errors whenever you want to get the phone number's value. Your methods can accept a `PhoneNumber` type from here on out, and just by looking at the method signatures you know that you're dealing with a valid phone number.

6.3.2   *try?*

You can prevent propagation in other ways as well. If you create a `PhoneNumber` type, you can treat it as an optional instead so that you can avoid an error from propagating higher up.

Once a function is a throwing function, but you're not interested in the reasons for failure, you can consider turning the result of the throwing function into an optional via the `try?` keyword, as shown here.

Listing 6.17   Applying the `try?` keyword

```
let phoneNumber = try? PhoneNumber("(123) 123-1234")
print(phoneNumber) // Optional(PhoneNumber(contents: "(123) 123-1234"))
```

By using `try?`, you stop error propagation. You can use `try?` to reduce various reasons for errors into a single optional. In this case, a `PhoneNumber` could not be created for multiple reasons, and with `try?` you indicate that you're not interested in the reason or error, just that the creation succeeded or not.

6.3.3   *try!*

You can assert that an error won't occur. In that case, like when you force unwrap, either you're right or you get a crash.

If you were to use `try!` to create a `PhoneNumber`, you assert that the creation won't fail.

Listing 6.18   Applying the `try!` keyword.

```
let phoneNumber = try! PhoneNumber("(123) 123-1234")
print(phoneNumber) // PhoneNumber(contents: "(123) 123-1234")
```

The try! keyword saves you from unwrapping an optional. But if you're wrong, the application crashes:

```
let phoneNumber = try! PhoneNumber("Not a phone number") // Crash
```

As with force unwrapping, only use try! when you know better than the compiler. Otherwise, you're playing Russian Roulette.

6.3.4 Returning optionals

Optionals are a way of error handling: either there is a value, or there is not. You can use optionals to signal something is wrong, which is an elegant alternative to throwing errors.

Let's say you want to load a file from Swift's playgrounds, which can fail, but the reason for failure doesn't matter. To remove the burden of error handling for your callers, you can choose to make your function return an optional Data value on failure.

Listing 6.19 Returning an optional

```
                                                   The function returns an
                                                   optional Data value.
func loadFile(name: String) -> Data? {      ◄──┘
    let url = playgroundSharedDataDirectory.appendingPathComponent(name)
    return try? Data(contentsOf: url)       ◄──┐
}                                               You catch any errors that
                                                come from Data and turn
                                                it into an optional.
```

If a function has a single reason for failure and the function returns a value, a rule of thumb is to return an optional instead of throwing an error. If a cause of failure does matter, you can choose to throw an error.

If you're unsure of what a caller is interested in, and you don't mind introducing error types, you can still throw an error. The caller can always decide to turn an error into an optional if needed via the try? keyword.

6.3.5 Exercise

5 Can you name at least three ways to make throwing APIs easier for developers to use?

6.4 Closing thoughts

As you've seen, error handling may sound simple on paper, but applying best practices when dealing with errors is important. One of the worst cases of error handling is that errors get swallowed or ignored. By applying best practices in this chapter, I hope that you've acquired a good arsenal of techniques to combat—and adequately handle—these errors. If you have a taste for more error-handling techniques, you're in luck—chapter 11 covers errors in an asynchronous environment.

Summary

- Even though errors are usually enums, any type can implement the `Error` protocol.

- Inferring from a function which errors it throws isn't possible, but you can use Quick Help to soften the pain.

- Keep throwing code in a predictable state for when an error occurs. You can achieve a predictable state via immutable functions, working with copies or temporary values, and using `defer` to undo any mutations that may occur before an error is thrown.

- You can handle errors four ways: do `catch`, `try?` and `try!`, and propagating them higher in the stack.

- If a function doesn't catch all errors, any error that occurs gets propagated higher up the stack.

- An error can contain technical information to help to troubleshoot. User-facing messages can be deduced from the technical information, by implementing the `LocalizedError` protocol.

- By implementing the `CustomNSError` you can bridge an error to `NSError`.

- A good practice for handling errors is via centralized error handling. With centralized error handling, you can easily change how to handle errors.

- You can prevent throwing errors by turning them into optionals via the `try?` keyword.

- If you're certain that an error won't occur, you can turn to retrieve a value from a throwing function with the `try!` keyword, with the risk of a crashing application.

- If there is a single reason for failure, consider returning an optional instead of creating a throwing function.

- A good practice is to capture validity in a type. Instead of having a throwing function you repeatedly use, create a type with a throwing initializer and pass this type around with the confidence of knowing that the type is validated.

Answers

1 Can you name one or more downsides of how Swift handles errors, and how to compensate for them?

  Functions are marked as throwing, so it places the burden on the developer to handle them. But functions don't reveal which errors are thrown.

  You can add a Quick Help annotation to functions to share which errors can be thrown.

2 Can you name three ways to make sure throwing functions return to their original state after throwing errors?

  – Use immutable functions.

  – Work on copies or temporary values.

  – Use `defer` to reverse mutation that happened before an error is thrown.

3 What's the downside of passing messages for the user inside an error?

Because then it's harder to differentiate between technical information for debugging and information to display to the user.

4 What two changes to loadFile can you make to make the code compile? (without resorting to try! and try?)

Make loadFile catch all errors and not just a specific one. Or make load-File throwing to repropagate the error.

5 Can you name at least three ways to make throwing APIs easier for developers to use?

– Capture an error when creating a type, so an error is handled only on the creation of a type and not passing of a value.

– Return an optional instead of throwing an error when there is a single failing reason.

– Convert an error into an optional with the try? keyword and return the optional.

– Prevent propagation with the try! keyword.

Generics

Generics are a core component of Swift, and they can be tricky to understand at first. There is no shame if you've been staying away from generics, perhaps because they are sometimes intimidating or confusing. Like a carpenter can do work without a hammer, so can you develop software without generics. But making generics part of your regular software routine sure does help, because by using generics you can create code that works on current and future requirements, and it saves much repetition. By using generics, your code ends up more succinct, hard-hitting, boilerplate-reducing, and future-proof.

This chapter starts by looking at the benefits of generics and when and how to apply them. It starts slow, but then ramps up the difficulty by looking at more complex use cases. Generics are a cornerstone of Swift, so it's good to internalize them because they're going to pop up a lot, both in the book and while reading and writing Swift out in the wild.

After enough exposure and "aha" moments, you'll start to feel comfortable in using generics to write hard-hitting, highly reusable code.

You'll discover the purpose and benefits of generics and how they can save you from writing duplicate code. Then, you'll take a closer look at what generics do behind the scenes, and how you can reason about them. At this point, generics should be a little less scary.

In Swift, generics and protocols are vital in creating polymorphic code. You'll find out how to use protocols to *constrain* generics, which enables you to create generic functions with specific behavior. Along the way, this chapter introduces two essential protocols that often coincide with generics: Equatable and Comparable.

Then, to step up your generics game, you'll find out how to constrain generics with multiple protocols, and you'll see how to improve readability with a where clause. The Hashable protocol is introduced, which is another essential protocol that you see often when working with generics.

It all comes together when you create a flexible struct. This struct contains multiple constrained generics and implements the Hashable protocol. Along the way, you'll get a glimpse of a Swift feature called *conditional conformance.*

To further cement your knowledge of generics, you'll learn that generics don't always mix with subclasses. When using both techniques at the same time, you'll need to be aware of a few special rules.

Once generics become part of your toolbox, you may find yourself slimming down your codebase with elegant and highly reusable code. Let's take a look.

7.1 The benefits of generics

JOIN ME! It's more educational and fun if you can check out the code and follow along with the chapter. You can download the source code at http://mng .bz/nQE8.

Let's start small to get a feel for generics. Imagine that you have a function called firstLast that extracts the first and last elements from an array of integers.

> **Listing 7.1 First and last**

```
let (first, last) = firstLast(array: [1,2,3,4,5])
print(first) // 1
print(last) // 5
```

```
func firstLast(array: [Int]) -> (Int, Int) {
    return (array[0], array[array.count-1])
}
```

Now, you'd like the same for arrays containing String. In the following listing, you're defining a similar function, except it's specified to the String type. Swift knows which similarly named function to pick.

Listing 7.2   firstLast with an array of strings

```
func firstLast(array: [String]) -> (String, String) {
    return (array[0], array[array.count-1])
}

let (first, last) = firstLast(array: ["pineapple", "cherry", "steam locomotive"])
print(first) // "pineapple"
print(last) // "steam locomotive"
```

Having to create a new function for each type doesn't quite scale. If you want this method for an array of Double, UIImage, or custom Waffle types, you would have to create new functions every time.

Alternatively, you can write a single function that works with Any, but then the return value of the tuple would be (Any, Any), not (String, String) or (Int, Int). You would have to downcast (Any, Any) to (String, String) or (Int, Int) at runtime.

Reducing boilerplate and avoiding Any is where generics can help. With generics, you can create a function that is polymorphic at compile time. Polymorphic code means that it can work on multiple types. With a generic function, you need to define the function only once, and it works with Int, String, and any other type, including custom types that you introduce or haven't even written yet. With generics, you would not work with Any, saving you from downcasting at runtime.

7.1.1   *Creating a generic function*

Let's compare the nongeneric and the generic version of the firstLast function.

You're adding a generic <T> type parameter to your function signature. Adding a <T> helps you introduce a generic to your function, which you can refer to in the rest of your function. Notice how all you do is define a <T> and replace all occurrences of Int with T.

Listing 7.3   Comparing a generic versus nongeneric function signature

```
// Nongeneric version
func firstLast(array: [Int]) -> (Int, Int) {
    return (array[0], array[array.count-1])
}

// Generic version
func firstLast<T>(array: [T]) -> (T, T) {
    return (array[0], array[array.count-1])
}
```

A CUP OF T? Usually a generic is often defined as type T, which stands for *Type*. Generics tend to be called something abstract such as T, U, or V as a convention. Generics can be words, too, such as Wrapped, as used in Optional.

By declaring a generic T via the <T> syntax, you can refer to this T in the rest of the function—for example, array: [T] and its return type (T, T).

You can refer to T in the body, which is showcased by expanding the body of the function, as shown here.

Listing 7.4 Referencing a generic from the body

```
func firstLast<T>(array: [T]) -> (T, T) {
    let first: T = array[0]
    let last: T = array[array.count-1]
    return (first, last)
}
```

You can see your generic function in action. Notice how your function works on multiple types. You could say your function is type-agnostic.

Listing 7.5 The generic function in action

```
let (firstString, lastString) = firstLast(array: ["pineapple", "cherry",
    "steam locomotive"])
print(firstString) // "pineapple"
print(lastString) // "steam locomotive"
```

If you were to inspect the values firstString or lastString, you could see that they are of type String, as opposed to Any. You can pass custom types, too, as demonstrated next by the Waffle struct shown here.

Listing 7.6 Custom types

```
// Custom types work, too
struct Waffle {
    let size: String
}

let (firstWaffle: Waffle, lastWaffle: Waffle) = firstLast(array: [
    Waffle(size: "large"),
    Waffle(size: "extra-large"),
    Waffle(size: "snack-size")
    ])

print(firstWaffle) // Waffle(size: "large")
print(lastWaffle) // Waffle(size: "snack-size")
```

That's all it takes. Thanks to generics, you can use one function for an array holding Int, String, Waffle, or anything else, and you're getting concrete types back. You aren't juggling with Any or downcasting at runtime; the compiler declares everything at compile time.

WHY NOT WRITE GENERICS STRAIGHT AWAY? Starting with a nongeneric function and later replacing all types with a generic is easier than starting to write a generic function from the get-go. But if you're feeling confident, go ahead and write a generic function right away!

7.1.2 *Reasoning about generics*

Reasoning about generics can be hard and abstract. Sometimes a T is a String, and at a different time it's an Int, and so forth. You can wrap both an integer and a string inside an array via the use of a generic function as shown here.

Listing 7.7 Wrapping a value inside an array

```
func wrapValue<T>(value: T) -> [T] {
    return [value]
}

wrapValue(value: 30) // [30]
wrapValue(value: "Howdy!") // ["Howdy!"]
```

But you can't specialize the type from *inside* the function body; this is to say, you can't pass a T and turn it into an Int value from inside the function body.

Listing 7.8 A faulty generic function

```
func illegalWrap<T>(value: T) -> [Int] {
    return [value]
}
```

Listing 7.8 produces a Swift compiler error:

```
Cannot convert value of type 'T' to expected element type 'Int'.
```

When working with generics, Swift generates specialized code at compile time. You can think of it as the generic `wrapValue` function turning into specialized functions for you to use, sort of like a prism where a white light goes in, and colors come out (see figure 7.1 and the listing that follows).

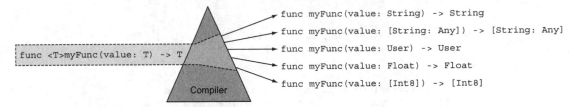

Figure 7.1 **Generic code is turned to specialized code at compile time.**

Listing 7.9 The `wrapValue` function

```
// Given this generic function...
func wrapValue<T>(value: T) -> [T] { ... }

// ... you get access to specialized functions.
func wrapValue(value: Int) -> [Int] { ... }
func wrapValue(value: String) -> [String] { ... }
func wrapValue(value: YourOwnType) -> [YourOwnType] { ... }
```

Swift creates multiple `wrapValue` functions behind the scenes—a process called *monomorphization* where the compiler turns polymorphic code into concrete singular code. Swift is clever enough to prevent tons of code generation to prevent large binaries. Swift uses various tricks involving metadata to limit the amount of code generation. In this case, the compiler creates a low-level `wrapValue` function. Then, for relevant types, Swift generates metadata, called *value witness tables*. At runtime, Swift passes the corresponding metadata to the low-level representation of `wrapValue` when needed.

The compiler is smart enough to minimize the amount of metadata generated. Because Swift can make smart decisions about when and how to generate code, you don't have to worry about large binary files—also known as *code bloat*—or extra-long compilation times!

Another significant benefit of generics in Swift is that you know what values you're dealing with at compile time. If you were to inspect the return value of `wrapValue`—by Alt-clicking it in Xcode—you could already see that it returns a `[String]` or `[Int]`, or anything that you put in there. You can inspect types before you even consider running the application, making it easier to reason about polymorphic types.

7.1.3 *Exercise*

1 Which of the following functions compile? Confirm this by running the code:

```
func wrap<T>(value: Int, secondValue: T) -> ([Int], U) {
    return ([value], secondValue)
}
```

```
func wrap<T>(value: Int, secondValue: T) -> ([Int], T) {
    return ([value], secondValue)
}

func wrap(value: Int, secondValue: T) -> ([Int], T) {
    return ([value], secondValue)
}

func wrap<T>(value: Int, secondValue: T) -> ([Int], Int) {
    return ([value], secondValue)
}

func wrap<T>(value: Int, secondValue: T) -> ([Int], Int)? {
    if let secondValue = secondValue as? Int {
        return ([value], secondValue)
    } else {
        return nil
    }
}
```

2   What's the benefit of using generics over the Any type (for example, writing a function as func<T>(process: [T]) versus func(process:[Any]))?

7.2   *Constraining generics*

Earlier, you saw how you worked with a generic type T, which could be anything. The generic T in your previous examples is an *unconstrained* generic. But when a type can be anything you also can't do much with it.

You can narrow down what a generic represents by constraining it with a protocol; let's see how this works.

7.2.1   *Needing a constrained function*

Imagine that you want to write a generic function that gives you the lowest value inside an array. This function is set up generically so that it works on an array with any type, as shown here.

Listing 7.10   **Running the** `lowest` **function**

```
lowest([3,1,2]) // Optional(1)
lowest([40.2, 12.3, 99.9]) // Optional(12.3)
lowest(["a","b","c"]) // Optional("a")
```

The lowest function can return nil when the passed array is empty, which is why the values are optional.

Your first attempt is to create the function with a generic parameter of type T. But you'll quickly discover in the following code that the function signature is lacking something.

Listing 7.11 The `lowest` function (will compile soon, but not yet)

```
// The function signature is not finished yet!
func lowest<T>(_ array: [T]) -> T? {
    let sortedArray = array.sorted { (lhs, rhs) -> Bool in
        return lhs < rhs
    }
    return sortedArray.first
}

lowest([1,2,3])
```

Sort an array by passing it a closure.

This line of code compares two values inside the array. If lhs is considered lower than rhs, you end up with an ascending array.

The lowest function returns the lowest compared value.

LHS AND RHS lhs stands for "left hand side." rhs stands for "right hand side." This is a convention when comparing two of the same types.

Unfortunately, listing 7.11 won't work. Swift throws the following error:

```
error: binary operator '<' cannot be applied to two 'T' operands
        if lowest < value {
        ~~~~~~ ^ ~~~~~
```

The error occurs because T could be anything. Still, you're performing actions on it, such as comparing the T with another T via the < operator. But since T represents anything, the lowest function doesn't know it can compare T values.

Let's find out how you can fix lowest with a protocol. First, you'll take a little detour to learn about two key protocols, which you'll need to finish the lowest function.

7.2.2 The Equatable and Comparable protocols

Protocols define an interface with requirements, such as which functions or variables to implement. Types that conform to a protocol implement the required functions and variables. You've already observed this in earlier chapters when you made types conform to the CustomStringConvertible protocol or the RawRepresentable protocol.

The prevalent Equatable protocol allows you to check if two types are equal. Such types can be integers, strings, and many others, including your custom types:

```
5 == 5 // true
30231 == 2 // false
"Generics are hard!" == "Generics are easy!" // false
```

When a type conforms to the Equatable protocol, that type needs to implement the static == function, as shown here.

Listing 7.12 Equatable

```
public protocol Equatable {
    static func == (lhs: Self, rhs: Self) -> Bool
}
```

NOTE For structs and enums, Swift can synthesize the Equatable implementation for you, which saves you from manually implementing the == method.

Another common protocol that Swift offers is `Comparable`. Types conforming to `Comparable` can be compared with each other, to see which value is more, or less, than the other value:

```
5 > 2 // true
3.2 <= 1.3 // false
"b" > "a" // true
```

Interestingly, `Comparable` also consists of static functions, but that's not a requirement for protocols.

Listing 7.13 Comparable

```
public protocol Comparable : Equatable {     <──┐
    static func < (lhs: Self, rhs: Self) -> Bool
    static func <= (lhs: Self, rhs: Self) -> Bool
    static func >= (lhs: Self, rhs: Self) -> Bool
    static func > (lhs: Self, rhs: Self) -> Bool
}
```

Types implementing Comparable will also need to implement Equatable.

When a type conforms to Comparable, the <, <=, >=, and > plus == become available for use on a type.

Both `Comparable` and `Equatable` are highly prevalent, and both live in the core Swift library.

7.2.3 *Constraining means specializing*

Back to the problem. Your `lowest` function was comparing two T types, but T is not yet `Comparable`. You can specialize the `lowest` function by indicating that T conforms to `Comparable`, as shown here.

Listing 7.14 Constraining a generic

```
// Before. Didn't compile.
func lowest<T>(_ array: [T]) -> T? {

// After. The following signature is correct.
func lowest<T: Comparable>(_ array: [T]) -> T? {
```

Inside the `lowest` function scope, T represents anything that conforms to `Comparable`. The code compiles again and works on multiple `Comparable` types, such as integers, floats, strings, and anything else that conforms to `Comparable`.

Here's the full `lowest` function.

Listing 7.15 The `lowest` function

```
func lowest<T: Comparable>(_ array: [T]) -> T? {
    let sortedArray = array.sorted { (lhs, rhs) -> Bool in
        return lhs < rhs
    }
    return sortedArray.first
}
```

You earlier recognized how sorted takes two values and returns a Bool. But sorted can use the power of protocols if all its elements are Comparable. You only need to call the sorted method without arguments, making the function body much shorter.

Listing 7.16 The lowest function (shortened)

```
func lowest<T: Comparable>(_ array: [T]) -> T? {
    return array.sorted().first
}
```

7.2.4 Implementing Comparable

You can apply lowest to your types, too. First, create an enum conforming to Comparable. This enum represents three royal ranks that you can compare. Then, you'll pass an array of this enum to the lowest function.

Listing 7.17 The RoyalRank enum, adhering to Comparable

```
enum RoyalRank: Comparable {        ◄──┐  The RoyalRank enum
    case emperor                         implements the
    case king                            Comparable protocol.
    case duke

    static func <(lhs: RoyalRank, rhs: RoyalRank) -> Bool {   ◄──┐ Implement <
        switch (lhs, rhs) {        ◄──┐                             to conform to
            case (king, emperor): return true    Pattern match      Comparable.
            case (duke, emperor): return true    to see if one
            case (duke, king): return true       case is lower
            default: return false                than the other.
        }
    }
}
```

To make RoyalRank adhere to Comparable, you usually would need to implement == from Equatable. Luckily, Swift synthesizes this method for you, saving you from writing an implementation. On top of this, you also would need to implement the four methods from Comparable. But you only need to implement the < method, because with the implementations for both the < and == methods, Swift can deduce all other implementations for Comparable. As a result, you only need to implement the < method, saving you from writing some boilerplate.

You made RoyalRank adhere to Comparable—and indirectly to Equatable—so now you can compare ranks against each other, or pass an array of them to your lowest function as in the following.

Listing 7.18 Comparable in action

```
let king = RoyalRank.king
let duke = RoyalRank.duke

duke < king // true
duke > king // false
duke == king // false
```

```
let ranks: [RoyalRank] = [.emperor, .king, .duke]
lowest(ranks) // .duke
```

One of the benefits of generics is that you can write functions for types that don't even exist yet. If you introduce new `Comparable` types in the future, you can pass them to `lowest` without extra work!

7.2.5   *Constraining vs. flexibility*

Not all types are `Comparable`. If you passed an array of Booleans, for instance, you'd get an error:

```
lowest([true, false])
```

```
error: in argument type '[Bool]', 'Bool' does not conform to expected type
    'Comparable'
```

Booleans do not conform to `Comparable`. As a result, the `lowest` function won't work on an array with Booleans.

Constraining a generic means trading flexibility for functionality. A constrained generic becomes more specialized but is less flexible.

7.3   *Multiple constraints*

Often, one single protocol won't solve all your problems when constraining to it.

Imagine a scenario where you not only want to keep track of the lowest values inside an array but also their occurrences. You would have to compare the values and probably store them in a dictionary to keep track of their occurrences. If you need a generic that can be compared and stored in a dictionary, you require that the generic conforms to both the `Comparable` and `Hashable` protocols.

You haven't looked at the `Hashable` protocol yet; do that now before seeing how to constrain a generic to multiple protocols.

7.3.1   *The Hashable protocol*

Types conforming to the `Hashable` protocol can be reduced to a single integer called a *hash value*. The act of hashing is done via a hashing function, which turns a type into an integer (see figure 7.2).

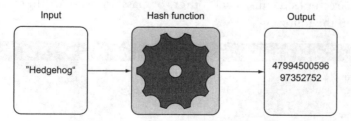

Figure 7.2   In Swift, a hashing function turns a value into an integer.

NOTE Hashing functions are a complex topic. Providing a deep understanding of them is outside the scope of this book.

Hashable types can be used as dictionary keys, or part of a Set, amongst other use cases. One common Hashable type is String.

Listing 7.19 A String as a dictionary key

```
let dictionary = [
    "I am a key": "I am a value",
    "I am another key": "I am another value",
]
```

Integers are also Hashable; they can also serve as dictionary keys or be stored inside a Set:

```
let integers: Set = [1, 2, 3, 4]
```

Many built-in types that are Equatable are also Hashable, such as Int, String, Character, and Double.

TAKING A CLOSER LOOK AT THE HASHABLE PROTOCOL

The Hashable protocol defines a method that accepts a hasher; the implementing type can then feed values to this hasher. Note in this example that the Hashable protocol extends Equatable.

Listing 7.20 The Hashable protocol

```
public protocol Hashable : Equatable {     ◁——  Types conforming to Hashable also
    func hash(into hasher: inout Hasher)         have to conform to Equatable.
    // ... details omitted               ◁——  Types conforming to Hashable must
}                                                offer the func hash (into hasher:
                                                 inout Hasher) method.
```

Types adhering to Hashable need to offer the static == method from Equatable and the func hash(into hasher: inout Hasher) method from Hashable.

NOTE Just like it can with Equatable, Swift can synthesize implementations for Hashable for free on structs and enums, which is showcased in section 4.4.

7.3.2 Combining constraints

To create the lowestOccurences function as mentioned earlier, you need a generic type that conforms both to Hashable and Comparable. Conforming to two protocols is possible when you constrain a generic to multiple types, as shown in figure 7.3 and listing 7.21.

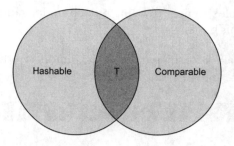

Figure 7.3 A generic that conforms to two protocols.

The lowestOccurrence function has a generic T type which is constrained to both the Comparable and Hashable protocols with the help of the & operator.

Listing 7.21   Combining constraints

```
func lowestOccurrences<T: Comparable & Hashable>(values: [T]) -> [T: Int] {
    // ... snip
}
```

Now T can be compared and put inside a dictionary inside the function body.

If a generic signature gets a bit hard to read, you can use a where clause, as an alternative, which goes at the end of a function, as shown here.

Listing 7.22   where clause

```
func lowestOccurrences<T>(values: [T]) -> [T: Int]       ◁   You still write a
    where T: Comparable & Hashable {       ◁─┐               generic as before.
    // ... snip                               │
}                       The constraints go at the
                           end of the function
                         inside a where clause. │
```

These are two different styles of writing generic constraints, but they both work the same.

7.3.3 *Exercises*

3 Write a function that, given an array, returns a dictionary of the occurrences of each element inside the array.

4 Create a logger that prints a generic type's description and debug description when passed.

Hint: Besides CustomStringConvertible, which makes sure types implement a description property, Swift also offers CustomDebugStringConvertible, which makes type implement a debugDescription property.

7.4   *Creating a generic type*

Thus far, you've been applying generics to your functions. But you can also make *types* generic.

In chapter 4, you delved into how Optional uses a generic type called Wrapped to store its value, as shown in the following listing.

Listing 7.23 The generic type `Wrapped`

```
public enum Optional<Wrapped> {
  case none
  case some(Wrapped)
}
```

Another generic type is `Array`. You write them as `[Int]` or `[String]` or something similar, which is syntactic sugar. Secretly, the syntax is `Array<Element>`, such as `Array<Int>`, which also compiles.

Let's use this section to create your generic struct that helps you combine `Hashable` types. The goal is to make clear how to juggle multiple generics at once while you work with the `Hashable` protocol.

7.4.1 *Wanting to combine two Hashable types*

Unfortunately, using two `Hashable` types as a key for a dictionary isn't possible, even if this key consists out of two `Hashable` types. In particular, you can combine two strings—which are `Hashable`—into a tuple and try to pass it as a dictionary key as shown here.

Listing 7.24 Using a tuple as a key for a dictionary

```
let stringsTuple = ("I want to be part of a key", "Me too!")
let anotherDictionary = [stringsTuple: "I am a value"]
```

But Swift quickly puts a stop to it.

Listing 7.25 Error when using a tuple as a key

```
error: type of expression is ambiguous without more context
let anotherDictionary = [stringsTuple: "I am a value"]
                         ^~~~~~~~~~~~~~~~~~~~~~~~~~~~~~~
```

As soon as you put two `Hashable` types inside a tuple, that tuple isn't `Hashable` anymore. Swift doesn't offer a way to combine the two hash values from a tuple. You'll solve this problem by creating a `Pair` type that contains two `Hashable` properties.

7.4.2 *Creating a Pair type*

You can combine two `Hashable` types by introducing a new generic struct that you'll call `Pair`. The `Pair` type accepts two `Hashable` types and will be made `Hashable` itself, too, as shown in this listing.

Listing 7.26 `Pair` type in action

```
let keyPair = Pair("I want to be part of a key", "Me too!")
let anotherDictionary = [keyPair: "I am a value"] // This works.
```

`Pair` can store two types, which are `Hashable`. A first naive approach may be to declare a single generic T, as shown in the next listing.

Listing 7.27   Introducing `Pair`

```
struct Pair<T: Hashable> {
    let left: T
    let right: T

    init(_ left: T, _ right: T) {
      self.left = left
      self.right = right
    }
}
```

The Pair struct contains a pair of T types, which are constrained to Hashable.

The first Hashable property of the pair

The second Hashable property of the pair

Pair isn't Hashable yet, but you'll get to that shortly. First, there is a different problem—can you guess it?

7.4.3   Multiple generics

Since T is used for both values, `Pair` gets specialized to types such as the following.

Listing 7.28   `Pair` is specialized: the `left` and `right` properties are of the same type

```
struct Pair {
  let left: Int
  let right: Int
}

struct Pair {
  let left: String
  let right: String
}
```

Currently, you can't have a `Pair` where the `left` property is one type—such as a `String`—and the right property is something else, such as an `Int`.

POP QUIZ   Before continuing, can you guess how to fix `Pair` so that it accepts two separate types?

You can make sure that `Pair` accepts two separate (or the same) types by defining two different generics on `Pair`.

Listing 7.29   `Pair` accepts two generics

```
struct Pair<T: Hashable, U: Hashable> {
    let left: T
    let right: U

    init(_ left: T, _ right: U) {
      self.left = left
      self.right = right
    }
}
```

The right property is now a U type.

Pair now accepts two generic types, T and U. Both are constrained to Hashable.

The initializer is also updated to accept a U type.

Now `Pair` can accept two different types, such as a `String` and `Int`, but also two similar types as shown here.

Listing 7.30 `Pair` accepts mixed types

```
// Pair accepts mixed types
let pair = Pair("Tom", 20)

// Same types such as two strings are still okay
let pair = Pair("Tom", "Jerry")
```

By introducing multiple generic types, `Pair` becomes more flexible because the compiler separately specializes the `T` and `U` types.

7.4.4 Conforming to Hashable

Currently, `Pair` isn't `Hashable` yet—you'll fix that now.

To create a hash value for `Pair`, you have two options: you can let Swift synthesize the implementation for you, or you can create your own. First, do it the easy way where Swift synthesizes the `Hashable` implementation for you, saving you from writing boilerplate.

Introduced in version 4.1, Swift has a fancy technique called *conditional conformance*, which allows you to automatically conform certain types to the `Hashable` or `Equatable` protocol. If all its properties conform to these protocols, Swift synthesizes all the required methods for you. For instance, if all properties are `Hashable`, `Pair` can automatically be `Hashable`.

In this case, all you need to do is make `Pair` conform to `Hashable`, and you don't need to give an implementation; this works as long as both `left` and `right` are `Hashable`, as in this example.

Listing 7.31 `Pair` accepts two generics

```
struct Pair<T: Hashable, U: Hashable>: Hashable {      ◁─┐  Pair now conforms
    let left: T                                           │  to Hashable as well.
    let right: U        ┐  You don't need to do anything
                        │  special because left and right
    // ... snip         │  are Hashable, too.
}
```

Swift now creates a hash value for `Pair`. With little effort, you can use `Pair` as a `Hashable` type, such as adding them to a `Set`.

Listing 7.32 Adding a `Pair` to a `Set`

```
let pair = Pair<Int, Int>(10, 20)
print(pair.hashValue) // 5280472796840031924

let set: Set = [
  Pair("Laurel", "Hardy"),
  Pair("Harry", "Lloyd")
]
```

BEING EXPLICIT   Notice how you can explicitly specify the types inside the `Pair` by using the `Pair<Int, Int>` syntax.

Since `Pair` is `Hashable`, you can pass it a hasher, which `Pair` updates with values, as shown here.

Listing 7.33   Passing a hasher to `Pair`

```
let pair = Pair("Madonna", "Cher")

var hasher = Hasher()
hasher.combine(pair)
// alternatively: pair.hash(into: &hasher)
let hash = hasher.finalize()
print(hash) // 4922525492756211419
```

You can also create a manual hasher and pass it to Pair.

You can pass hasher to pair in a different manner, too.

Once you call finalize(), you obtain a hash value.

There isn't one winning hasher. Some hashers are fast, some are slow but more secure, and some are better at cryptography. Because you can pass custom hashers, you keep control of how and when to hash types. Then a `Hashable` type such as `Pair` keeps control of what to hash.

MANUALLY IMPLEMENTING HASHABLE

Swift can synthesize a `Hashable` implementation for structs and enums. But synthesizing `Equatable` and `Hashable` implementations won't work on classes. Also, perhaps you'd like more control over them.

In these cases, implementing `Hashable` manually makes more sense. Let's see how.

You can consolidate the hash values from the two properties inside `Pair` by implementing the `func hash(into hasher: inout Hasher)` method. In this method, you call `combine` for each value you want to include in the hashing operation. You also implement the static `==` method from `Equatable`, in which you compare both values from two pairs.

Listing 7.34   Implementing `Hashable` manually

```
struct Pair<T: Hashable, U: Hashable>: Hashable {

    // ... snip

    func hash(into hasher: inout Hasher) {
        hasher.combine(left)
        hasher.combine(right)
    }

    static func ==(lhs: Pair<T, U>, rhs: Pair<T, U>) -> Bool {
        return lhs.left == rhs.left && lhs.right == rhs.right
    }

}
```

For Pair to conform to Hashable, Pair needs to implement the func hash(into hasher: inout Hasher) method.

Compare two Pair types by comparing their left and right properties.

Call combine on the supplied hasher for each value you want to hash.

To conform to Hashable, you must also conform to Equatable. Do this by implementing the static == method where you compare two Pair types.

Writing `Pair` took some steps, but you have a type that is flexible and highly reusable across projects. Which other generic structs can make your life easier? Perhaps a parser that turns a dictionary into a concrete type, or a struct that can write away any type to a file.

7.4.5   Exercise

5   Write a generic cache that allows you to store values by `Hashable` keys.

7.5   Generics and subtypes

This section covers subclassing mixed with generics. It's a bit theoretical, but it does shed a little light on some tricky situations if you want to understand generics on a deeper level.

Subclassing is one way to achieve polymorphism; generics are another. Once you start mixing the two, you must be aware of some rules, because generics become unintuitive once you intertwine these two polymorphism mechanisms. Swift hides many complexities behind polymorphism, so you usually don't have to worry about theory. But you're going to hit a wall sooner or later once you use subclassing in combination with generics, in which case a little theory can be useful. To understand subclassing and generics, you need to dive into a bit of theory called *subtype polymorphism* and *variance*.

7.5.1   Subtyping and invariance

Imagine that you're modeling data for an online education website where a subscriber can start specific courses. Consider the following class structure: the `OnlineCourse` class is a superclass for courses, such as `SwiftOnTheServer`, which inherits from `OnlineCourse`. You're omitting the details to focus on generics, as given here.

Listing 7.35   Two classes

```
class OnlineCourse {
    func start() {
        print("Starting online course.")
    }
}

class SwiftOnTheServer: OnlineCourse {
    override func start() {
        print("Starting Swift course.")
    }
}
```

As a small reminder of subclassing in action: whenever an `OnlineCourse` is defined, such as on a variable, you can assign it to a `SwiftOnTheServer`, as shown in the next listing, since they both are of type `OnlineCourse`.

Listing 7.36   Assigning a subclass to superclass

```
var swiftCourse: SwiftOnTheServer = SwiftOnTheServer()
var course: OnlineCourse = swiftCourse // is allowed
course.start() // "Starting Swift course".
```

You could state that `SwiftOnTheServer` is a *subtype* of `OnlineCourse`. Usually, subtypes refer to subclassing. But sometimes a subtype isn't about subclassing. For instance, an `Int` is a subtype of an optional `Int?`, because whenever an `Int?` is expected, you can pass a regular `Int`.

7.5.2   *Invariance in Swift*

Passing a subclass when your code expects a superclass is all fine and dandy. But once a generic type wraps a superclass, you lose subtyping capabilities. For example, you're introducing a generic `Container` holding a value of type `T`. Then you try to assign `Container<SwiftOnTheServer>` to `Container<OnlineCourse>`, just like before where you assigned `SwiftOnTheServer` to `OnlineCourse`. Unfortunately, you can't do this, as shown in figure 7.4.

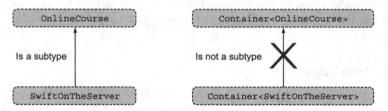

Figure 7.4   Subtyping doesn't apply to `Container`

Even though `SwiftOnTheServer` is a subtype of `OnlineCourse`, `Container<Swift-OnTheServer>` is not a subtype of `Container<OnlineCourse>`, as demonstrated in this listing.

Listing 7.37   `Container`

```
struct Container<T> {}

var containerSwiftCourse: Container<SwiftOnTheServer> =
➥ Container<SwiftOnTheServer>()
var containerOnlineCourse: Container<OnlineCourse> = containerSwiftCourse

error: cannot convert value of type 'Container<SwiftOnTheServer>' to
➥ specified type 'Container<OnlineCourse>'
```

Let's see this shortcoming in a scenario slightly closer to real life. Imagine a generic `Cache` that stores data. You'd like to refresh a cache that holds online courses via the `refreshCache` method, as follows.

Listing 7.38   Cache

```
struct Cache<T> {
    // methods omitted
}
func refreshCache(_ cache: Cache<OnlineCourse>) {
    // ... snip
}
```

But here it shows again that, you can only pass `Cache<OnlineCourse>` types, but not `Cache<SwiftOnTheServer>`.

Listing 7.39   Invariance in action

```
refreshCache(Cache<OnlineCourse>()) // This is allowed
refreshCache(Cache<SwiftOnTheServer>()) // error: cannot convert
➡ value of type 'Cache<SwiftOnTheServer>' to expected argument type
➡ 'Cache<OnlineCourse>'
```

Swift's generics are *invariant*, which states that just because a generic type wraps a subclass, it does *not* make it a subtype of a generic wrapping its superclass. My best guess why this is? Because Swift is relatively young, and invariance is a safe way to handle polymorphism until the language gets fleshed out more.

7.5.3   *Swift's generic types get special privileges*

To make things even more confusing, Swift's generic types, such as `Array` or `Optional`, do allow for subtyping with generics. In other words, Swift's types from the standard library do not have the limitation you just witnessed. Only the generics that you define yourself have the limitations.

For better comparison, write out optionals as their true generic counterpart; for example, `Optional<OnlineCourse>` instead of the syntactic sugar `OnlineCourse?`. Then you'll pass an `Optional<SwiftOnTheServer>` to a function accepting an `Optional<OnlineCourse>`. Remember, this was illegal for your generic `Container`, but now it's fine.

Listing 7.40   Swift's types are covariant

```
func readOptionalCourse(_ value: Optional<OnlineCourse>) {
    // ... snip
}

readOptionalCourse(OnlineCourse()) // This is allowed.
readOptionalCourse(SwiftOnTheServer()) // This is allowed, Optional is covariant.
```

Swift's built-in generic types are *covariant*, which means that generic types can be subtypes of other generic types. Covariance explains why you can pass an `Int` to a method expecting an `Int?`.

You're flying economy while Swift's types are enjoying extra legroom in the business class. Hopefully, it's only a matter of time until your generic types can be covariant, too.

At first thought, it might be frustrating when you're running into a situation where you want to mix generics and subclasses. Honestly, you can get pretty far without subclassing. In fact, if you're not using specific frameworks that depend on subclassing, such as UIKit, you can deliver a complete application without subclassing at all. Making your classes `final` by default can also help to disincentivize subclassing and stimulate protocols and extensions to add functionality to classes. This book highlights multiple alternatives to subclassing that Swift offers.

7.6 *Closing thoughts*

Having read this chapter, I hope you feel confident in your ability to create generic components in your projects.

Abstractions come at a cost. Code becomes a bit more complicated and harder to interpret with generics. But you gain a lot of flexibility in return. With a bit of practice, it may seem like the *Matrix* (if you're familiar with the film), where looking at these `T`, `U`, and `V` types will turn them into blondes, brunettes, and redheads, or perhaps `String`, `Int`, and `Float`.

The more comfortable you are with generics, the easier it is to shrink the size of your codebase and write more reusable components. I can't express enough how important understanding generics on a fundamental level is, because generics keep returning in other chapters and in many Swift types in the wild.

Summary

- Adding an unconstrained generic to a function allows a function to work with all types.
- Generics can't be specialized from inside the scope of a function or type.
- Generic code is converted to specialized code that works on multiple types.
- Generics can be constrained for more specialized behavior, which may exclude some types.
- A type can be constrained to multiple generics to unlock more functionality on a generic type.
- Swift can synthesize implementations for the `Equatable` and `Hashable` protocols on structs and enums.
- Synthesizing default implementations doesn't work on classes.
- Generics that you write are invariant, and therefore you cannot use them as subtypes.
- Generic types in the standard library are covariant, and you can use them as subtypes.

Answers

1 Which of the functions will compile? Confirm this by running the code.

This one will work:

```swift
func wrap<T>(value: Int, secondValue: T) -> ([Int], T) {
    return ([value], secondValue)
}
```

Also, this one will work:

```swift
func wrap<T>(value: Int, secondValue: T) -> ([Int], Int)? {
    if let secondValue = secondValue as? Int {
        return ([value], secondValue)
    } else {
        return nil
    }
}
```

2 What's the benefit of using generics over the `Any` type (for example, writing a function as `func<T>(process: [T])` versus `func(process: [Any])`)?

By using a generic, code is made polymorphic at compile time. By using `Any`, you have to downcast at runtime.

3 Write a function that, given an array, returns a dictionary of the occurrences of each element inside the array:

```swift
func occurrences<T: Hashable>(values: [T]) -> [T: Int] {
    var groupedValues = [T: Int]()

    for element in values {
        groupedValues[element, default: 0] += 1
    }

    return groupedValues
}

print(occurrences(values: ["A", "A", "B", "C", "A"])) // ["C": 1,
    "B": 1, "A": 3]
```

4 Create a logger that will print a generic type's description and `debugDescription` when passed:

```swift
struct CustomType: CustomDebugStringConvertible, CustomStringConvertible {
    var description: String {
        return "This is my description"
    }

    var debugDescription: String {
        return "This is my debugDescription"
    }
}
```

```
struct Logger {
    func log<T>(type: T)
        where T: CustomStringConvertible & CustomDebugStringConvertible {
            print(type.debugDescription)
            print(type.description)
    }
}

let logger = Logger()
logger.log(type: CustomType())
```

5 Write a generic cache that allows you to store values by Hashable keys:

```
class MiniCache<T: Hashable, U> {

    var cache = [T: U]()

    init() {}

    func insert(key: T, value: U) {
        cache[key] = value
    }

    func read(key: T) -> U? {
        return cache[key]
    }

}

let cache = MiniCache<Int, String>()
cache.insert(key: 100, value: "Jeff")
cache.insert(key: 200, value: "Miriam")
cache.read(key: 200) // Optional("Miriam")
cache.read(key: 99) // Optional("Miriam")
```

Putting the pro in protocol-oriented programming

This chapter covers

- The relationship and trade-offs between generics and using protocols as types
- Understanding associated types
- Passing around protocols with associated types
- Storing and constraining protocols with associated types
- Simplifying your API with protocol inheritance

Protocols bring a lot of power and flexibility to your code. Some might say it's Swift's flagship feature, especially since Apple markets Swift as a *protocol-oriented-programming* language. But as lovely as protocols are, they can become difficult fast. Plenty of subtleties are involved, such as using protocols at runtime or compile time, and constraining protocols with associated types.

This chapter's goal is to lay down a solid foundation regarding protocols; it will shed light on using protocols as an interface versus using protocols to constrain generics. This chapter also aims to carry you over the hump of what can be considered advanced protocols, which are protocols with associated types. The end goal is to make sure you understand why, when, and how to apply protocols (and generics) in multiple scenarios. The only requirements are that you're at least a little bit

145

familiar with protocols and that you have read chapter 7, "Generics." After this chapter, protocols and associated types will repeatedly return, so I recommend not to skip this one!

First, you'll take a look to see how protocols fare by themselves, versus using protocols to constrain generics. You'll look at both sides of the coin and take on two approaches. One approach uses generics, and the other does not. The aim of this chapter is that you'll be able to make trade-offs and decide on a proper approach in day-to-day programming.

In the second section, you'll move on to the more difficult aspect of protocols, which is when you start using associated types. You can consider protocols with associated types as generic protocols, and you'll discover why you would need them and when you can apply them in your applications.

Once you start passing around protocols with associated types, you're working with very flexible code. But things will get tricky. You'll take a closer look to see how to pass protocols with associated types around, and how to create types that store them with constraints. On top of that, you'll apply a nice trick to clean up your APIs by using a technique called protocol inheritance.

8.1   Runtime versus compile time

So far, this book has covered generics extensively and how they relate to protocols. With generics, you create polymorphic functions defined at compile time. But protocols don't always have to be used with generics if you want to gain particular runtime—also known as *dynamic dispatch*—benefits. In this section, you're going to create a protocol, and then you'll see how to make trade-offs between generics constrained by protocols, and how to use protocols as types without using generics.

8.1.1   Creating a protocol

> **JOIN ME!** It's more educational and fun if you can check out the code and follow along with the chapter. You can download the source code at http://mng .bz/qJZ2.

You'll start building a cryptocoin portfolio that can hold coins such as Bitcoin, Ethereum, Litecoin, Neo, Dogecoin, and a bazillion others.

You don't want to write a portfolio or function for each coin, especially with the hundreds of other coins that your application may support. You've seen before how you can use enums to work with polymorphism, which is often a suitable approach. But enums, in this case, would be too restrictive. You would have to declare a case for each coin (which could be hundreds!). Alternatively, what if you offer a framework, but then implementers can't add more cases to the types of coins? In these cases, you can use protocols, which are a more flexible way to achieve polymorphism. If you introduce a protocol, you and others can adhere to this protocol for each coin.

To showcase this method, you'll introduce a protocol, as shown in the following listing, called `CryptoCurrency`, with four properties called `name`, `symbol`, and `price` (for the current price in the user's currency setting) and `holdings` (representing the number of coins a user has).

Listing 8.1 A `CryptoCurrency` protocol

```
import Foundation

protocol CryptoCurrency {
    var name: String { get }
    var symbol: String { get }
    var holdings: Double { get set }
    var price: NSDecimalNumber? { get set }
}
```

You are taking advantage of commonalities where you define the minimum properties that each coin should have. Protocols are like blueprints in this way; you can write functions and properties that work only on a `CryptoCurrency` protocol, not needing to know about the coin that's passed to it.

As a next step, you declare a few coins that adhere to this protocol.

Listing 8.2 Declaring coins

```
struct Bitcoin: CryptoCurrency {
    let name = "Bitcoin"
    let symbol = "BTC"
    var holdings: Double
    var price: NSDecimalNumber?
}

struct Ethereum: CryptoCurrency {
    let name = "Ethereum"
    let symbol = "ETH"
    var holdings: Double
    var price: NSDecimalNumber?
}
```

VAR OR LET Whenever you declare properties on a protocol, they are always a var. The implementer can then choose to make it a `let` or `var` property. Also, if the protocol has a `get set` modifier on a property, the implementer has to offer a var to allow for mutation.

8.1.2 *Generics versus protocols*

Let's build a portfolio that can hold some coins for a customer. You've seen before how you can use generics to work with a protocol. You'll start with the next listing by taking the generics approach and quickly see the problem that accompanies it.

Listing 8.3   Introducing a portfolio (won't fully work yet!)

```
final class Portfolio<Coin: CryptoCurrency> {          Declare a
    var coins: [Coin]                                   generic.
                                     Store the coins
    init(coins: [Coin]) {            with generic
        self.coins = coins           type Coin.
    }

    func addCoin(_ newCoin: Coin) {
        coins.append(newCoin)
    }

    // ... snip. We are leaving out removing coins, calculating the total
     value, and other functionality.
}
```

The previous code is a small segment of a larger `Portfolio` class, which can have more functionality, such as removing coins, tracking gains and losses, and other use cases.

POP QUIZ   The `Portfolio` class has a problem. Can you detect it?

8.1.3   A trade-off with generics

There's a shortcoming. The Coin generic represents a single type, so you can only add one type of coin to your portfolio.

Listing 8.4   Trying to add different coins to the `Portfolio`

An Ethereum coin is created, with a value of 500.
(Normally it would be retrieved from live data).

```
let coins = [
    Ethereum(holdings: 4, price: NSDecimalNumber(value: 500)),
    // If we mix coins, we can't pass them to Portfolio
    // Bitcoin(holdings: 4, price: NSDecimalNumber(value: 6000))      Portfolio can't
 ]                                                                    accept an array
let portfolio = Portfolio(coins: coins)                              with different coins.
```

Currently, the portfolio contains an Ethereum coin. Because you used a generic, `Coin` inside the portfolio is now pinned to Ethereum coins. Because of generics, if you add a different coin, such as Bitcoin, you're stopped by the compiler, as shown in this listing.

Listing 8.5   Can't mix protocols with generics

```
let btc = Bitcoin(holdings: 3, price: nil)
portfolio.addCoin(btc)

error: cannot convert value of type 'Bitcoin' to expected argument type 'Ethereum'
```

The compiler smacks you with an error. At compile time, the `Portfolio` initializer resolves the generic to `Ethereum`, which means that you can't add different types to the portfolio. You can confirm as well by checking the type of coins that `Portfolio` holds, as shown in this example.

Listing 8.6 Checking the type of coins

```
print(type(of: portfolio)) // Portfolio<Ethereum>
print(type(of: portfolio.coins)) // Array<Ethereum>
```

TYPE(OF:) By using `type(of:)` you can inspect a type.

Generics give you benefits, such as knowing what types you're dealing with at compile time. The compiler can also apply performance optimizations because of this extra information.

But in this case, you don't want to pin down the `Coin` type at compile time. You want to mix and match coins and even add new coins at runtime. To meet this requirement, you're going to move from compile time to runtime, so it's time to step away from generics. Not to worry; you'll keep using the `CryptoCurrency` protocol.

8.1.4 Moving to runtime

You move to runtime by removing the generic. In th next example, you'll refactor `Portfolio` so that it holds coins that adhere to `CryptoCurrency`.

Listing 8.7 A dynamic `Portfolio`

```
// Before
final class Portfolio<Coin: CryptoCurrency> {
    var coins: [Coin]

    // ... snip
}

// After
final class Portfolio {                 ◄——  Remove the generic
    var coins: [CryptoCurrency]              definition on Portfolio.
                                        ◄——  The coins array is now of
    // ... snip                               type CryptoCurrency
}                                            instead of the generic Coin.
```

The portfolio has no generic and holds only `CryptoCurrency` types. You can mix and match the types inside the `CryptoCurrency` array, as indicated next by adding multiple types of coins.

Listing 8.8 Mixing and match coins

```
// No need to specify what goes inside of portfolio.
let portfolio = Portfolio(coins: [])    ◄——  You don't need to specify
                                             any generic parameter.
// Now we can mix coins.
let coins: [CryptoCurrency] = [
```

```
        Ethereum(holdings: 4, price: NSDecimalNumber(value: 500)),
        Bitcoin(holdings: 4, price: NSDecimalNumber(value: 6000))
]
portfolio.coins = coins        ◁─┤  You can add different
                                    types of coins.
```

By stepping away from generics, you gain flexibility back.

8.1.5 *Choosing between compile time and runtime*

It's a subtle distinction, but these examples showcase how generics are defined in the compile-time world and how protocols as types live in the runtime world.

If you use a protocol at runtime, you could think of them as interfaces or types. As shown in the following example, if you check the types inside the coins array, you get an array of CryptoCurrency, whereas before the array resolved to one type, namely [Ethereum] and potentially others.

Listing 8.9 Checking an array

```
print(type(of: portfolio)) // Portfolio

let retrievedCoins = portfolio.coins
print(type(of: retrievedCoins)) // Array<CryptoCurrency>
```

Using a protocol at runtime means you can mix and match all sorts of types, which is a fantastic benefit. But the type you're working with is a CryptoCurrency protocol. If Bitcoin has a special method called bitcoinStores(), you wouldn't be able to access it from the portfolio unless the protocol has the method defined as well, which means all coins now have to implement this method. Alternatively, you could check at runtime if a coin is of a specific type, but that can be considered an anti-pattern and doesn't scale with hundreds of possible coins.

8.1.6 *When a generic is the better choice*

Let's consider another scenario that showcases another difference between protocols as a type and using protocols to constrain generics. This time, constraining a generic with a protocol is the better choice.

For example, you can have a function called retrievePrice. You pass this function a coin, such as a Bitcoin struct or Ethereum struct, and you receive the same coin but updated with its most recent price. Next, you can see two similar functions: one with a generic implementation for compile time use, and one with a protocol as a type for runtime use.

Listing 8.10 A generic protocol vs. a runtime protocol

```
func retrievePriceRunTime(coin: CryptoCurrency, completion: ((CryptoCurrency)
    -> Void) ) {          ◁─┐
                            │  The retrievePriceRuntime function is using a runtime protocol.
                            │  You return a CryptoCurrency protocol inside the closure.
```

```
        // ... snip. Server returns coin with most-recent price.
        var copy = coin
        copy.price = 6000
        completion(copy)
    }

    func retrievePriceCompileTime<Coin: CryptoCurrency>(coin: Coin,
    ➡   completion: ((Coin) -> Void)) {
        // ... snip. Server returns coin with most-recent price.
        var copy = coin
        copy.price = 6000
        completion(copy)
    }
```

The retrievePriceCompileTime function, but this time it works on a generic constrained to the CryptoCurrency protocol. The completion handler also used the Coin generic.

```
    let btc = Bitcoin(holdings: 3, price: nil)
    retrievePriceRunTime(coin: btc) { (updatedCoin: CryptoCurrency) in
        print("Updated value runtime is \(updatedCoin.price?.doubleValue ?? 0)")
    }

    retrievePriceCompileTime(coin: btc) { (updatedCoin: Bitcoin) in
        print("Updated value compile time is \(updatedCoin.price?.doubleValue
        ?? 0)")
    }
```

Notice how the completion handler passed a value of type CryptoCurrency. Inside the closure, you don't know what the concrete type is until runtime.

But you know what to expect with the generic version. The function passes a Bitcoin type, the same type you passed into the function.

Thanks to generics, you know exactly what type you're working with inside the closure. You lose this benefit when using a protocol as a type.

Having generics appear inside your application may be wordy, but I hope you're encouraged to use them because of their benefits compared to runtime protocols.

Generally speaking, using a protocol as a type speeds up your programming and makes mixing and swapping things around easier. Generics are more restrictive and wordy, but they give you performance benefits and compile-time knowledge of the types you're implementing. Generics are often the better (but harder) choice, and in some cases they're the only choice, which you'll discover next when implementing protocols with associated types.

8.1.7   Exercises

1   Given this protocol

```
    protocol AudioProtocol {}
```

what is the difference between the following statements?

```
    func loadAudio(audio: AudioProtocol) {}
    func loadAudio<T: AudioProtocol>(audio: T) {}
```

2   How would you decide to use a generic or nongeneric protocol in the following example?

```
protocol Ingredient {}
struct Recipe<I: Ingredient> {
    let ingredients: [I]
    let instructions: String
}
```

3   How would you decide to use a generic or nongeneric protocol in the following struct?

```
protocol APIDelegate {
    func load(completion:(Data) -> Void)
}

struct ApiLoadHandler: APIDelegate {
    func load(completion: (Data) -> Void) {
        print("I am loading")
    }
}

class API {
    private let delegate: APIDelegate?

    init(delegate: APIDelegate) {
        self.delegate = delegate
    }
}

let dataModel = API(delegate: ApiLoadHandler())
```

8.2   *The why of associated types*

Let's go more in-depth and work with what may be considered *advanced protocols*, also known as protocols with associated types—or PATs for short, to go easy on the finger-joints of yours truly.

Protocols are abstract as they are, but with PATs, you're making your protocols generic, which makes your code even more abstract and exponentially complex.

Wielding PATs is a useful skill to have. It's one thing to hear about them, nod, and think that they may be useful for your code one day. But I aim to make you understand PATs profoundly and feel comfortable with them, so that at the end of this section, PATs don't intimidate you, and you feel ready to start implementing them (when it makes sense to do so).

In this section, you start by modeling a protocol and keep running into shortcomings, which you ultimately will solve with associated types. Along the way, you get to experience the reasoning and decision making of why you want to use PATs.

8.2.1   *Running into a shortcoming with protocols*

Imagine that you want to create a protocol resembling a piece of work that it needs to perform. It could represent a job or task, such as sending emails to all customers, migrating a database, resizing images in the background, or updating statistics by gathering information. You can model this piece of code via a protocol you'll call `Worker`.

The first type you'll create and conform to Worker is MailJob. MailJob needs a
String email address for its input, and returns a Bool for its output, indicating whether
the job finished successfully. You'll start naïvely and reflect the input and output of
MailJob in the Worker protocol. Worker has a single method, called start, that takes a
String for its input and a Bool for its output, as in the following listing.

Listing 8.11   The Worker protocol

```
protocol Worker {

    @discardableResult
    func start(input: String) -> Bool
}

class MailJob: Worker {
    func start(input: String) -> Bool {
        // Send mail to email address (input can represent an email address)
        // On finished, return whether or not everything succeeded
        return true
    }
}
```

Ignore the start method's output; you can suppress
compiler warnings with @discardableResult.

The Worker protocol
has a single method.

The MailJob class
adheres to Worker.

NOTE Normally you may want to run a worker implementation in the background, but for simplicity you keep it in the same thread.

But Worker does not cover all the requirements. Worker fits the needs for MailJob,
but doesn't scale to other types that may not have String and Bool as their input
and output.

Let's introduce another type that conforms to Worker and specializes in removing
files and call it FileRemover. FileRemover accepts a URL type as input for its directory,
removes the files, and returns an array of strings representing the files it deleted.
Since FileRemover accepts a URL and returns [String], it can't conform to Worker
(see figure 8.1).

Unfortunately, the protocol doesn't *scale* well. Try two different approaches before
heading to the solution involving protocols with associated types.

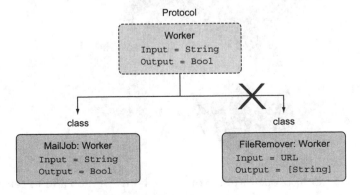

Figure 8.1   Trying to conform to Worker

8.2.2 Trying to make everything a protocol

Before you solve your problem with associated types, consider a solution that involves more protocols. How about making Input and Output a protocol, too? This seems like a valid suggestion—it allows you to avoid PATs altogether. But this approach has issues, as you are about to witness.

Listing 8.12 Worker without associated types

```
protocol Input {}        Declare two protocols: one for
protocol Output {}       Input and one for Output.

protocol Worker {                                The start method now accepts
    @discardableResult                           Input and Output as protocols,
    func start(input: Input) -> Output    <──    instead of associated types.
}
```

This approach works. But for *every* type you want to use for the input and output, you'd have to make multiple types adhere to the Input and Output protocols. This approach is a surefire way to end up with boilerplate, such as making String, URL, and [URL] adhere to the Input protocol, and again for the Output protocol. Another downside is that you're introducing a new protocol for each parameter and return type. On top of that, if you were to introduce a new method on Input or Output, you would have to implement it on *all* the types adhering to these protocols. Making everything a protocol is viable on a smaller project, but it won't scale nicely, causes boilerplate, and puts a burden on the developers that conform to your protocol.

8.2.3 Designing a generic protocol

Let's take a look at another approach where you'd like both MailJob and FileRemover to conform to Worker. In the next listing, you'll first approach your solution naïvely (which won't compile), but it highlights the motivation of associated types. Then, you'll solve your approach with associated types.

The Worker protocol wants to make sure that each implementation can decide for itself what the input and output represents. You can attempt this by defining two generics on the protocol, called Input and Output. Unfortunately, your approach won't work yet—let's see why.

Listing 8.13 A Worker protocol (won't compile yet!)

```
protocol Worker<Input, Output> {                    ◁——⌐  You can't declare
    @discardableResult                                  │  generics on a protocol.
    func start(input: Input) -> Output      ◁——————————⌐
}                                            The Worker starts a job with some
                                             input and returns some output.
```

Swift quickly stops you:

```
error: protocols do not allow generic parameters; use associated types instead
```

Swift doesn't support protocols with generic parameters. If Swift would support a generic protocol, you would need to define a concrete type on the protocol on an implementation. For instance, let's say you model the MailJob class with the Input generic set to String and the Output generic set to Bool. Its implementation would then be class MailJob: Worker<String, Bool>. Since the Worker protocol would be generic, you theoretically could implement Worker multiple times on MailJob. Multiple implementations of the same protocol, however, do not compile, as shown in this listing.

Listing 8.14 Not supported: a MailJob implementing Worker multiple times

```
// Not supported: Implementing a generic Worker.
class MailJob: Worker<String, Bool> {          ◁——⌐  Theoretically you could
    // Implementation omitted                       implement Worker for different
}                                                   types, such as <String, Bool>,
                                                    or <Int, [String]>.
class MailJob: Worker<Int, [String]> {         ◁——⌐
    // Implementation omitted
}

// etc
```

At the time of writing, Swift doesn't support multiple implementations of the same protocol. What Swift does support, however, is that you can implement a protocol only once for each type. In other words, MailJob gets to implement Worker once. Associated types give you this balance of making sure that you can implement a protocol once while working with generic values. Let's see how this works.

8.2.4   *Modeling a protocol with associated types*

You've seen two alternatives that were not the real solutions to your problem. You'll create a viable solution to the problem. You're going to follow the compiler's advice and use associated types. You can rewrite `Worker` and use the `associatedtype` keyword, where you declare both the `Input` and `Output` generics as associated types.

```
Listing 8.15   Worker with associated types
```

```
                                    The Worker protocol doesn't
                                    have a generics declaration.
protocol Worker {        ◁──────┐
    associatedtype Input         │  Declare associated types via
    associatedtype Output        │  the associatedtype keyword.

    @discardableResult                       In the rest of the protocol
    func start(input: Input) -> Output  ◁──  signature, you can reference
}                                            the associated types.
```

Now the `Input` and `Output` generics are declared as associated types. Associated types are similar to generics, but they are defined *inside* a protocol. Notice how `Worker` does not have the `<Input, Output>` notation. With `Worker` in place, you can start to conform to it for both `MailJob` and `FileRemover`.

8.2.5   *Implementing a PAT*

The `Worker` protocol is ready to be implemented. Thanks to associated types, both `Mailjob` and `FileRemover` can successfully conform to `Worker`. `MailJob` sets the `Input` and `Output` to `String` and `Bool`, whereas `FileRemover` sets the `Input` and `Output` to `URL` and `[String]` (see figure 8.2).

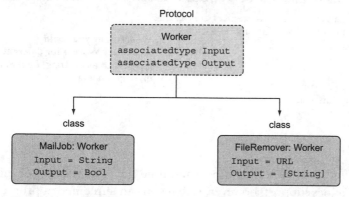

Figure 8.2   `Worker` implemented

Looking at the details of `MailJob` in the next listing, you can see that it sets the `Input` and `Output` to concrete types.

Listing 8.16 `MailJob` (implementation omitted)

```
class MailJob: Worker {
    typealias Input = String        ← For MailJob, the Input associated
    typealias Output = Bool           type is defined as String.

                                    ← For MailJob, the Output associated
    func start(input: String) -> Bool {  type is defined as Bool.
        // Send mail to email address (input can represent an email address)
        // On finished, return whether or not everything succeeded
        return true
    }
}
```

Now, `MailJob` always uses `String` and `Bool` for its `Input` and `Output`.

> **NOTE** Each type conforming to a protocol can only have a single implementation of a protocol. But you still get generic values with the help of associated types. The benefit is that each type can decide what these associated values represent.

The implementation of `FileRemover` is different than `MailJob`, and its associated types are also of different types. Note, as shown in the following, that you can omit the typealias notation if Swift can infer the associated types.

Listing 8.17 The `FileRemover`

```
class FileRemover: Worker {
//    typealias Input = URL           You can choose to omit the types if the
//    typealias Output = [String]     compiler can infer the types from the
                                      method and property signatures.
    func start(input: URL) -> [String] {
        do {
            var results = [String]()
            let fileManager = FileManager.default
            let fileURLs = try fileManager.contentsOfDirectory(at: input,
    includingPropertiesForKeys: nil)
                                                            ← The FileRemover finds
            for fileURL in fileURLs {                         the directory and
                try fileManager.removeItem(at: fileURL)   ← iterates through the
                results.append(fileURL.absoluteString)       files to remove them.
            }

            return results
        } catch {
            print("Clearing directory failed.")
            return []
        }
    }
}
```

When using protocols with associated types, multiple types can conform to the same protocol; yet, each type can define what an associated type represents.

> **TIP** Another way to think of an associated type is that it's a generic, except it's a generic that lives inside a protocol.

8.2.6   *PATs in the standard library*

Swift uses associated types all around the standard library, and you've been using a few already!

The most common uses of a PAT are the `IteratorProtocol`, `Sequence`, and `Collection` protocols. These protocols are conformed to by `Array`, `String`, `Set`, `Dictionary`, and others, which use an associated type called `Element`, representing an element inside the collection. But you've also seen other protocols, such as `RawRepresentable` on enums where an associated type called `RawValue` allows you to transform any type to an enum and back again.

SELF REQUIREMENTS

Another flavor of an associated type is the `Self` keyword. A common example is the `Equatable` protocol, which you saw in chapter 7. With `Equatable`, two of the same types—represented by `Self`—are compared. As shown in this listing, `Self` resolves to the type that conforms to `Equatable`.

```
Listing 8.18   Equatable
```

```swift
public protocol Equatable {
    static func == (lhs: Self, rhs: Self) -> Bool      ⟵─┤ Equatable has Self
}                                                          requirements.
```

8.2.7   *Other uses for associated types*

Bending your mind around PATs can be tough. A protocol with an associated type is a generic protocol, making it harder to reason about. Introducing associated types starts making sense when conformers of a protocol use different types in their implementation. Generally speaking, PATs tend to pop up more often in frameworks because of a higher chance of reusability.

Here are some use cases for associated types:

- A *Recording protocol*—Each recording has a duration, and it could also support scrubbing through time via a `seek()` method, but the actual data could be different for each implementation, such as an audio file, video file, or YouTube stream.
- A *Service protocol*—It loads data; one type could return JSON data from an API, and another could locally search and return raw string data.
- A *Message protocol*—It's on a social media tool that tracks posts. In one implementation, a message represents a Tweet; in another, a message represents a Facebook direct message; and in another, it could be a message on WhatsApp.
- A *SearchQuery protocol*—It resembles database queries, where the result is different for each implementation.

- A `Paginator` *protocol*—It can be given a page and offset to browse through a database. Each page could represent some data. Perhaps it has some users in a user table in a database, or perhaps a list of files, or a list of products inside a view.

8.2.8   Exercise

4   Consider the following subclassing hierarchy for a game, where you have enemies that can attack with a specific type of damage. Can you replace this subclassing hierarchy with a protocol-based solution?

```
class AbstractDamage {}

class AbstractEnemy {
    func attack() -> AbstractDamage {
        fatalError("This method must be implemented by subclass")
    }
}

class Fire: AbstractDamage {}
class Imp: AbstractEnemy {
    override func attack() -> Fire {
        return Fire()
    }
}

class BluntDamage: AbstractDamage {}
class Centaur: AbstractEnemy {
    override func attack() -> BluntDamage {
        return BluntDamage()
    }
}
```

8.3   Passing protocols with associated types

Let's see the ways you can pass a protocol with associated types around. You'll use the `Worker` protocol from the last section with two associated types named `Input` and `Output`.

Imagine that you want to write a generic function or method that accepts a single worker and an array of elements that this worker must process. By passing an array of type [W.Input], where W represents a Worker, you make sure that the Input associated type is the exact type the Worker can handle (see figure 8.5). PATs can only be implemented as generic constraints—with some complicated exceptions aside—so you'll use generics to stay in the world of compile-time code.

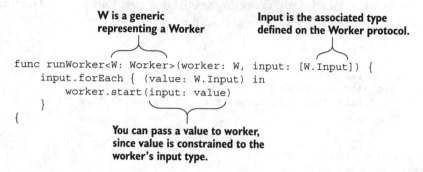

Figure 8.3   Passing the same input to multiple workers

NOTE   You can safely omit any references to W.Output in runWorker because you're not doing anything with it.

With runWorker in place, you can pass it multiple Worker types, such as a MailJob or a FileRemover, as shown in the next listing. Make sure that you pass matching Input types for each worker; you pass strings for MailJob and URLs to FileRemover.

Listing 8.19   Passing multiple workers

```
let mailJob = MailJob()
runWorker(worker: mailJob, input: ["grover@sesamestreetcom", "bigbird@sesames
    treet.com"])                                                    ◁── Pass the MailJob to
                                                                        runWorker with a
                                                                        list of emails.
let fileRemover = FileRemover()
runWorker(worker: fileRemover, input: [                     ◁──
    URL(fileURLWithPath: "./cache", isDirectory: true),         Pass a FileRemover
    URL(fileURLWithPath: "./tmp", isDirectory: true),           instance to runWorker
    ])                                                          with a list of URLs.
```

NOTE   Like generics, associated types get resolved at compile time, too.

8.3.1   Where clauses with associated types

You can constrain associated types in functions with a *where* clause, which becomes useful if you want to specialize functionality somewhat. Constraining associated types is very similar to constraining a generic, yet the syntax is slightly different.

For instance, let's say you want to process an array of users; perhaps you need to strip empty spaces from their names or update other values. You can pass an array of

users to a single worker. You can make sure that the `Input` associated type is of type
`User` with the help of a *where* clause so that you can print the users' names the worker
is processing. By constraining an associated type, the function is specialized to work
only with users as input.

Listing 8.20 Constraining the `Input` associated type

```
final class User {                        ⊲──┐  Define a User.
    let firstName: String
    let lastName: String
    init(firstName: String, lastName: String) {
        self.firstName = firstName
        self.lastName = lastName
    }
}

func runWorker<W>(worker: W, input: [W.Input])
where W: Worker, W.Input == User {        ⊲──
    input.forEach { (user: W.Input) in
        worker.start(input: user)
        print("Finished processing user \(user.firstName) \(user.lastName)")  ⊲──┐
    }
}
```

Inside runWorker, you
constrain the Input associated
type to User. Note that you can
constrain W here as well.

Now you can reference users
by their properties inside
the body of the function.

8.3.2 *Types constraining associated types*

You just saw how associated types get passed via functions. Now focus on how associated types work with types such as structs, classes, or enums.

As an example, you could have an `ImageProcessor` class that can store a `Worker`
type (see figure 8.6). Workers in this context could be types that crop an image, resize
an image, or turn them to sepia. What exactly this `ImageProcessor` does depends on
the `Worker`. The added value of the `ImageProcessor` is that it can batch process a large
number of images by getting them out of a store, such as a database.

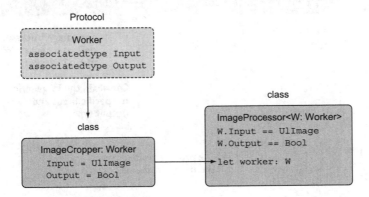

Figure 8.4 `ImageProcessor`

The `ImageProcessor` accepts an `ImageCropper` that is of type `Worker`.

```
let cropper = ImageCropper(size: CGSize(width: 200, height: 200))
let imageProcessor: ImageProcessor<ImageCropper> = ImageProcessor(worker:
    cropper)
```

Here you explicitly define the generic type inside
ImageProcessor, via ImageProcessor<ImageCropper>.

First you'll introduce the `Worker`, which in this case is `ImageCropper`. The implementation is omitted to focus on the protocol conformance.

```
final class ImageCropper: Worker {

    let size: CGSize
    init(size: CGSize) {
        self.size = size
    }

    func start(input: UIImage) -> Bool {
        // Omitted: Resize image to self.size
        // return bool to indicate that the process succeeded
        return true
    }
}
```

Here is where you'll create the `ImageProcessor` type. `ImageProcessor` accepts a generic `Worker`. But this `Worker` has two constraints: the first constraint sets the `Input` to type `UIImage`, and the `Output` is expected to be a Boolean, which reflects whether the job of the `Worker` was completed successfully or not.

You can constrain the associated types of `Worker` with a *where* clause. You can write this *where* clause before the opening brackets of `ImageProcessor`, as shown here.

```
final class ImageProcessor<W: Worker>
 where W.Input == UIImage, W.Output == Bool {

    let worker: W

    init(worker: W) {
        self.worker = worker
    }

    private func process() {
        // start batches
        var results = [Bool]()

        let amount = 50
        var offset = 0
```

The ImageProcessor
defines a generic W
of type Worker.

Constrain the W generic
to specific Input and
Output types.

The process method runs
the ImageProcessor.

```
        var images = fetchImages(amount: amount, offset: offset)
        var failedCount = 0
        while !images.isEmpty {

            for image in images {
                if !worker.start(input: image) {
                    failedCount += 1
                }
            }

            offset += amount
            images = fetchImages(amount: amount, offset: offset)
        }

        print("\(failedCount) images failed")
    }

    private func fetchImages(amount: Int, offset: Int) -> [UIImage] {
        // Not displayed: Return images from database or harddisk
        return [UIImage(), UIImage()]
    }
}
```

> **Loop through the store's images, and process them, until you run out of images.**

> **For each image, the worker's start method is called to process the image. If it fails, you bump the failedCount by one.**

> **In the example, you mock the returning of images, but in a real-world scenario, it would work with a real data-store.**

By accepting a generic `Worker`, the `ImageProcessor` class can accept different types, such as image croppers, resizers, or one that makes an image black and white.

8.3.3 Cleaning up your API with protocol inheritance

Depending on how generic this application turns out, you may end up passing a generic `Worker` around. Redeclaring the same constraints—such as `where W.Input == UIImage, W.Output == Bool`—may get tiresome, though.

For convenience, you can apply protocol inheritance to further constrain a protocol. Protocol inheritance means that you create a new protocol that inherits the definition of another protocol. Think of it like subclassing a protocol.

You can create an `ImageWorker` protocol that inherits all the properties and functions from the `Worker` protocol, but with one big difference: the `ImageWorker` protocol constrains the `Input` and `Output` associated types with a *where* clause, as shown here.

Listing 8.24 The `ImageWorker`

```
protocol ImageWorker: Worker where Input == UIImage, Output == Bool {
    // extra methods can go here if you want
}
```

PROTOCOL EXTENSION In this case, `ImageWorker` is empty, but note that you can add extra protocol definitions to it if you'd like. Then types adhering to `ImageWorker` must implement these on top of the `Worker` protocol.

With this protocol, the *where* clause is implied, and passing an `ImageWorker` around means that types don't need to manually constrain to `Image` and `Bool` anymore. The `ImageWorker` protocol can make the API of `ImageProcessor` a bit cleaner.

Listing 8.25 No need to constrain anymore

```
// Before:
final class ImageProcessor<W: Worker>
where W.Input == UIImage, W.Output == Bool { ... }

// After:
final class ImageProcessor<W: ImageWorker> { ... }
```

8.3.4 Exercises

5 You have the following types:

```
// A protocol representing something that can play a file at a location.
protocol Playable {
    var contents: URL { get }
    func play()
}

// A Movie struct that inherits this protocol.
final class Movie: Playable {
    let contents: URL

    init(contents: URL) {
        self.contents = contents
    }

    func play() { print("Playing video at \(contents)") }
}
```

You introduce a new `Song` type, but instead of playing a file at a URL, it uses an `AudioFile` type. How would you deal with this? See if you can make the protocol reflect this change:

```
struct AudioFile {}

final class Song: Playable {
    let contents: AudioFile

    init(contents: AudioFile) {
        self.contents = contents
    }

    func play() { print("Playing song") }
}
```

6 Given this playlist that first could only play movies, how can you make sure it can play either movies or songs?

```
final class Playlist {

    private var queue: [Movie] = []

    func addToQueue(playable: Movie) {
        queue.append(playable)
    }

    func start() {
        queue.first?.play()
    }
}
```

8.4 Closing thoughts

Protocols with associated types and generics unlocks abstract code, but forces you to reason about types during compile time. Although it's sometimes challenging to work with, getting your highly reusable abstract code to compile can be rewarding. You don't always have to make things difficult, however. Sometimes a single generic or concrete code is enough to give you what you want. Now that you have seen how associated types work, you're prepared to take them on when they return in upcoming chapters.

Summary

- You can use protocols as generic constraints. But protocols can also be used as a type at runtime (dynamic dispatch) when you step away from generics.
- Using protocols as a generic constraint is usually the way to go, until you need dynamic dispatch.
- Associated types are generics that are tied to a protocol.
- Protocols with associated types allow a concrete type to define the associated type. Each concrete type can specialize an associated type to a different type.
- Protocols with `Self` requirements are a unique flavor of associated types referencing the current type.
- Protocols with associated types or `Self` requirements force you to reason about types at compile time.
- You can make a protocol inherit another protocol to further constrain its associated types.

Answers

1 What is the difference between the statements?
   - The nongeneric function uses dynamic dispatch (runtime).
   - The generic function is resolved at compile time.
2 How would you decide to use a generic or nongeneric protocol in the struct?
       A recipe requires multiple different ingredients. By using a generic, you can use only one type of ingredient. Using eggs for everything can get boring, so, in this case, you should step away from generics.

3 How would you decide to use a generic or nongeneric protocol in the struct?

The delegate is a single type; you can safely use a generic here. You get compile-time benefits, such as extra performance, and seeing at compile time which type you'll use. The code could look like this:

```
protocol APIDelegate {
    func load(completion:(Data) -> Void)
}

struct ApiLoadHandler: APIDelegate {
    func load(completion: (Data) -> Void) {
        print("I am loading")
    }
}

class API<Delegate: APIDelegate> {
    private let delegate: Delegate?

    init(delegate: Delegate) {
        self.delegate = delegate
    }
}

let dataModel = API(delegate: ApiLoadHandler())
```

4 Consider the subclassing hierarchy for a game, where you have enemies that can attack with a certain type of damage. Can you replace this subclassing hierarchy with a protocol-based solution?

```
protocol Enemy {
    associatedtype DamageType
    func attack() -> DamageType
}

struct Fire {}
class Imp: Enemy {
    func attack() -> Fire {
        return Fire()
    }
}

struct BluntDamage {}
class Centaur: Enemy {
    func attack() -> BluntDamage {
        return BluntDamage()
    }
}
```

5 You introduce a new Song type, but instead of playing a file at a URL, it uses an AudioFile type. How would you deal with this? See if you can make the protocol reflect this.

Answer: You introduce an associated type, such as Media. The contents property is now of type Media, which resolves to something different for each implementation:

```
protocol Playable {
    associatedtype Media
    var contents: Media { get }
    func play()
}

final class Movie: Playable {
    let contents: URL

    init(contents: URL) {
        self.contents = contents
    }

    func play() { print("Playing video at \(contents)") }
}

struct AudioFile {}
final class Song: Playable {
    let contents: AudioFile

    init(contents: AudioFile) {
        self.contents = contents
    }

    func play() { print("Playing song") }
}
```

6 Given the playlist that first could only play movies, how can you make sure it can play either movies or songs?

```
final class Playlist<P: Playable> {

    private var queue: [P] = []

    func addToQueue(playable: P) {
        queue.append(playable)
    }

    func start() {
        queue.first?.play()
    }
}
```

NOTE You can't mix movies and songs, but you can create a playlist for songs (or a playlist for movies).

Iterators, sequences, and collections

9

This chapter covers

- Taking a closer look at iteration in Swift
- Showing how `Sequence` is related to `IteratorProtocol`
- Learning useful methods that `Sequence` supplies
- Understanding the different collection protocols
- Creating data structures with the `Sequence` and `Collection` protocols.

You use iterators, sequences, and collections all the time when programming Swift. Whenever you use an `Array`, `String`, `stride`, `Dictionary`, and other types, you're working with something you can iterate over. Iterators enable the use of *for* loops. They also enable a large number of methods, including, but not limited to, `filter`, `map`, `sorted`, and `reduce`.

In this chapter, you're going to see how these iterators work, learn about useful methods (such as `reduce` and `lazy`), and see how to create types that conform to the `Sequence` protocol. The chapter also covers the `Collection` protocol and its many subprotocols, such as `MutableCollection`, `RandomAccessCollection`, and others. You'll find out how to implement the `Collection` protocol to get a lot of free methods on your types. Being comfortable with `Sequence` and `Collection` will give you a deeper understanding of how iteration works, and how to create custom types powered up by iterators.

You'll start at the bottom and build up from there. You'll get a look at how *for* loops work and how they are syntactic sugar for methods on `IteratorProtocol` and `Sequence`.

Then, you'll take a closer look at `Sequence`, and find out how it produces iterators and why this is needed.

After that, you'll learn some useful methods on `Sequence` that can help expand your iterator vocabulary. You'll get acquainted with `lazy`, `reduce`, `zip`, and others.

To best show that you understand `Sequence`, you'll create a custom type that conforms to `Sequence`. This sequence is a data structure called a `Bag` or `MultiSet`, which is like a `Set`, but for multiple values.

Then you'll move on to `Collection` and see how it's different from `Sequence`. You'll see all the different types of `Collection` protocols that Swift offers and their unique traits.

As a final touch, you'll integrate `Collection` on a custom data structure. You don't need to be an algorithm wizard to reap the benefits of `Collection`. Instead, you'll learn a practical approach by taking a regular data structure and power it up with `Collection`.

I made sure that you won't fall asleep during this chapter either. Besides some theory, this chapter contains plenty of practical use cases.

9.1 Iterating

When programming Swift, you're looping (iterating) through data all the time, such as retrieving elements inside of an array, obtaining individual characters inside a string, processing integers inside a range—you name it. Let's start with a little bit of theory, so you know the inner workings of iteration in Swift. Then you'll be ready to apply this newfound knowledge on practical solutions.

> **JOIN ME!** It's more educational and fun if you can check out the code and follow along with the chapter. You can download the source code at http://mng .bz/7JPy.

9.1.1 IteratorProtocol

Every time you use a *for in* loop, you're using an iterator. For example, you can loop over an array regularly via *for in*.

Listing 9.1 Using *for in*

```
let cheeses = ["Gouda", "Camembert", "Brie"]

for cheese in cheeses {
    print(cheese)
}
```

```
// Output:
"Gouda"
"Camembert"
"Brie"
```

But *for in* is syntactic sugar. Actually, what's happening under the hood is that an iterator is created via the `makeIterator()` method. Swift walks through the elements via a *while* loop, shown here.

> **Listing 9.2   Using `makeIterator()`**

```
var cheeseIterator = cheeses.makeIterator()     ⟵
while let cheese = cheeseIterator.next() {       ⟵
    print(cheese)
}

// Output:
"Gouda"
"Camembert"
"Brie"
```

An iterator is created; notice how it's mutable and requires a var.

Behind the scenes, Swift continuously calls next() on the iterator until it's exhausted and ends the loop.

Although a *for* loop calls `makeIterator()` under the hood, you can pass an iterator directly to a *for* loop:

```
var cheeseIterator = cheeses.makeIterator()
for element in cheeseIterator {
    print(cheese)
}
```

The `makeIterator()` method is defined in the `Sequence` protocol, which is closely related to `IteratorProtocol`. Before moving on to `Sequence`, let's take a closer look at `IteratorProtocol` first.

9.1.2   The IteratorProtocol

An iterator implements `IteratorProtocol`, which is a small, yet powerful component in Swift. `IteratorProtocol` has an associated type called `Element` and a `next()` method that returns an optional `Element` (see figure 9.1 and the listing that follows). Iterators generate values, which is how you can loop through multiple elements.

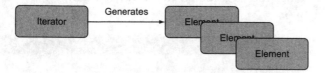

Figure 9.1   `IteratorProtocol` produces elements

Listing 9.3 `IteratorProtocol` in Swift

```
public protocol IteratorProtocol {
    /// The type of element traversed by the iterator.
    associatedtype Element          ◁────┐   An Element associated type is
                                          │   defined, representing an element
    mutating func next() -> Element?  ────┘   that an iterator product
}
```

NOTE If you've ever seen `Array` extensions, this is the same `Element` the extension uses.

Every time you call `next` on an iterator, you get the next value an iterator produces until the iterator is exhausted, on which you receive `nil`.

An iterator is like a bag of groceries— you can pull elements out of it, one by one. When the bag is empty, you're out. The convention is that after an iterator depletes, it returns `nil` and any subsequent `next()` call is expected to return `nil`, too, as shown in this example.

Listing 9.4 Going through an iterator

```
let groceries = ["Flour", "Eggs", "Sugar"]
var groceriesIterator: IndexingIterator<[String]> = groceries.makeIterator()
print(groceriesIterator.next()) // Optional("Flour")
print(groceriesIterator.next()) // Optional("Eggs")
print(groceriesIterator.next()) // Optional("Sugar")
print(groceriesIterator.next()) // nil
print(groceriesIterator.next()) // nil
```

NOTE Array returns an `IndexingIterator`, but this could be different per type.

9.1.3 The Sequence protocol

Closely related to `IteratorProtocol`, the `Sequence` protocol is implemented all over Swift. In fact, you've been using sequences all the time. `Sequence` is the backbone behind any other type that you can iterate over. `Sequence` is also the superprotocol of `Collection`, which is inherited by `Array`, `Set`, `String`, `Dictionary`, and others, which means that these types also adhere to `Sequence`.

9.1.4 Taking a closer look at Sequence

A `Sequence` can produce iterators. Whereas an `IteratorProtocol` is exhaustive, after the elements inside an iterator are consumed, the iterator is depleted. But that's not a problem for `Sequence`, because `Sequence` can create a new iterator for a new loop. This way, types conforming to `Sequence` can repeatedly be iterated over (see figure 9.2).

Notice in listing 9.5 that the `Sequence` protocol has an associated type called `Iterator`, which is constrained to `IteratorProtocol`. `Sequence` also has a make-Iterator method that creates an iterator.

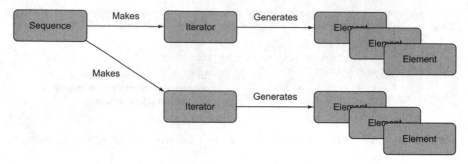

Figure 9.2 Sequence produces iterators

Sequence is a large protocol with a great number of default methods, but this chapter covers only the crucial elements.

Listing 9.5   Sequence protocol (not complete)

Sequence makes sure that the Element associated type is the same as the one from IteratorProtocol.

```
public protocol Sequence {

    associatedtype Element          ◁
```
An Element associated type is defined, representing an element that an iterator produces.

```
    associatedtype Iterator: IteratorProtocol where Iterator.Element == Element   ◁
```
An associated type is defined and constrained to IteratorProtocol.

A Sequence can keep producing iterators.
```
    func makeIterator() -> Iterator

    func filter(
        _ isIncluded: (Element) throws -> Bool
    ) rethrows -> [Element]
```
Many methods are defined on Sequence, such as filter and forEach, to name a few.

```
    func forEach(_ body: (Element) throws -> Void) rethrows   ◁

// ... snip
}
```

NO 'SEQUENCEPROTOCOL'? Sequence is not SequenceProtocol. Yet, Sequence constrains Iterator to IteratorProtocol, which might explain why Iterator-Protocol is named this way. Quirky, but so be it.

To implement Sequence, you merely have to implement makeIterator(). Being able to produce iterators is the secret sauce to how a Sequence can be iterated over repeatedly, such as looping over an array multiple times. Sequence may seem like an iterator factory, but don't let this code snippet fool you. Sequence packs quite the punch, because it offers many default methods, such as filter, map, reduce, flatMap, forEach, dropFirst, contains, regular looping with *for in*, and much more. Having a type conform to Sequence means that it gets a lot of functionality for free. Sequence is not reserved for Swift types; you can create custom types that adhere to Sequence, too.

Let's take a look at some essential methods on Sequence.

9.2   *The powers of Sequence*

Types that implement Sequence gain many useful methods for free. This book doesn't rehash all methods because you're probably familiar with some of them (and I'd like to try to keep this book under 1,000 pages). Let's take this opportunity to shed light on some useful or tricky methods to build your iterative vocabulary.

9.2.1   *filter*

Swift doesn't shy away from taking ideas from *functional programming* concepts, such as map, filter, or reduce methods. The filter method is a common method that Sequence offers.

As an example, filter on Sequence filters data depending on the closure you pass it. For each element, filter passes each element to the closure function and expects a Boolean in return.

The filter method returns a new collection, except it keeps the elements from which you return true in the passed closure.

To illustrate, notice how filter is being applied to filter values of an array. It returns an array with all values higher than 1.

Listing 9.6   filter is a higher-order function

```
let result = [1,2,3].filter { (value) -> Bool in
    return value > 1
}

print(result) // [2, 3]
```

9.2.2   *forEach*

Eating pasta every day gets boring—same with using *for* loops every day. If boredom strikes, you can use forEach instead; it's a good alternative to a regular *for* loop to indicate that you want a so-called side effect. A side effect happens when some outside state is altered—such as saving an element to a database, printing, rendering a view, you name it—indicated by forEach not returning a value.

For instance, you can have an array of strings where for each element the `deleteFile` function gets called.

Listing 9.7   Using `forEach`

```
["file_one.txt", "file_two.txt"].forEach { path in
    deleteFile(path: path)
}

func deleteFile(path: String) {
    // deleting file ....
}
```

With `forEach` you have a nice shorthand way to call a function. In fact, if the function only accepts an argument and returns nothing, you can directly pass it to `forEach` instead. Notice in this listing how curly braces {} are replaced by parentheses (), because you're directly passing a function.

Listing 9.8   Using `forEach` by passing a function

```
["file_one.txt", "file_two.txt"].forEach(deleteFile)
```

9.2.3   *enumerated*

When you want to keep track of the number of times you looped, you can use the enumerated method, as shown in the following listing. It returns a special `Sequence` called `EnumeratedSequence` that keeps count of the iterations. The iteration starts at zero.

Listing 9.9   `enumerated`

```
["First line", "Second line", "Third line"]
    .enumerated()
    .forEach { (index: Int, element: String) in
        print("\(index+1): \(element)")
    }

// Output:
1: First line
2: Second line
3: Third line
```

> The enumerated() method returns a special EnumeratedSequence, which produces the element with an offset (index).

> Use the index to prefix the text with a line number. You add 1 to the index so that your list starts at 1 because index starts at 0.

Notice how `forEach` fits well once you chain sequence methods.

9.2.4   *Lazy iteration*

Whenever you're calling methods on a sequence, such as `forEach`, `filter`, or others, the elements are iterated *eagerly*. Eager iteration means that the elements inside the sequence are accessed immediately once you iterate. In most scenarios, an eager approach is the one you need. But in some scenarios this is not ideal. For example, if you have extremely large (or even infinite) resources, you may not want to traverse the whole sequence, but only some elements at a time.

For this case, Swift offers a particular sequence called LazySequence, which you obtain via the lazy keyword.

For example, you could have a range, going from 0 to the massive Int.max number. You want to filter on this range to keep all even numbers, and then get the last three numbers. You'll use lazy to prevent a full iteration over a gigantic collection. Because of lazy, this iteration is quite cheap, because a lazy iterator calculates only a select few elements.

Notice in this listing that no actual work is done by LazySequence until you start reading the elements, which you do in the last step.

Listing 9.10 Using lazy

```
let bigRange = 0..<Int.max          ◄──┐ Define an enormous range.

let filtered = bigRange.lazy.filter { (int) -> Bool in
    return int % 2 == 0
}                                   ◄──  Define the filtered elements;
                                         note that no elements have
                                         been evaluated yet.
let lastThree = filtered.suffix(3)  ◄──
                                         Get the last three elements;
for value in lastThree {                 note that (again) no elements
    print(value)                    ◄──┐ have been evaluated.
}
                                         Now that you act on the
// Output:                               elements, the lazy code
9223372036854775802                      is evaluated.
9223372036854775804
9223372036854775806
```

Using lazy can be a great tool for large collections when you're not interested in all the values. One downside is that lazy closures are @escaping and temporarily store a closure. Another downside of using lazy is that every time you access the elements, the results are recalculated on the fly. With an eager iteration, once you have the results, you're done.

9.2.5 *reduce*

The reduce method may be one of the trickier methods on Sequence to understand. With its foundation in functional programming, you may see it appear in other languages. It could be called fold, like in Kotlin or Rust, or it could be called inject in Ruby. To make it even more challenging, Swift offers two variants of the reduce method, so you have to decide which one to pick for each scenario. Let's take a look at both variants.

With reduce you iterate over each element in a Sequence, such as an Array, and you accumulatively build an object. When reduce is done, it returns the finalized object. In other words, with reduce you turn multiple elements into a new object.

Most commonly, you're turning an array into something else, but reduce can also be called on other types.

REDUCE IN ACTION

Here, you'll apply reduce to see it in action. String conforms to Sequence, so you can call reduce on it and iterate over its characters. For instance, imagine that you want to know the number of line breaks on a String. You'll do this by iterating over each character, and increase the count if a character equals "\n".

To start off, you have to supply a start value to reduce. Then, for each iteration, you update this value. In the next scenario, you want to count the number of line breaks, so you pass an integer with a value of zero, representing the count. Then your final result is the number of line breaks you measured, stored in numberOf-LineBreaks.

Listing 9.11 Preparing for a reduce

```
let text = "It's hard to come up with fresh exercises.\nOver and over again.\
    nAnd again."
let startValue = 0
let numberOfLineBreaks = text.reduce(startValue) { // ... snip
  // ... Do some work here
}
print(numberOfLineBreaks) // 2
```

With each iteration, reduce passes two values via a closure: one value is the element from the iteration, the other is the integer (startValue) you passed to reduce.

Then, for each iteration, you check for a newline character, represented by "\n", and you increase the integer by one if needed. You do this by returning a new integer (see figure 9.3).

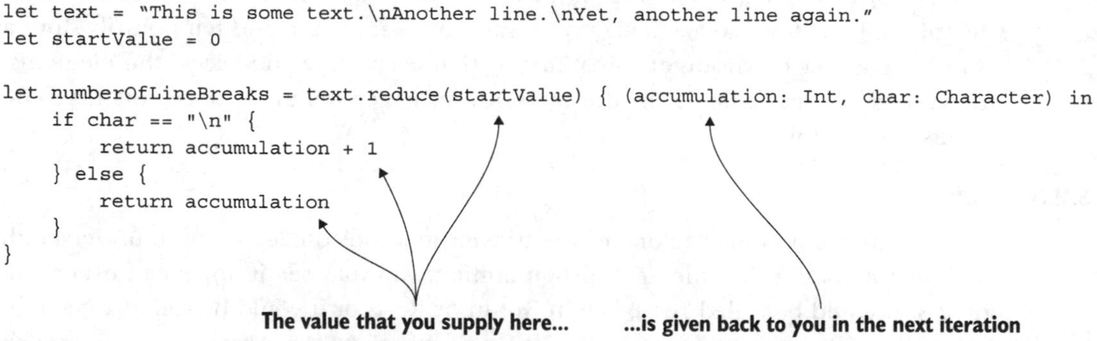

```
let text = "This is some text.\nAnother line.\nYet, another line again."
let startValue = 0

let numberOfLineBreaks = text.reduce(startValue) { (accumulation: Int, char: Character) in
    if char == "\n" {
        return accumulation + 1
    } else {
        return accumulation
    }
}
```

The value that you supply here...   ...is given back to you in the next iteration

Figure 9.3 How reduce passes values

But reduce does something clever: in each iteration, you get the next character and the new integer you just updated in the previous iteration.

You return the accumulation value inside the closure, and reduce gives it right back again in the next iteration, allowing you to keep updating the accumulation integer. This way, you iterate over all elements while you update a single value. After reduce has finished iterating, it returns the final value you created—in this case numberOfLineBreaks.

9.2.6 *reduce into*

Imagine that you're reducing the number of student grades into a dictionary that counts the number of grades, resolved to A, B, C, or D. You would be updating this dictionary in each iteration. The problem, however, is that you would have to create a mutable copy of this dictionary for every iteration. A copy occurs whenever you reference a dictionary, because Dictionary is a *value type*. Let's see in this next listing how this works with reduce, before improving the code with reduce(into:).

> **Listing 9.12   reduce with less performance**

You're reducing, with a start value of [:], which is an empty dictionary. Swift can deduce which type it is, saving you from explicitly writing [Character: Int]().

```
let grades = [3.2, 4.2, 2.6, 4.1]
let results = grades.reduce([:]) { (results: [Character: Int], grade: Double) in
    var copy = results
    switch grade {
    case 1..<2: copy["D", default: 0] += 1
    case 2..<3: copy["C", default: 0] += 1
    case 3..<4: copy["B", default: 0] += 1
    case 4...: copy["A", default: 0] += 1
    default: break
    }

    return copy
}

print(results) // ["C": 1, "B": 1, "A": 2]
```

Create a mutable copy with var to be able to mutate a dictionary.

Increment a counter by matching on the grades.

Return a copy for every iteration.

In the end, you have a dictionary with the grades collected.

Because you're copying the dictionary for every iteration with var copy = results, you incur a performance hit. Here is where reduce(into:) comes in. With the into variant, you can keep mutating the same dictionary, as shown here.

> **Listing 9.13   reduce(into:)**

```
let results = grades.reduce(into: [:]) { (results: inout [Character: Int],
    grade: Double) in
    switch grade {
    case 1..<2: results["D", default: 0] += 1
    case 2..<3: results["C", default: 0] += 1
    case 3..<4: results["B", default: 0] += 1
    case 4...: results["A", default: 0] += 1
    default: break
    }
}
```

The into variant of reduce

NOTE You aren't returning anything from the closure when using reduce
(into:).

When you're working with larger value types—such as dictionaries or arrays—consider using the into variant for added performance.

Using reduce may look a bit foreign, because you might as well use a *for* loop as an alternative. But reduce can be a very concise way to build a value accumulatively. You could also state that reduce shows intent. With a *for* loop, you have to play the compiler to see if you're filtering or transforming data or doing something else. If you see a reduce, you can quickly deduce (poetry intended) that you're turning multiple values into something new.

Reduce is abstract enough that you can do many things with it. But reduce is most elegant when converting a list of elements into one thing. Whether that thing is a simple integer or a complex class or struct, reduce is your friend.

9.2.7 zip

To close off this section, let's look at zip. Zipping allows you to zip (pair) two iterators. If one iterator depletes, zip stops iterating.

Notice in this next listing how you iterate both from a to c and 1 to 10. Since the array with strings is the shortest, zip ends after three iterations.

Listing 9.14 `zip`

```
for (integer, string) in zip(0..<10, ["a", "b", "c"]) {
    print("\(integer): \(string)")
}
// Output:
// 0: a
// 1: b
// 2: c
```

NOTE zip is a free-standing function and not called on a type.

Many more methods exist, including, but not limited to, map, flatMap, and compactMap, which have the privilege of their own chapter (chapter 10). Let's move on and see how to create a type conforming to Sequence, which gets all these methods for free.

9.2.8 Exercises

1 What is the difference between reduce and reduce(into:)?
2 How would you choose between the two?

9.3 Creating a generic data structure with Sequence

Earlier you survived the theory lesson of how Sequence and IteratorProtocol work under the hood. Now, you'll focus on building something with the newly acquired knowledge.

In this section, you're building a data structure called a `Bag`, also known as a multi-set. You'll be using `Sequence` and `IteratorProtocol` so that you get free methods on `Bag`, such as `contains` or `filter`.

A `Bag` is like a `Set`: it stores elements in an unordered way and has quick insertion and lookup capabilities. But a `Bag` can store the same element multiple times, whereas a `Set` doesn't.

Foundation has `NSCountedSet`, which is similar, but it's not a native Swift type with a Swift-like interface. The one you build here is smaller in functionality, but Swifty all over and a good exercise.

9.3.1 Seeing bags in action

First, let's see how a bag works (see figure 9.4). You can insert objects just like `Set`, but with one big difference: you can store the same object multiple times. `Bag` has one optimization trick up its sleeve, though, because it keeps track of the number of times an object is stored and doesn't physically store an object multiple times. Storing an element only once keeps memory usage down.

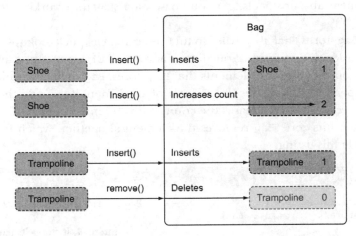

Figure 9.4 How Bag stores data

Let's see your `Bag` in action in this next listing. Its interface is similar to that of `Set`, but notice how you can add the same string multiple times. Also note that `Bag` is generic, just like `Set`, indicated by `Bag` storing strings, integers, or anything `Hashable`.

Listing 9.15 Using `Bag`

```
var bag = Bag<String>()
bag.insert("Huey")
bag.insert("Huey")
bag.insert("Huey")

bag.insert("Mickey")
```

You can insert elements into Bag.

```
bag.remove("Huey")
```
◄────── **You can also remove elements from Bag.**

```
bag.count // 3
```

```
print(bag)
// Output:
// Huey occurs 2 times
// Mickey occurs 1 time
```

```
let anotherBag: Bag = [1.0, 2.0, 2.0, 3.0, 3.0, 3.0]
 print(anotherBag)
// Output:
// 2.0 occurs 2 times
// 1.0 occurs 1 time
// 3.0 occurs 3 times
```
◄─── **You can create a Bag the same way you would create a Set. You'll see how to do this with the help of the ExpressibleByArrayLiteral protocol.**

NOTE   A bag can store anything that's `Hashable`. Even though a bag can store anything, it can't simply mix and match types—such as strings and integers—just like with `Array` or `Set`.

Before you implement any protocols, get your base data structure working to keep things simple.

Like `Set`, your `Bag` stores `Hashable` types so that you can have quick lookups by putting an element inside a dictionary. You define a generic `Element` constrained to `Hashable` for this, representing the elements that `Bag` stores. `Bag` stores each element inside a `store` property, and increases the counter of an element if you add the same element again. Conversely, `Bag` decreases the counter if you remove an element from it. When the counter hits zero, `Bag` removes the element altogether, which frees up memory, as shown in this listing.

Listing 9.16   Looking inside `Bag`

```
struct Bag<Element: Hashable> {           ◄──────  Bag stores Hashable elements.
    private var store = [Element: Int]()   ◄─
                                                  Internally it stores its data inside
    mutating func insert(_ element: Element) {    a dictionary with elements and
        store[element, default: 0] += 1    ◄─     their counts for values.
    }
                                                  When you insert an element, you
                                                  increase its count by 1. If an element
    mutating func remove(_ element: Element) {    doesn't exist in the store yet, it gets
        store[element]? -= 1                       added with a default value of 0, which
        if store[element] == 0 {                   you immediately increase as well.
            store[element] = nil
        }
    }
                                                  If an element's count is 0, you
    var count: Int {                              remove the element from Bag.
        return store.values.reduce(0, +)   ◄─
    }                                             Reduce the
}                                                 collective counts
                                                  into a total count.
```

When you remove an element, you decrease its count.

Now, with the basic functionality in place, start implementing some useful protocols. To help peek inside the bag, implement `CustomStringConvertible`. Whenever you print your bag, the `description` property supplies a custom string of the elements inside and their occurrences, as shown in this listing.

Listing 9.17 Making `Bag` conform to `CustomStringConvertible`

```
extension Bag: CustomStringConvertible {
    var description: String {
        var summary = String()
        for (key, value) in store {
            let times = value == 1 ? "time" : "times"
            summary.append("\(key) occurs \(value) \(times)\n")
        }
        return summary
    }
}
```

This is how you got the output as before:

```
let anotherBag: Bag = [1.0, 2.0, 2.0, 3.0, 3.0, 3.0]
print(anotherBag)
// Output:
// 2.0 occurs 2 times
// 1.0 occurs 1 time
// 3.0 occurs 3 times
```

9.3.2 Creating a BagIterator

You can already use `Bag` as is. But you can't iterate over it until you implement `Sequence`. To implement `Sequence`, you need an iterator, which you'll creatively call `BagIterator`.

Inside `Bag`, a `store` property holds the data. `Bag` passes `store` to the `Iterator-Protocol` so that `IteratorProtocol` can produce values one by one. Sending a copy to `IteratorProtocol` means that it can mutate its copy of the `store` without affecting `Bag`.

Since `store` is a value type, it gets copied to `IteratorProtocol` when `Bag` passes the store to `IteratorProtocol`—but not to worry: Swift optimizes this to make sure a copy is cheap.

You need to apply a little trick because `Bag` is lying. It isn't holding the number of elements that it says it does; it's merely holding the element with a counter. So you'll apply a trick: `BagIterator` returns the same element a multiple of times depending on the element's count. This way, an outsider doesn't need to know about the tricks `Bag` uses, and yet it gets the correct amount of elements.

Every time you call `next` on `BagIterator`, the iterator returns an element and lowers its count. Once the count hits nil, `BagIterator` removes the element. If no elements are left, the iterator is depleted and returns nil, signaling that `BagIterator` has finished iteration. The following listing gives an example of this.

Listing 9.18 Creating a `BagIterator`

The BagIterator conforms to IteratorProtocol, and also has a generic Element like Bag for its elements.

```
struct BagIterator<Element: Hashable>: IteratorProtocol {
```

BagIterator has its copy of the store from Bag.

```
    var store = [Element: Int]()

    mutating func next() -> Element? {
        guard let (key, value) = store.first else {
            return nil
        }
        if value > 1 {
            store[key]? -= 1
        } else {
            store[key] = nil
        }
        return key
    }
}
```

The next method from IteratorProtocol is called to supply elements.

If the store is empty, the iterator is depleted and returns nil.

If the value has some counts left, you decrease its count.

If the value has no more counts left, you remove it from the dictionary.

At the end, you return the element.

You're almost there. With `BagIterator` in place, you can extend `Bag` and make it conform to `Sequence`, as shown in the following listing. All that you need to do is implement `makeIterator` and return a freshly made `BagIterator`, which gets a fresh copy of store.

Listing 9.19 Implementing `Sequence`

Bag now conforms to Sequence.

You only need to implement the makeIterator method.

```
extension Bag: Sequence {
    func makeIterator() -> BagIterator<Element> {
        return BagIterator(store: store)
    }
}
```

You create and return a new BagIterator, but not before you supply it a copy of your store.

That was it; you now have unlocked the powers of `Sequence`, and `Bag` has plenty of free functionality. You can call `filter`, `lazy`, `reduce`, `contains`, and many other methods on a `Bag` instance.

Listing 9.20 Wielding the power of `Sequence`

```
bag.filter { $0.count > 2}
bag.lazy.filter { $0.count > 2}
bag.contains("Huey") // true
bag.contains("Mickey") // false
```

`Bag` is complete and wields the power of `Sequence`. Still, you can implement at least two more optimizations, related to `AnyIterator` and `ExpressibleByArrayLiteral`. Let's go over them now.

9.3.3   *Implementing AnyIterator*

For Bag, you had very little work to do when extending Sequence. All you did was create an instance of BagIterator and return it. In a scenario like this, you can decide to return AnyIterator to save you from creating a BagIterator altogether.

AnyIterator is a *type erased* iterator, which you can think of as a generalized iterator. AnyIterator accepts a closure when initialized; this closure is called whenever next is called on the iterator. In other words, you can put the next functionality from BagIterator inside the closure you pass to AnyIterator.

The result is that you can extend Bag by conforming to Sequence, return a new AnyIterator there, and then you can delete BagIterator.

Listing 9.21   Using `AnyIterator`

```
extension Bag: Sequence {                              The makeIterator
    func makeIterator() -> AnyIterator<Element> {      method now returns
        var exhaustiveStore = store // create copy     an AnyIterator.

        return AnyIterator<Element> {
            guard let (key, value) = exhaustiveStore.first  else {
                return nil
            }                                       You create an AnyIterator while
            if value > 1 {                           you pass it a closure, which
                exhaustiveStore[key]? -= 1          depletes the exhaustiveStore.
            } else {
                exhaustiveStore[key] = nil
            }
            return key
        }
    }
}
```

Whether you want to use AnyIterator depends on your situation, but it can be an excellent alternative to a custom iterator to remove some boilerplate.

9.3.4   *Implementing ExpressibleByArrayLiteral*

Earlier, you saw how to create a bag from an array literal syntax. Notice how you create a bag, even though you use an array-like notation:

```
let colors: Bag = ["Green", "Green", "Blue", "Yellow", "Yellow", "Yellow"]
```

To obtain this syntactic sugar, you can implement ExpressibleByArrayLiteral. By doing so, you implement an initializer that accepts an array of elements. You can then use these elements to propagate the store property of Bag. You'll use the reduce method on the array to reduce all elements into one store dictionary.

Listing 9.22 Implementing `ExpressibleByArrayLiteral`

Make Bag conform to
ExpressibleByArrayLiteral.

To conform to
ExpressibleByArrayLiteral,
you have to implement an
initializer to accept an
array of elements.

```
extension Bag: ExpressibleByArrayLiteral {
    typealias ArrayLiteralElement = Element
    init(arrayLiteral elements: Element...) {
        store = elements.reduce(into: [Element: Int]()) {
            (updatingStore, element) in
                updatingStore[element, default: 0] += 1
        }
    }
}
```

Use reduce to convert
the elements array into
a dictionary.

Increment the value of each
element inside the dictionary by
one, with a default value of zero.

```
let colors: Bag = ["Green", "Green", "Blue", "Yellow", "Yellow", "Yellow"]
print(colors)
// Output:
// Green occurs 2 times
// Blue occurs 1 time
// Yellow occurs 3 times
```

Now you can use the array syntax to
create a bag. Notice how colors is of
type Bag so Swift knows that colors
is not an array.

The `Bag` type has a Swift-friendly interface. In its current state, `Bag` is ready to use, and you can keep adding to it, such as by adding `intersection` and `union` methods to make it more valuable. Generally speaking, you won't have to create a custom data structure every day, but it does have use once in a while. Knowing about `Sequence` lays down an essential foundation because it's the base for the `Collection` protocol, which is a bit higher-level. The next section introduces the `Collection` protocol.

9.3.5 *Exercise*

3   Make an infinite sequence. This sequence keeps looping over the sequence you pass. An infinite sequence is handy to generate data, such as when zipping. The infinite sequence keeps going, but the other sequence could deplete, thus stopping the iteration.

For example, this code

```
let infiniteSequence = InfiniteSequence(["a","b","c"])
for (index, letter) in zip(0..<100, infiniteSequence) {
    print("\(index): \(letter)")
}
```

outputs the following:

```
0: a
1: b
2: c
3: a
4: b

... snip
```

```
95: c
96: a
97: b
98: c
99: a
```

9.4 The Collection protocol

It's time to move on to the next level of the iteration trifecta: besides `IteratorProtocol` and `Sequence`, there is the `Collection` protocol.

The `Collection` protocol is a subprotocol of `Sequence`—meaning that `Collection` inherits all functionality from `Sequence`. One major difference between `Collection` and `Sequence` is that collection types are indexable. In other words, with collection types, you can directly access an element at a specific position, such as via a subscript; for example, you can use `myarray[2]` or `myset["monkeywrench"]`.

Another difference is that `Sequence` doesn't dictate whether or not it's destructive, meaning that two iterations may not give the same results, which can potentially be a problem if you want to iterate over the same sequence multiple times.

As an example, if you break an iteration and continue from where you left off, you won't know if a `Sequence` continues where it stopped, or if it restarted from the beginning.

Listing 9.23 Resuming iteration on a `Sequence`

```
let numbers = // Let's say numbers is a Sequence but not a Collection
for number in numbers {
  if number == 10 {
    break
  }
}

for number in numbers {
  // Will iteration resume, or start from the beginning?
}
```

`Collection` does guarantee to be nondestructive, and it allows for repeated iteration over a type with the same results every time.

The most common `Collection` types that you use every day are `String`, `Array`, `Dictionary`, and `Set`. You'll start by taking a closer look at all available `Collection` protocols.

9.4.1 The Collection landscape

With collections, you gain indexing capabilities. For example, on `String` you can use indices to get elements, such as getting the words before and after a space character, as shown in the following listing.

Listing 9.24　Indexing a `String`

```
let strayanAnimals = "Kangaroo Koala"
if let middleIndex = strayanAnimals.index(of: " ") {          ⟵─┤ Obtain the index of a
    strayanAnimals.prefix(upTo: middleIndex) // Kangaroo           Character inside a String.
    strayanAnimals.suffix(from: strayanAnimals.index(after: middleIndex)) //
     Koala
}
```

Besides offering indexing capabilities, `Collection` has multiple subprotocols, which each offer restrictions and optimizations on top of `Collection`. For instance, `Mutable-Collection` allows for mutation of a collection, but it doesn't allow you to change its length. Alternatively, `RangeReplaceableCollection` allows the length of a collection to change. `BidirectionalCollection` allows a collection to be traversed backwards. `RandomAccessCollection` promises performance improvements over `Bidirectional-Collection` (see figure 9.5).

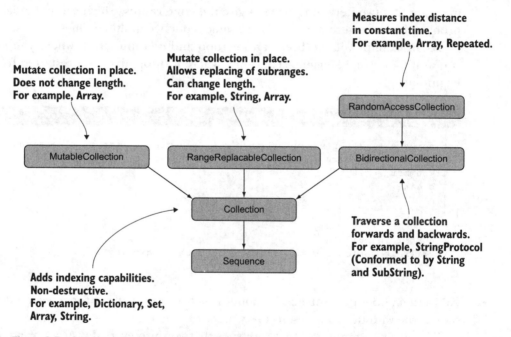

Figure 9.5　An overview of the `Collection` protocols

9.4.2　*MutableCollection*

`MutableCollection` offers methods that mutate elements in place without changing the length of a collection. Because the methods of `MutableCollection` don't change the length, the protocol can offer guarantees and performance improvements. The most common type that adheres to `MutableCollection` is `Array`.

　　`MutableCollection` adds a few special methods. To obtain these methods, you need to have a variable `Array`—as opposed to a constant—by using the `var` keyword.

With a `MutableCollection` you can sort in place:

```
var mutableArray = [4, 3, 1, 2]
mutableArray.sort() // [1, 2, 3, 4]
```

Another intriguing method that `MutableCollection` offers is `partition`. The partition method reshuffles the array in two parts that you define. On top of that, `partition` returns the index of where the array is split up. You can, as shown in this example, choose to partition an array of integers into odd and even numbers.

> **Listing 9.25 Partitioning**

```
var arr = [1,2,3,4,5]
let index = arr.partition { (int) -> Bool in        Partition the array
    return int % 2 == 0                             by even numbers.
}
                                                    The array is reshuffled;
                                                    the even numbers are
print(arr) // [1, 5, 3, 4, 2]                       now at the end.
 print(index) // 3
                                                    This is the index of the
                                                    cutoff point between odd
arr[..<index] // [1, 5, 3]                           and even numbers.
 arr[index...] // [4, 2]
                                                    The first numbers until
       The numbers after the                        the partitioned index are
       partitioned index are                        odd numbers.
       even numbers.
```

Other methods, such as `reverse()` and `swapAt()`, come in handy, too. I recommended experimenting with them and making them part of your iterator vocabulary.

STRING DOESN'T CONFORM TO MUTABLECOLLECTION

Perhaps surprisingly, `String` doesn't conform to `MutableCollection`, because the length of `String` can change if you were to reorder characters. Changing the length of a collection is something that `MutableCollection` doesn't allow.

The length of `String` changes when you reorder characters, because of its underlying structure; a character can be composed out of multiple unicode *scalars*. For instance, the character é could exist out of the scalars e and the acute accent '; swapping them around could turn é into 'e. Because moving scalars could potentially create different characters, `String` can change length, which is why `String` does *not* conform to `MutableCollection`.

9.4.3 *RangeReplaceableCollection*

Next up in the list of contenders is `RangeReplaceableCollection`, which allows you to swap out ranges and change its length. `Array` and `String` conform to `RangeReplaceableCollection`. Moreover, it brings you some handy methods, such as concatenation via the + method.

If the array is defined mutably by `var` (not to be confused with `MutableCollection`), you can use the += keyword to append in place. Notice in the next listing how you can change the length of the array with the methods offered by RangeReplaceable-Collection.

Listing 9.26   Mutating length of an array

```
var muppets = ["Kermit", "Miss Piggy", "Fozzie bear"]

muppets += ["Statler", "Waldorf"]
print(muppets) // ["Kermit", "Miss Piggy", "Fozzie bear", "Statler", "Waldorf"]

muppets.removeFirst() // "Kermit"
print(muppets) // ["Miss Piggy", "Fozzie bear", "Statler", "Waldorf"]

muppets.removeSubrange(0..<2)
print(muppets) // ["Statler", "Waldorf"]
```

Since `String` adheres to RangeReplaceableCollection, you can mutate strings in place and change its length.

Listing 9.27   Mutating `String`

```
var matrix = "The Matrix"
matrix += " Reloaded"
print(matrix) // The Matrix Reloaded
```

REMOVEALL

RangeReplaceableCollection also has a useful method called `removeAll(where:)`. With this method, you can quickly remove elements from a collection, such as Array (for instance, when you want to remove "Donut" from an array of healthy food items, as shown in the following code).

Listing 9.28   `removeAll` in action

```
var healthyFood = ["Donut", "Lettuce", "Kiwi", "Grapes"]
healthyFood.removeAll(where:{ $0 == "Donut" })
print(healthyFood) // ["Lettuce", "Kiwi", "Grapes"]
```

You may be tempted to use `filter` instead, but when removing values, special optimizations can be applied, making it faster to use the `removeAll` method on variable collections.

> **NOTE** The removeAll method is only available if your collection is a variable, as indicated with var.

9.4.4   *BidirectionalCollection*

With a `BidirectionalCollection` you can traverse a collection backwards from an index, as in the following example. You can get the index before another index, which allows you to access a previous element (such as obtaining previous characters on a string).

Listing 9.29 Iterating backwards

```
var letters = "abcd"
var lastIndex = letters.endIndex
while lastIndex > letters.startIndex {
    lastIndex = letters.index(before: lastIndex)
    print(letters[lastIndex])
}

// Output:
// d
// c
// b
// a
```

Using index(before:) is a bit low level for regular use. Idiomatically, you can use the reversed() keyword to reverse a collection.

Listing 9.30 Using reversed() instead

```
var letters = "abcd"
for value in letters.reversed() {
    print(value)
}
```

But index(before:) does help if you want to iterate backwards only a specific number of times. By using reversed(), the iterator keeps looping until you break the loop.

9.4.5 *RandomAccessCollection*

The RandomAccessCollection inherits from BidirectionalCollection and offers some performance improvements for its methods. The major difference is that it can measure distances between indices in constant time. In other words, RandomAccessCollection poses more restrictions on the implementer, because it must be able to measure the distances between indices without traversal. Potentially, traversing a collection can be expensive when you advance indices—for example, using index(_offsetBy:)—which is not the case for RandomAccessCollection.

Array conforms to all collection protocols, including RandomAccessCollection, but a more esoteric type that conforms to RandomAccessCollection is the Repeated type. This type is handy to enumerate over a value multiple times. You obtain a Repeated type by using the repeatElement function, as shown here.

Listing 9.31 Repeated type

```
for element in repeatElement("Broken record", count: 3) {
    print(element)
}

// Output:
// Broken record
```

```
// Broken record
// Broken record
```

You can use `repeatElement` to quickly generate values, which is useful for use cases such as generating test data. You can even zip them together, as in the following example, for more advanced iterations.

Listing 9.32   Using `zip`

```
zip(repeatElement("Mr. Sniffles", count: 3), repeatElement(100, count:
    3)).forEach { name, index in
  print("Generated \(name) \(index)")
}

Generated Mr. Sniffles 100
Generated Mr. Sniffles 100
Generated Mr. Sniffles 100
```

9.5   *Creating a collection*

Let's face it, in most of your programming you're not inventing a new collection type every day. You can usually get by with `Set`, `Array`, and others that Swift offers. That isn't to say that knowing about `Collection` is a waste of time, though. More often than not you have some data structure that could benefit from `Collection`. With a little bit of code, you can make your types conform to `Collection` and reap all the benefits without knowing how to balance binary search trees or by implementing other fancy algorithms.

9.5.1   *Creating a travel plan*

You'll start by making a data structure called `TravelPlan`. A travel plan is a sequence of days, consisting of one or more activities. For instance, a travel plan could be visiting Florida, and it could contain multiple activities, such as visiting Key West, being chased by alligators on the golf course, or having breakfast at the beach.

First, you'll create the data structures, and then you'll adhere `TravelPlan` to `Collection` so that you can iterate over `TravelPlan` and obtain indexing behavior. You'll start with the `Activity` and `Day` before you move on to `TravelPlan`.

As shown in this listing, `Activity` is nothing more than a timestamp and a description.

Listing 9.33   `Activity`

```
struct Activity: Equatable {
    let date: Date
    let description: String
}
```

`Day` is slightly more intricate than `Activity`. `Day` has a date, but since it covers a whole day, you can strip the time, as in this next listing. Then you can make `Day` conform to `Hashable` so that you can store it in a dictionary as a key later.

Listing 9.34   Day

```
struct Day: Hashable {                        Conform Day
    let date: Date                            to Hashable.

    init(date: Date) {
        // Strip time from Date
        let unitFlags: Set<Calendar.Component> = [.day, .month, .year]
        let components = Calendar.current.dateComponents(unitFlags, from: date)
        guard let convertedDate = Calendar.current.date(from: components) else {
            self.date = date
            return
        }
        self.date = convertedDate
    }

}
```

Create a new date without the time.

You care only about the day, month, and year components of a date, not the time.

The `TravelPlan` stores days as keys, and their activities as values. This way, a travel plan can have multiple days, where each day can have multiple activities. Having multiple activities per day is reflected by a dictionary inside `TravelPlan`. Since you refer to this dictionary multiple times, you introduce a `typealias` for convenience called `DataType`.

Also, you add an initializer that accepts activities. You can then group activities by days and store them in the dictionary. In this next listing, you'll use the `grouping` method on `Dictionary` to turn `[Activity]` into `[Day: [Activity]]`.

Listing 9.35   TravelPlan

```
struct TravelPlan {

    typealias DataType = [Day: [Activity]]          DataType is a type alias to
                                                    save you from repeatedly
    private var trips = DataType()                  typing [Day: [Activity]].

    init(activities: [Activity]) {
        self.trips = Dictionary(grouping: activities) { activity -> Day in
            Day(date: activity.date)
        }                              You can create a dictionary
    }                                  out of an array of activities
}                                      by using the grouping
                                       initializer on Dictionary.
```

`grouping` works by passing it a sequence—such as `[Activity]`—and a closure. Then grouping calls the closure for each element. You return a `Hashable` type inside the closure, and then every value of the array is added to the corresponding key. You end up with the keys—the ones you return in the closure—and an array of values for each key.

9.5.2 Implementing Collection

Now, your `TravelPlan` data structure is functional, but you can't iterate over it yet. Instead of conforming `TravelPlan` to `Sequence`, you'll make `TravelPlan` conform to `Collection`.

Surprisingly enough, you don't need to implement `makeIterator`. You could, but `Collection` supplies a default `IndexingIterator`, which is a nice benefit of adhering to `Collection`.

To adhere to `Collection`, you need to implement four things: two variables (`startIndex` and `endIndex`) and two methods (`index(after:)` and `subscript(index:)`).

Because you're not coming up with your own algorithm and you're encapsulating a type that conforms to `Collection`—in this case, a dictionary—you can use the methods of the underlying dictionary instead, as shown in this listing. In essence, you're forwarding the underlying methods of a dictionary.

Listing 9.36 Implementing `Collection`

```
extension TravelPlan: Collection {

    typealias KeysIndex = DataType.Index          Make two aliases
    typealias DataElement = DataType.Element       for convenience.

    var startIndex: KeysIndex { return trips.keys.startIndex }
    var endIndex: KeysIndex { return trips.keys.endIndex }

    func index(after i: KeysIndex) -> KeysIndex {
        return trips.index(after: i)
    }

    subscript(index: KeysIndex) -> DataElement {
        return trips[index]
    }

}
```

Forward the startIndex and endIndex properties from the underlying dictionary.

Forward the index(after:) and subscript(index:) methods from the underlying dictionary.

That's all it took! Now `TravelPlan` is a full-fledged `Collection` and you can iterate over it.

Listing 9.37 `TravelPlan` iteration

```
for (day, activities) in travelPlan {
    print(day)
    print(activities)
}
```

You don't have to come up with a custom iterator. `Collection` supplies `IndexingIterator` for you.

Listing 9.38 A default iterator

```
let defaultIterator: IndexingIterator<TravelPlan> = travelPlan.makeIterator()
```

9.5.3 Custom subscripts

By adhering to `Collection`, you gain subscript capabilities, which let you access a collection via square brackets [].

But since you're forwarding the one from a dictionary, you'd have to use an esoteric dictionary index type. In the next listing, you'll create a few convenient subscripts instead, which allows you to access elements via a useful subscript syntax.

Listing 9.39 Implementing subscripts

```
extension TravelPlan {
    subscript(date: Date) -> [Activity] {
        return trips[Day(date: date)] ?? []
    }

    subscript(day: Day) -> [Activity] {
        return trips[day] ?? []
    }
}

// Now, you can access contents via convenient subscripts.

travelPlan[Date()]           ⟵───┤ You can subscript
                                  │ with a Date.

let day = Day(date: Date())
travelPlan[day]              ⟵───┤ You can subscript
                                  │ with a Day.
```

Another critical aspect of `Collection` is that the subscript is expected to give back a result instantaneously unless stated otherwise for your type. Instant access is also referred to as *constant-time* or $O(1)$ performance in Big-O notation. Since you're forwarding method calls from a dictionary, `TravelPlan` is returning values in constant time. If you were to traverse a full collection to get a value, access would not be instantaneous, and you would have a so-called $O(n)$ performance. With $O(n)$ performance, longer collections mean that lookup times increase linearly. Developers that use your collection may not expect that.

9.5.4 ExpressibleByDictionaryLiteral

Like you did with the `Bag` type in section 9.3.4, "Implementing ExpressibleByArray-Literal", you can implement the `ExpressibleByArrayLiteral` protocol for convenient initializing. To conform to this protocol, you merely have to adopt an initializer that accepts multiple elements. As shown in this listing, inside the body of the initializer, you can relay the method by calling an existing initializer.

Listing 9.40 Implementing `ExpressibleByArrayLiteral`

```
extension TravelPlan: ExpressibleByArrayLiteral {
    init(arrayLiteral elements: Activity...) {
        self.init(activities: elements)
```

```
        }
    }
```

Another protocol you can implement for convenience is ExpressibleByDictionary-Literal. It's similar to ExpressibleByArrayLiteral, but it allows you to create a TravelPlan from a dictionary notation instead. You implement an initializer that supplies an array of tuples. Then you can use the uniquingKeysWith: method on Dictionary to turn the tuples into a dictionary. The closure you pass to uniquing-KeysWith: is called when a conflict of two keys occurs. In this case, you choose one of the two conflicting values, as shown in the following code.

> **Listing 9.41   Implementing ExpressibleByDictionaryLiteral**

```
extension TravelPlan: ExpressibleByDictionaryLiteral {        Pass an array of tuples to
    init(dictionaryLiteral elements: (Day, [Activity])...) {   a Dictionary initializer.
        self.trips = Dictionary(elements, uniquingKeysWith: { (first: Day, ) in  ◄
            return first // Choose one when a Day is duplicate.   ◄
        })
    }
}                                                    If two days are equal, you
                                                     have a conflict. You use the
                                                     closure to decide to use one
                                                     of the two days.

let adrenalineTrip = Day(date: Date())
let adrenalineActivities = [
    Activity(date: Date(), description: "Bungee jumping"),
    Activity(date: Date(), description: "Driving in rush hour LA"),
    Activity(date: Date(), description: "Sky diving")
]


let adrenalinePlan = [adrenalineTrip: activities] // You can now create a
    TravelPlan from a dictionary
```

9.5.5   Exercise

4   Make the following type adhere to the Collection protocol:

```
struct Fruits {
    let banana = "Banana"
    let apple = "Apple"
    let tomato = "Tomato"
}
```

9.6   Closing thoughts

You've successfully—and relatively painlessly—created a custom type that adheres to Collection. The real power lies in recognizing when you can implement these iteration protocols. Chances are that you might have some types in your projects that can gain extra functionality by adhering to Collection.

You've also taken a closer look at Sequence and IteratorProtocol to get a deeper understand of how iteration works in Swift. You don't need to be an algorithmic wizard to power up your types, which come in handy in day-to-day work. You also discovered a handful of widespread and useful iterator methods you can find on `Sequence`. If you want more iteration tips, check out chapter 10, which covers `map`, `flatMap`, and `compactMap`.

Summary

- Iterators produce elements.
- To iterate, Swift uses a while loop on `makeIterator()` under the covers.
- Sequences produce iterators, allowing them to be iterated over repeatedly.
- Sequences won't guarantee the same values when iterated over multiple times.
- `Sequence` is the backbone for methods such as `filter`, `reduce`, `map`, `zip`, `repeat`, and many others.
- `Collection` inherits from `Sequence`.
- `Collection` is a protocol that adds subscript capabilities and guarantees nondestructive iteration.
- `Collection` has subprotocols, which are more-specialized versions of `Collection`.
- `MutableCollection` is a protocol that offers mutating methods without changing the length of a collection.
- `RangeReplaceableCollection` is a protocol that restricts collections for easy modification of part of a collection. As a result, the length of a collection may change. It also offers useful methods, such as `removeAll(where:)`.
- `BidirectionalCollection` is a protocol that defines a collection that can be traversed both forward and backward.
- `RandomAccessCollection` restricts collections to constant-time traversal between indices.
- You can implement `Collection` for regular types that you use in day-to-day programming.

Answers

1 What is the difference between reduce and `reduce(into:)`?

With `reduce(into:)` you can prevent copies for each iteration.

2 How would you choose between the two?

`reduce` makes sense when you aren't creating expensive copies for each iteration, such as when you're reducing into an integer. `reduce(into:)` makes more sense when you're reducing into a struct, such as an array or dictionary.

3 Make an infinite sequence. This sequence will keep looping over the sequence you pass:

```
// If you implement both Sequence and IteratorProtocol, you only need
➥ to implement the next method.
struct InfiniteSequence<S: Sequence>: Sequence, IteratorProtocol {
```

```
        let sequence: S
        var currentIterator: S.Iterator
        var isFinished: Bool = false

        init(_ sequence: S) {
            self.sequence = sequence
            self.currentIterator = sequence.makeIterator()
        }

        mutating func next() -> S.Element? {
            guard !isFinished else {
                return nil
            }

            if let element = currentIterator.next() {
                return element
            } else {
                self.currentIterator = sequence.makeIterator()
                let element = currentIterator.next()
                if element == nil {
                    // If sequence is still empty after creating a new one,
                    then the sequence is empty to begin with; you will need to protect
                    against this in case of an infinite loop.
                    isFinished = true
                }
                return element
            }
        }

    }

    let infiniteSequence = InfiniteSequence(["a","b","c"])
    for (index, letter) in zip(0..<100, infiniteSequence) {
        print("\(index): \(letter)")
    }
```

4 Make the following type adhere to Collection:

```
    struct Fruits {
        let banana = "Banana"
        let apple = "Apple"
        let tomato = "Tomato"
    }

    extension Fruits: Collection {
        var startIndex: Int {
            return 0
        }

        var endIndex: Int {
            return 3 // Yep, it's 3, not 2. That's how Collection wants it.
        }

        func index(after i: Int) -> Int {
            return i+1
        }
```

```
    subscript(index: Int) -> String {
        switch index {
        case 0: return banana
        case 1: return apple
        case 2: return tomato
        default: fatalError("The fruits end here.")
        }
    }

}

let fruits = Fruits()
fruits.forEach { (fruit) in
    print(fruit)
}
```

10

Understanding map, flatMap, and compactMap

This chapter covers

- Mapping over arrays, dictionaries, and other collections
- When and how to `map` over optionals
- How and why to `flatMap` over collections
- Using `flatMap` on optionals
- Chaining and short-circuiting computations
- How to mix `map` and `flatMap` for advanced transformations

Modern languages like Swift borrow many concepts from the functional programming world, and `map` and `flatMap` are powerful examples of that. Sooner or later in your Swift career, you'll run into (or write) code that applies `map` and `flatMap` operations on arrays, dictionaries, and even optionals. With `map` and `flatMap`, you can write hard-hitting, succinct code that is immutable—and therefore safer. Moreover, since version 4.1, Swift introduces `compactMap`, which is another refreshing operation that helps you perform effective transformations on optionals inside collections.

In fact, you may even be familiar with applying `map` and `flatMap` now and then in your code. This chapter takes a deep dive to show how you can apply `map` and flatMap in many ways. Also, it compares these operations against alternatives and looks at the trade-offs that come with them, so you'll know exactly how to decide between a functional programming style or an imperative style.

This chapter flows well after reading chapter 9. If you haven't read it yet, I recommend going back to that chapter before reading this one.

First, you'll see how map works on arrays and how you can easily perform effective transformations via a pipeline. Also, you'll find out how iterative *for* loops fare against the functional map method, so you'll have some rules of thumb to pick between each style.

Then you'll learn about mapping over dictionaries, and other types conforming to the Sequence protocol for an in-depth look.

After covering mapping over collections, you'll find out more about mapping over optionals, which allows you to delay unwrapping of optionals and program a happy path in your program. Then you'll see that map is an abstraction and how it's beneficial to your code.

Being able to apply flatMap on optionals is the next big subject. You'll see how map doesn't always cut it when dealing with nested optionals, but luckily, flatMap can help.

Then, you'll see how flatMap can help you fight nested *if let* unwrapping of optionals—sometimes referred to as the pyramid of doom. You'll discover how you can create powerful transformations while maintaining high code readability.

Like map, flatMap is also defined on collections. This chapter covers Collection types, such as arrays and strings, to show how you can harness flatMap for succinct operations.

Taking it one step further, you'll get a look at how optionals and collections are affected with compactMap. You'll see how you can filter nils while transforming collections.

As a cherry on top, you'll explore the differences and benefits after you start nesting map, flatMap, and compactMap operations.

The goal of this chapter is to make sure you're confident incorporating map, flatMap, and compactMap often in your daily programming. You'll see how to write more concise code, as well as more immutable code, and learn some cool tips and tricks along the way, even if you've already been using map or flatMap from time to time. Another reason to get comfortable with map and flatMap is to prepare you for asynchronous error-handling in chapter 11, where map and flatMap will return.

10.1   *Becoming familiar with map*

> **JOIN ME!**   It's more educational and fun if you can check out the code and follow along with the chapter. You can download the source code at http://mng .bz/mzr2.

Receiving an array, looping over it, and transforming its values is a routine operation.

Suppose that you have the names and git commits of people on a project. You could create a more readable format to see if some developers are involved in a project. To transform the names and commits to a readable format, you start with a *for* loop to iterate over each value and use that to fill up the array you want.

Listing 10.1   Transforming an array

Inside the resolveCounts function, you create a temporary array that you'll return.

An array of tuples as data to work with

```
let commitStats = [
    (name: "Miranda", count: 30),
    (name: "Elly", count: 650),
    (name: "John", count: 0)
]

let readableStats = resolveCounts(statistics: commitStats)
print(readableStats) // ["Miranda isn't very active on the project", "Elly
    is quite active", "John isn't involved in the project"]

func resolveCounts(statistics: [(String, Int)]) -> [String] {
    var resolvedCommits = [String]()
    for (name, count) in statistics {
        let involvement: String

        switch count {
        case 0: involvement = "\(name) isn't involved in the project"
        case 1..<100: involvement =  "\(name) isn't active on the project"
        default: involvement =  "\(name) is active on the project"
        }

        resolvedCommits.append(involvement)
    }
    return resolvedCommits
}
```

Pass the array of tuples to the resolveCounts function.

To iterate over the tuples, name and count are bound to constants.

Create an involvement string which will be populated with a value.

Depending on the count, you set the involvement string.

Append each string to the resolvedCommits variable.

When all is done, the resolvedCommits variable is returned as the transformed result.

The *for* loop is a good start, but you have some boilerplate. You need a new variable array (`resolvedCommits`), which could theoretically be mutated by accident.

Now that the function is in place, you can easily refactor its body without affecting the rest of the program. Here, you'll use map to turn this imperative style of looping into a map operation.

With map, you can iterate over each element and pass it to a closure that returns a new value. Then, you end up with a new array that contains the new values (see figure 10.1).

In code, this means you're passing a closure to map, which gets called for each element in the array. In the closure, you return a new string, and the new array is built with these strings. After map finishes, `resolveCounts` returns this new mapped array.

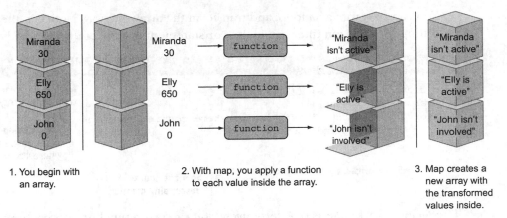

1. You begin with an array.

2. With map, you apply a function to each value inside the array.

3. Map creates a new array with the transformed values inside.

Figure 10.1   A map operation on an array

Listing 10.2   Refactoring a *for* loop with map

You still match on the count to determine the string.

A closure is passed to map on the statistics array. After map is done, resolveCounts returns a new array.

```
func resolveCounts(statistics: [(String, Int)]) -> [String] {
    return statistics.map { (name: String, count: Int) -> String in
        switch count {
        case 0: return "\(name) isn't involved in the project."
        case 1..<100: return "\(name) isn't very active on the project."
        default: return "\(name) is active on the project."
        }
    }
}
```

A new string is returned in the closure for each iteration.

Notice how the structure of the new array is intact. You end up with a new Array, with the same length, except its inner values are transformed.

Both the map approach and the *for* loop give the same results, but the map operation is shorter and immutable, which are two benefits. Another difference with a *for* loop is that with *for* you're responsible for creating a new array, instead of letting the map function handle this for you.

10.1.1   Creating a pipeline with map

Pipelines are an expressive way to describe the steps of data transformations. Let's discover how this works.

Imagine that you have a function that again takes the names and commit counts. It returns only the counts, but sorted and with empty counts filtered out, such as the following:

[(name: "Miranda", count: 30), (name: "Elly", count: 650), (name: "John", count: 0)] turns into [650, 30].

You can start with a *for* loop, and transform the array that way. Notice in the following listing how you can filter inside the *for* statement outside of the loop body.

Listing 10.3   Transforming data with a `for` loop

```
func counts(statistics: [(String, Int)]) -> [Int] {
    var counts = [Int]()
    for (name, count) in statistics where count > 0 {
        counts.append(count)
    }

    return counts.sorted(by: >)
}
```

Again, you create a temporary array.

Filter during iteration via a where statement.

Sort the counts in descending manner.

The *for* loop works fine as is. Alternatively, you can take a pipeline approach where you separately describe each step. Notice how for every step, a value goes in, and a value goes out, allowing you to connect the pieces of a pipeline in a modular fashion. You can express the intent of the operations quite elegantly, as shown here.

Listing 10.4   Transforming data with a pipeline

```
func counts(statistics: [(String, Int)]) -> [Int] {
    return statistics
        .map { $0.1 }
        .filter { $0 > 0 }
        .sorted(by: >)
}
```

When transformations are done, the result is returned.

map over the tuples inside the statistics array, returning only the counts.

Sort the counts.   Filter out any empty counts.

The `map` method is a crucial component in constructing a pipeline because it returns a new array. It helps you transform data while you can keep chaining, such as by sorting and filtering operations you apply.

A pipeline defines a clear and immutable way of transforming your data into separate steps. In contrast, if you perform many operations inside a single *for* loop, you risk ending up with a more complex loop and mutable arrays. The second downside of a *for* loop is that many actions can muddy up the loop, where you end up with hard-to-maintain or even buggy code.

The downside of this pipeline approach is that you perform at least two loops on this array: one for `filter`, one for `map`, and some iterations used by the `sorted` method, which doesn't need to perform a full iteration. With a *for* loop, you can be more efficient by combining the `map` and `filter` in one loop (and also sorting if you want to reinvent the wheel). Generally speaking, a pipeline is performant enough and worth the expressive and immutable nature—Swift is fast, after all. But when absolute performance is vital, a *for* loop might be the better approach.

Another benefit of a *for* loop is that you can stop an iteration halfway with `continue`, `break`, or `return`. But with `map` or a pipeline, you'd have to perform a complete iteration of an array for every action.

Generally speaking, readability and immutability are more crucial than performance optimizations. Use what fits your scenario best.

10.1.2 *Mapping over a dictionary*

An array isn't the only type of collection you can map over. You can even map over dictionaries. For instance, if you have the commits data in the shape of a dictionary, you can again transform these into string values.

Before you work with dictionaries, as a tip, you can effortlessly turn your array of tuples into a dictionary via the uniqueKeysWithValues initializer on Dictionary, as shown in this code.

Listing 10.5 Turning tuples into a dictionary

```
print(commitStats) // [(name: "Miranda", count: 30), (name: "Elly", count:
    650), (name: "John", count: 0)]
let commitsDict = Dictionary(uniqueKeysWithValues: commitStats)
print(commitsDict) // ["Miranda": 30, "Elly": 650, "John": 0]
```

> **UNIQUE KEYS** If two tuples with the same keys are passed to Dictionary (uniqueKeysWithValues:), a runtime error occurs. For instance, if you pass [(name: "Miranda", count: 30), name: "Miranda", count 40)], an application could crash. In that case, you may want to use Dictionary(_:uniquing-KeysWith:).

Now that you own a dictionary, you can map over it, as shown here.

Listing 10.6 Mapping over a dictionary

```
print(commitsDict) // ["Miranda": 30, "Elly": 650, "John": 0]

let mappedKeysAndValues = commitsDict.map { (name: String, count: Int) ->
    String in
    switch count {
    case 0: return "\(name) isn't involved in the project."
    case 1..<100: return "\(name) isn't very active on the project."
    default: return "\(name) is active on the project."
    }
}

print(mappedKeysAndValues) // ["Miranda isn't very active on the project",
➥ "Elly is active on the project", "John isn't involved in the project"]
```

> **FROM DICTIONARY TO ARRAY** Be aware that going from a dictionary to an array means that you go from an unordered collection to an ordered collection, which may not be the correct ordering you'd like.

With map, you turned both a key and value into a single string. If you want, you can only map over a dictionary's values. For instance, you can transform the counts into strings, while keeping the names in the dictionary, as in the next example.

Listing 10.7   Mapping over a dictionary's values

```
let mappedValues = commitsDict.mapValues { (count: Int) -> String in
    switch count {
    case 0: return "Not involved in the project."
    case 1..<100: return "Not very active on the project."
    default: return "Is active on the project"
    }
}

print(mappedValues) // ["Miranda": "Very active on the project", "Elly":
➥ "Is active on the project", "John": "Not involved in the project"]
```

Note that by using `mapValues`, you keep owning a dictionary, but with `map` you end up with an array.

10.1.3   *Exercises*

1   Create a function that turns an array into a nested array. Make sure to use the map method. Given the following:

```
makeSubArrays(["a","b","c"]) // [[a], [b], [c]]
makeSubArrays([100,50,1]) // [[100], [50], [1]]
```

2   Create a function that transforms the values inside a dictionary for movies. Each rating, from 1 to 5, needs to be turned into a human readable format (for example, a rating of 1.2 is "Very low", a rating of 3 is "Average", and a rating of 4.5 is "Excellent"):

```
let moviesAndRatings: [String : Float] = ["Home Alone 4" : 1.2, "Who
➥ Framed Roger Rabbit?" : 4.6, "Star Wars: The Phantom Menace" : 2.2,
➥ "The Shawshank Redemption" : 4.9]

let moviesHumanRadable = transformRating(moviesAndRatings)

print(moviesHumanRadable) // ["Home Alone 4": "Weak", "Star Wars: The
➥ Phantom Menace": "Average", "Who Framed Roger Rabbit?": "Excellent",
➥ "The Shawshank Redemption": "Excellent"]
```

3   Still looking at movies and ratings, convert the dictionary into a single description per movie with the rating appended to the title. For example

```
let movies: [String : Float] = ["Home Alone 4" : 1.2, "Who framed Roger
➥ Rabbit?" : 4.6, "Star Wars: The Phantom Menace" : 2.2, "The Shawshank
➥ Redemption" : 4.9]
```

turns into

```
["Home Alone 4 (Weak)", "Star Wars: The Phantom Menace (Average)",
➥ "Who framed Roger Rabbit? (Excellent)", "The Shawshank Redemption
➥ (Excellent)"]
```

Try to use map if possible.

10.2 *Mapping over sequences*

You saw before how you could map over Array and Dictionary types. These types implement a Collection and Sequence protocol.

As an example, you can generate mock data—such as for tests or to fill up screens in a user interface—by defining some names, creating a Range of integers, and mapping over each iteration. In this case, you can quickly generate an array of names, as in this example.

Listing 10.8 Mapping over a Range sequence

```
let names = [          ◁──  Define a set of names      Measure the count once
    "John",                 to be generated.           (as opposed to in each
    "Mary",                                             iteration of map).
    "Elizabeth"
]
let nameCount = names.count   ◁────────────             map over a range, in
                                                        this case from 0 to 4.
let generatedNames = (0..<5).map { index in   ◁──
    return names[index % nameCount]   ◁──────           Using a modulus operator,
}                                                       you generate a value of either
                                                        0, 1, or 2. Then you pick a
                                                        name based on this value.

print(generatedNames) // ["John", "Mary", "Elizabeth", "John", "Mary"]
```

With a Range, you can generate numbers; but by mapping over a range, you can generate values that can be something other than numbers.

Besides ranges, you can also apply map on zip or stride because they conform to the Sequence protocol. With map, you can generate lots of useful values and instances. Performing map on sequences and collections always returns a new Array, which is something to keep in mind when working with map on these types.

10.2.1 *Exercise*

4 Generate an array of the letters "a", "b", and "c" 10 times. The end result should be ["a", "b", "c", "a", "b", "c", "a" ...] until the array is 30 elements long. Try to use map if you can.

10.3 *Mapping over optionals*

At first, applying map may seem like a fancy way to update values inside of collections. But the map concept isn't reserved for collections alone. You can also map over optionals. Strange, perhaps? Not really—it's a similar concept to transforming a value inside a container.

Mapping over an array means that you transform its inside values. In contrast, mapping over an optional means that you transform its *single* value (assuming it has one). Mapping over a collection versus mapping over an optional isn't so different after all. You're going to get comfortable with it and wield its power.

10.3.1 *When to use map on optionals*

Imagine that you're creating a printing service where you can print out books with social media photos and their comments. Unfortunately, the printing service doesn't support special characters, such as emojis, so you need to strip emojis from the texts.

Let's see how you can use map to clean up your code while stripping emojis. But before you map over an optional, you'll start with a way to strip emojis from strings, which you'll use in the mapping operation.

STRIPPING EMOJIS

First, you need a function that strips the emojis from a String; it does so by iterating over the unicodeScalars view of a String, and removes each scalar that's an emoji. You achieve this by passing the isEmoji method to the removeAll method, as shown here.

Listing 10.9   The `removeEmojis` function

Remove each scalar that is an emoji.

Convert the scalars back to a String again before returning it.

Create a mutable copy of the string's scalars. It needs to be mutable so that you can call removeAll.

The isEmoji function is a placeholder at this stage so that you can finish removeEmojis first.

```
func removeEmojis(_ string: String) -> String {
    var scalars = string.unicodeScalars
    scalars.removeAll(where: isEmoji)
    return String(scalars)
}

func isEmoji(_ scalar: Unicode.Scalar) -> Bool {
    // You'll fill the body. First, let's focus on the function signatures.
    return true
}
```

A useful approach when creating new functionality is to create dummy functions, such as isEmoji, so that you can finish up the high-level functions you want to create, such as removeEmojis, without losing focus over low-level functions.

At this stage, removeEmojis is ready and the code compiles. You're ready to focus on finishing the function body of isEmoji.

To create isEmoji, you check if a Unicode is part of an emoji range by pattern matching on the emoji range.

Listing 10.10   Detect if Unicode is in emoji range

```
/// Detect if Unicode is an emoji, based on Unicode tables
/// https://apps.timwhitlock.info/emoji/tables/unicode
func isEmoji(_ scalar: Unicode.Scalar) -> Bool {
    switch Int(scalar.value) {
    case 0x1F601...0x1F64F: return true // Emoticons
    case 0x1F600...0x1F636: return true // Additional emoticons
    case 0x2702...0x27B0: return true // Dingbats
    case 0x1F680...0x1F6C0: return true // Transport and map symbols
    case 0x1F681...0x1F6C5: return true // Additional transport and map symbols
    case 0x24C2...0x1F251: return true // Enclosed characters
    case 0x1F30D...0x1F567: return true // Other additional symbols
```

```
        default: return false
        }
}
```

With both functions complete, let's continue and see how you can embed this in a mapping operation to clean up your code.

10.3.2 *Creating a cover*

Back to your printing service. To create a printed photo book, you need to create a cover. This cover will always have an image, and it will have an optional title to display on top of the image.

The goal is to apply the `removeEmojis` function to the optional title, so that when a cover contains a title, the emojis will get stripped. This way, the emojis don't end up as squares on a printed photo book (see figure 10.2).

```
let cover = Cover(image: image, title: "🖤 OMG Cute ☆☆babypics☆☆! 😍🖤🍼👶")
print(cover.title) // Optional("OMG Cute babypics!")
```

Figure 10.2 Removing emojis from a cover title

In the following listing, you introduce the `Cover` class, which contains an optional `title` property. Because `removeEmojis` doesn't accept an optional, you'll first unwrap the title to apply the `removeEmojis` function.

Listing 10.11 The `Cover` class

```
class Cover {
    let image: UIImage
    let title: String?

    init(image: UIImage, title: String?) {
        self.image = image

        var cleanedTitle: String? = nil
        if let title = title {
            cleanedTitle = removeEmojis(title)
        }
        self.title = cleanedTitle
    }
}
```

- `var cleanedTitle: String? = nil` — **Create a temporary variable.**
- `if let title = title {` — **The optional title is unwrapped.**
- `cleanedTitle = removeEmojis(title)` — **The removeEmojis function is applied to the unwrapped title.**
- `self.title = cleanedTitle` — **The title on the class is set.**

You can condense (and improve) these four steps into a single step by mapping over the optional.

If you were to map over an optional, you'd apply the `removeEmojis()` function on the unwrapped value inside `map` (if there is one). If the optional is nil, the mapping operation is ignored (see figure 10.3).

In listing 10.12, you'll see how mapping over an optional would look like inside your `Cover`.

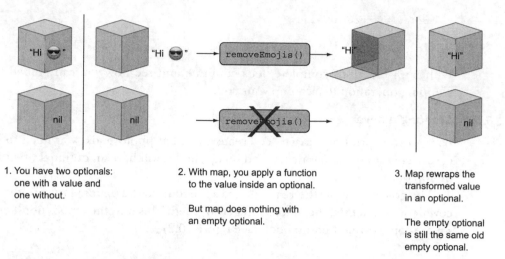

1. You have two optionals: one with a value and one without.

2. With map, you apply a function to the value inside an optional.

   But map does nothing with an empty optional.

3. Map rewraps the transformed value in an optional.

   The empty optional is still the same old empty optional.

Figure 10.3   A `map` operation on two optionals

Listing 10.12   Mapping over a title

```
class Cover {
    let image: UIImage
    let title: String?

    init(image: UIImage, title: String?) {
        self.image = image

        self.title = title.map { (string: String) -> String in
            return removeEmojis(string)
        }
    }
}
```

Pass a closure to map on the optional title.

Inside the closure you have a regular string, which you transform with removeEmojis.

Both operations give you the same output, which is a title without emojis, except you shortened the operation with map.

> **INSIDE MAP**   Notice how the value inside the map closure isn't an optional. That's the beauty of map: you don't have to worry about a value being optional or not.

10.3.3   A shorter map notation

You managed to shave off a few lines; big whoop, right? Let's see if you can shorten it further.

You can start by using the shorthand notation of a closure:

```
self.title = title.map { removeEmojis($0) }
```

But all map needs is a function, closure or not, that takes an argument and returns a value. So instead of creating a closure, you can pass your existing function remove-Emojis straight to map:

```
self.title = title.map(removeEmojis)
```

Passing removeEmojis directly to map works because it's a function that accepts one parameter and returns one parameter, which is exactly what map expects.

> **NOTE** The curly braces { } are replaced by parentheses ( ) because you're not creating a closure; you're passing a function reference as a regular argument.

The end result, as shown in this listing, is now much shorter.

Listing 10.13 Clean mapping

```
class Cover {
    let image: UIImage
    let title: String?

    init(image: UIImage, title: String?) {
        self.image = image
        self.title = title.map(removeEmojis)
    }
}
```

By using map, you turned your multiline unwrapping logic into a clean, immutable one-liner. The title property remains an optional string, but its values are transformed when the passed title argument has a value.

BENEFITS OF MAPPING OVER OPTIONALS

An optional has a context: namely, whether or not a value is nil. With map, you could think of mapping over this context. Considering optionals in Swift are everywhere, mapping over them is a powerful tool.

You can perform actions on the optional as if the optional were unwrapped; this way you can delay unwrapping the optional. Also, the function you pass to map doesn't need to know or deal with optionals, which is another benefit.

Applying map helps you remove boilerplate. Thanks to map, you're not fiddling with temporary variables or manual unwrapping anymore. Programming in an immutable way is good practice because it saves you from variables changing right under your nose.

Another benefit of map is that you can keep chaining, as shown in the following listing. For example, besides removing emojis, you can also remove whitespace from the title by mapping over it twice.

Listing 10.14 Chaining map operations

```
class Cover {
    let image: UIImage
    let title: String?
```

```
init(image: UIImage, title: String?) {
    self.image = image
    self.title = title.map(removeEmojis).map { $0.trimmingCharacters(in:
.whitespaces) }
    }
}
```

Listing 10.14 maps over the same optional twice. First, you pass a removeEmojis function, and then a closure to trim the whitespace. The second map operation is done via
a closure because you can't pass a function reference in this case. Also, notice how you
haven't unwrapped the optional once, yet you performed multiple actions on it.

You end up with a small pipeline where you immutably apply mapping operations
on the optional. Somewhere else in the application you can unwrap the optional to
read the value. But until then, you can pretend that the optional isn't nil and work
with its inner value.

10.3.4 *Exercise*

5 Given a contact data dictionary, the following code gets the street and city from
   the data and cleans up the strings. See if you can reduce the boilerplate (and be
   sure to use map somewhere):

```
let contact =
    ["address":

        [
            "zipcode": "12345",
            "street": "broadway",
            "city": "wichita"
        ]

    ]

func capitalizedAndTrimmed(_ string: String) -> String {
    return string.trimmingCharacters(in: .whitespaces).capitalized
}

// Clean up this code:
var capitalizedStreet: String? = nil
var capitalizedCity: String? = nil

if let address = contact["address"] {
    if let street = address["street"] {
        capitalizedStreet = capitalizedAndTrimmed(street.capitalized)
    }
    if let city = address["city"] {
        capitalizedCity = capitalizedAndTrimmed(city.capitalized)
    }
}

print(capitalizedStreet) // Broadway
print(capitalizedCity) // Wichita
```

10.4 map is an abstraction

With map, you can transform data while bypassing containers or contexts, such as arrays, dictionaries, or optionals.

Refer back to your method that strips emojis from a string, used in the previous section. Via the use of map, you can use the removeEmojis function on all types of containers, such as strings, dictionaries, or sets (see figure 10.4).

```
let omgBabies: String? = "💜 OMG Cute ⭐⭐babypics⭐⭐! 😎💜✏️😺"
print(omgBabies.map(removeEmojis)) // Optional(" OMG Cute babypics! ")

let food = ["Favorite Meal": "🍕 Pizza", "Favorite Drink": "☕ Coffee"]
print(food.mapValues(removeEmojis)) // ["Favorite Meal": " Pizza", "Favorite Drink": " Coffee"]

let set: Set<String> = ["Great job 👍", "Excellent 🙌"]
print(set.map(removeEmojis)) // ["Great job ", "Excellent "]
```

Figure 10.4 Removing emojis on multiple types

No matter whether you're dealing with dictionaries, arrays, optionals, or sets, the removeEmoji works on any type via the use of map. You don't need to write a removeEmojis function separately for each type.

The map abstraction is called a *functor*, which is a name coming from the field of mathematics and category theory. Mathematics is something you don't need to know about to use map. But it's interesting to see how a functor defines something that you can map over, and that Swift borrows the map function from the functional programming world.

10.5 Grokking flatMap

Understanding flatMap can be a rite of passage in Swift. At first, flatMap is like a monster under your bed: it's scary at first, but once you confront it, you'll see that flatMap isn't so bad.

This section's goal is for you to develop an understanding of `flatMap`—going for that feeling of "That was it?", like a magic trick being spoiled.

10.5.1 *What are the benefits of flatMap?*

Let's take the magic away: `flatMap` is a flatten operation after a `map` operation.

A flatten operation is useful when you're applying `map`, but you end up with a nested type. For instance, while mapping you end up with `Optional(Optional(4))`, but you wish it were `Optional(4)`. Alternatively, you end up with `[[1, 2, 3], [4, 5, 6]]`, but you need `[1, 2, 3, 4, 5, 6]`.

Simply put: with `flatMap` you combine nested structures.

It's a little more involved than that—such as the ability to sequence operations while carrying contexts, or when you want to program happy paths—but you'll get into that soon.

That's all the theory for now. That wasn't so bad, was it? Let's get right to the fun parts.

10.5.2 *When map doesn't cut it*

Let's take a look at how `flatMap` affects optionals.

Consider the following example where you want to transform an optional `String` to an optional `URL`. You naïvely try to use `map` and quickly see that it isn't suited for this situation.

Listing 10.15 Transforming a `String` to `URL`

```
// You received this data.
let receivedData = ["url": "https://www.clubpenguinisland.com"]

let path: String? = receivedData["url"]

let url = path.map { (string: String) -> URL? in
    let url = URL(string: string) // Optional(https://www.clubpenguinisland.com)
    return url // You return an optional string
}

print(url) // Optional(Optional(http://www.clubpenguinisland.com))
```

In this scenario, an optional `String` is given to you; you'd like to transform it into an optional `URL` object.

The problem, however, is that the creation of a `URL` can return a nil value. `URL` returns nil when you pass it an invalid `URL`.

When you're applying `map`, you're returning a `URL?` object in the mapping function. Unfortunately, you end up with two optionals nested in each other, such as `Optional(Optional(http://www.clubpenguinisland.com))`.

When you'd like to remove one layer of nesting, you can force unwrap the optional. Easy, right? See the results in the following code.

Listing 10.16 Removing double nesting with a force unwrap

```
let receivedData = ["url": "https://www.clubpenguinisland.com"]

let path: String? = receivedData["url"]

let url = path.map { (string: String) -> URL in          ⟵  You return a
    return URL(string: string)!                                regular URL now.
}                                               ⟵  You force unwrap—
                                                   dangerous!

print(url) // Optional(http://www.clubpenguinisland.com).  ⟵  The optional isn't
                                                               nested anymore.
```

Hold your ponies.

Even though this solves your double-nested optional problem, you've now introduced a possible crash by using a force unwrap. In this example, the code works fine because the URL is valid. But in real-world applications, that might not be the case. As soon as the URL returns nil, you're done for, and you have a crash.

Instead, as shown here, you can use flatMap to remove one layer of nesting.

Listing 10.17 Using flatMap to remove double-nested optional

```
let receivedData = ["url": "https://www.clubpenguinisland.com"]

let path: String? = receivedData["url"]

let url = path.flatMap { (string: String) -> URL? in     ⟵  You return
    return URL(string: string)                                URL? again.
}                                               ⟵  You return an
                                                   optional URL.!

print(url) // Optional(http://www.clubpenguinisland.com).  ⟵  The optional isn't
                                                               double-nested.
```

Note how you return a URL? again in the flatMap function. Just like with map, both closures are the same. But because you use flatMap, a flattening operation happens *after* the transformation. This flattening operation removes one layer of optional nesting.

FlatMap first performs a map, and then it flattens the optional. It can help to think of flatMap as mapFlat, because of the order of the operations.

By using flatMap, you can keep on transforming optionals and refrain from introducing those dreaded force unwraps.

10.5.3 *Fighting the pyramid of doom*

A pyramid of doom is code that leans to the right via indentation. This pyramid shape is a result of a lot of nesting, such as when unwrapping multiple optionals.

Here's another example when map won't be able to help, but flatMap comes in handy to fight this pyramid.

To showcase fighting the pyramid of doom, let's talk about the division of integers.

When you divide an integer, decimals get cut off:

```
print(5 / 2) // 2
```

When dividing an Int, dividing 5 by 2 returns 2 instead of 2.5, because Int doesn't have floating point precision, as Float does.

The function in listing 10.18 halves an Int only when it's even. If the Int is odd, the function returns nil.

The safe halving function takes a non-optional and returns an optional—for example, halving 4 becomes Optional(2). But halving 5 returns nil because decimals would be cut off.

Listing 10.18   Safe halving function

```
func half(_ int: Int) -> Int? { // Only half even numbers
    guard int % 2 == 0 else { return nil }
    return int / 2
}
print(half(4)) // Optional(2)
print(half(5)) // nil
```

Next, you're going to continuously apply this function.

You create a start value and halve it, which returns a new optional. If you halve the new value, you first have to unwrap the newly halved value before passing it on to half.

This chain of events creates a create a nasty tree of indented if let operations, also known as the pyramid of doom, as demonstrated here.

Listing 10.19   A pyramid of doom

```
var value: Int? = nil
let startValue = 80
if let halvedValue = half(startValue) {
```

```
    print(halvedValue) // 40
    value = halvedValue

    if let halvedValue = half(halvedValue) {
        print(halvedValue) // 20
        value = halvedValue

        if let halvedValue = half(halvedValue) {
            print(halvedValue) // 10
            if let halvedValue = half(halvedValue) {
                value = halvedValue
            } else {
                value = nil
            }

        } else {
            value = nil
        }
    } else {
        value = nil
    }
}

print(value) // Optional(5)
```

As you can see in this example, when you want to apply a function on a value continuously, you have to keep unwrapping the returned value. This nested unwrapping happens because half returns an optional each time.

Alternatively, you can group the *if let* statements in Swift, which is an idiomatic approach.

Listing 10.20 Combining *if let* statements

```
let startValue = 80
var endValue: Int? = nil

if
    let firstHalf = half(startValue),
    let secondHalf = half(firstHalf),
    let thirdHalf = half(secondHalf),
    let fourthHalf = half(thirdHalf) {
    endValue = fourthHalf
}
print(endValue) // Optional(5)
```

The downside of this approach is that you have to bind values to constants for each step, but naming each step can be cumbersome. Also, not all functions neatly accept one value and return another, which means that you would be chaining multiple closures, in which case the *if let* approach wouldn't fit.

Let's take a functional programming approach with flatMap and see if you can rewrite your code.

10.5.4   *flatMapping over an optional*

Now you're going to see how `flatMap` can be beneficial. Remember, `flatMap` is like `map`, except that it removes a layer of nesting after the mapping operation. You could, for example, have an `Optional(4)` and `flatMap` over it, applying the `half` function, which returns a new optional that `flatMap` flattens (see figure 10.5 and listing 10.21).

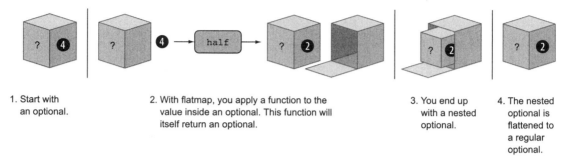

1. Start with an optional.

2. With flatmap, you apply a function to the value inside an optional. This function will itself return an optional.

3. You end up with a nested optional.

4. The nested optional is flattened to a regular optional.

Figure 10.5   A successful `flatMap` operation

You can see that if you `flatMap` the `half` function over `Optional(4)`, you end up with `Optional(2)`. With `map` you would end up with `Optional(Optional(2))`.

Listing 10.21   Halving with `flatMap`

```
let startValue = 8
let four = half(startValue) // Optional(4)
let two = four.flatMap { (int: Int) -> Int? in
    print(int) // 4
    let nestedTwo = half(int)
    print(nestedTwo) // Optional(2)
    return nestedTwo
}

print(two) // Optional(2)
```

The beauty of using `flatMap` is that you keep a regular optional, which means that you can keep chaining operations on it.

Listing 10.22   Multiple halving operations on `flatMap`

```
let startValue = 40
let twenty = half(startValue) // Optional(20)
let five =
    twenty
        .flatMap { (int: Int) -> Int? in
            print(int) // 20
            let ten = half(int)
            print(ten) // Optional(10)
            return ten
```

```
    }.flatMap { (int: Int) -> Int? in
        print(int) // 10
        let five = half(int)
        print(five) // Optional(5)
        return five
}

print(five) // Optional(5)
```

Because you never nest an optional more than once, you can keep chaining forever, or just twice, as in this example. You are getting rid of the ugly nested *if let* pyramid of doom. As a bonus, you aren't manually keeping track of a temporary value anymore while juggling *if let* statements.

SHORTCIRCUITING WITH FLATMAP

Because flatMap allows you to keep chaining nullable operations, you get another benefit: you can break off chains if needed.

When you return nil from a flatMap operation, you end up with a regular nil value instead. Returning nil from a flatMap operation means that subsequent flatMap operations are ignored.

In the next example, you halve 5 and flatMap over it. You end up with a nil; the result is the same as starting with a nil (see figure 10.6).

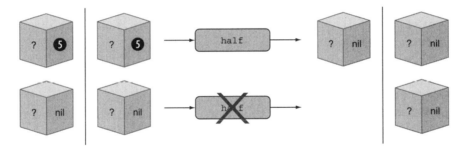

1. You have two optionals: one with a value and one without.

2. With flatmap, you apply a function to the value inside an optional. The function returns an optional. In the case of 5, it returns nil. So you end up with a nil value.

   But flatmap does nothing with an empty optional. The nil remains nil.

3. You end up a nil value either way.

Figure 10.6   flatMap **and nil values**

When you have a nil optional, subsequent flatMap operations are ignored. Because you can return nil from the flatMap closure, you can short-circuit a chained operation.

In the next example, see what happens if you keep on chaining, even when a flatMap operation returns nil.

Listing 10.23   Short-circuiting

```
let startValue = 40
let twenty = half(startValue) // Optional(20)
let someNil =
    twenty
        .flatMap { (int: Int) -> Int? in
            print(int) // 20
            let ten = half(int)
            print(ten) // Optional(10)
            return ten
        }.flatMap { (int: Int) -> Int? in
            print(int) // 10
            let five = half(int)
            print(five) // Optional(5)
            return five
        }.flatMap { (int: Int) -> Int? in
            print(int) // 5
            let someNilValue = half(int)
            print(someNilValue) // nil
            return someNilValue
        }.flatMap { (int: Int) -> Int? in
            return half(int)
        }

print(someNil) // nil
```

The closure in this flatMap returns a nil.

You're returning nil.

The closure in the last flatMap operation won't be called because the optional is nil before.

This code is never called because you're calling flatMap on a nil value.

flatMap ignores the passed closures as soon as a nil is found. This is the same as mapping over an optional, which also won't do anything if a nil is found.

Notice how the third flatMap operation returns nil, and how the fourth flatMap operation is ignored. The result remains nil, which means that flatMap gives you the power to break off chained operations.

You let flatMap handle any failed conversions, and you can focus on the happy path of the program instead!

Moreover, to finalize and clean up your code, you can use a shorter notation, as you did before, where you pass a named function to map. You can do the same with flatMap, as shown here.

Listing 10.24   A shorter notation

```
let endResult =
    half(80)
        .flatMap(half)
        .flatMap(half)
        .flatMap(half)

print(endResult) // Optional(5)
```

Generally, combining *if let* statements is the way to go because it doesn't require in-depth flatMap knowledge. If you don't want to create intermediate constants, or if you're working with multiple closures, you can use a flatMap approach for concise code.

As shown in the following example, imagine a scenario where you'd find a user by an id, find the user's favorite product, and see if any related product exists. The last step formats the data. Any of these steps could be a function or a closure. With flatMap and map, you can cleanly chain transformations without resorting to a big stack of if let constants and intermediary values.

Listing 10.25 Finding related products

```
let alternativeProduct =
    findUser(3)
      .flatMap(findFavoriteProduct)
      .flatMap(findRelatedProduct)
      .map { product in
        product.description.trimmingCharacters(in: .whitespaces)
      }
```

10.6 *flatMapping over collections*

You might have guessed that flatMap isn't reserved just for optionals, but for collections as well.

Just like flatMap ends up flattening two optionals, it also flattens a nested collection after a mapping operation.

For instance, you can have a function that generates a new array from each value inside an array—for example, turning [2, 3] into [[2, 2], [3, 3]]. With flatMap you can flatten these subarrays again to a single array, such as [2, 2, 3, 3] (see figure 10.7).

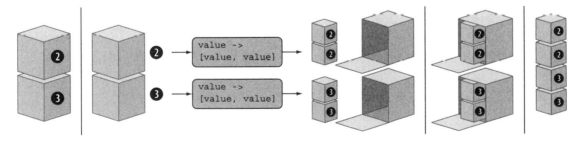

1. You have a regular array [2, 3].

2. With flatMap, you apply a function to each value inside the array. This function turns a value into [value, value], another array.

3. You end up with subarrays [[2, 2], [3, 3]].

flatMap flattens the nested arrays to [2, 2, 3, 3].

Figure 10.7   Flattening a collection with flatMap

In code this would look as follows.

Listing 10.26   Repeating values

```
let repeated = [2, 3].flatMap { (value: Int) -> [Int] in
    return [value, value]
}

print(repeated) // [2, 2, 3, 3]
```

Also, consider the following, where you start with a nested array of values. With flat-
Map, you flatten the subarrays to a single array.

Listing 10.27   Flattening a nested array

```
let stringsArr = [["I", "just"], ["want", "to"], ["learn", "about"],
    ["protocols"]]
let flattenedArray = stringsArr.flatMap { $0 }                          ◁───┐
 print(flattenedArray) // ["I", "just", "want", "to", "learn", "about",
    "protocols"]                        **Only the passed value is returned;**
                                        **no transformations are applied.**
```

Notice how you're not performing anything particular in the flatMap closure in this case.

10.6.1 *flatMapping over strings*

String is a collection, too. As you saw earlier, you can iterate over a view on a String,
such as unicodeScalars. Depending on the "view" of String you pick, you can also
iterate over the utf8 and utf16 code units of String.

   If you were to iterate over a String itself, you would iterate over its characters. Because
String conforms to the Collection protocol, you can flatMap over a String as well.

   For instance, you can create a succinct interspersed method on String, which
takes a Character and intersperses or weaves a character between each character of
the string (as in this example, turning "Swift" into "S-w-i-f-t").

Listing 10.28   `interspersed`

```
"Swift".interspersed("-") // S-w-i-f-t        String is extended with      You call flatMap the
                                               new functionality.                  String itself.
extension String {                    ◁──┘
    func interspersed(_ element: Character) -> String {
        let characters = self.flatMap { (char: Character) -> [Character] in   ◁──┘
            return [char, element]                ◁─┐
            }.dropLast()                      ◁──┐  The closure returns an array containing
                                                  a String character, and the passed
        return String(characters)      ◁──┐       element. Then flatMap flattens the array.
    }
}                      The array of characters        You don't need the element added
                       is converted to a String.      to the last character; you can drop
                                                       this element with dropLast().
```

You can write the method in a shorthanded manner, too, by omitting explicit types.

Listing 10.29 Shorthanded `interspersed` method

```
extension String {
    func interspersed(_ element: Character) -> String {
        let characters = self.flatMap { return [$0, element] }.dropLast()
        return String(characters)
    }
}
```

10.6.2 Combining flatMap with map

Once you start nesting `flatMap` with other `flatMap` or `map` operations, you can create powerful functionality with a few lines of code. Imagine that you need to create a full deck of cards. You can create this in very few lines once you combine `map` and `flatMap`.

First, you define the suits and faces. Then you iterate through the suits, and for each suit, you iterate through the faces. To create your deck, you're nesting `flatMap` and `map` so that you have access to both the suit and the face at the same time. This way, you can effortlessly create tuple pairs for each card.

As shown here, in the end, you use the `shuffle()` method, which shuffles `deckOf-Cards` in place.

Listing 10.30 Generating a deck of cards

Define the possible suits and faces.

```
let suits = ["Hearts", "Clubs", "Diamonds", "Spades"]
let faces = ["2", "3", "4", "5", "6", "7", "8", "9", "10", "J", "Q", "K", "A"]
```

Map over the possible faces.

```
var deckOfCards = suits.flatMap { suit in          ◁──  Iterate through suits
    faces.map { face in                                  with a flatMap operation,
        (suit, face)          ◁──                         because you're flattening
    }                               Because you're nesting,   an array.
}                                   both face and suit become
deckOfCards.shuffle()               available to create a new
print(deckOfCards) // [("Diamonds", "5"), ("Hearts", "8"), ("Hearts", "K"),
⇒ ("Clubs", "3"), ("Diamonds", "10"), ("Spades", "A"), ...
```

Because you're nesting, both face and suit become available to create a new type (in this case a tuple).

Shuffle the cards—otherwise the game gets boring. Note that deckOfCards is a var, allowing for in-place shuffling.

> **TIP** You shuffle `deckOfCards` in place, but you can also get a fresh copy with the `shuffled()` method.

The reason you use `flatMap` on the `suits` array is because mapping over `faces` returns an array, causing you to end up with nested arrays. With `flatMap` you remove one layer of nesting so that you neatly end up with an array of tuples.

10.6.3 Using compactMap

For collections, such as `Array`, `String`, or `Dictionary`, there is a little brother of `flat-Map` called `compactMap`. With `compactMap`, instead of flattening a nested collection, you can flatten optionals inside a collection.

In simpler terms, you can filter nils out of a collection. As you've seen before, not every `String` can be turned into a `URL`, resulting in an optional `URL` type, as in this example.

Listing 10.31   Creating optional URLs

```
let wrongUrl = URL(string: "OMG SHOES")
print(wrongUrl) // nil
let properUrl = URL(string: "https://www.swift.org")
print(properUrl) // Optional(https://www.swift.org)
```

If you were to fill up an array with strings and try to convert these to `URL` types via map, you would end up with an array of optional integers, as shown here.

Listing 10.32   Mapping over an array

```
let strings = [
    "https://www.duckduckgo.com",
    "https://www.twitter.com",
    "OMG SHOES",
    "https://www.swift.org"
]

let optionalUrls = strings.map { URL(string: $0) }
print(optionalUrls) // [Optional(https://www.duckduckgo.com),
➥ Optional(https://www.twitter.com), nil, Optional(https://www.swift.org)]
```

Notice how `"OMG SHOES"` can't be turned into an `URL`, resulting in a `nil` value inside the array.

Again, with `compactMap` you can flatten this operation, except this time, flattening the array means removing the nil optionals. This way, as shown in this listing, you end up with a non-optional list of URLs.

Listing 10.33   Flattening an optional array

```
let urls = strings.compactMap(URL.init)
print(urls) // [https://www.duckduckgo.com, https://www.twitter.com, https://
    www.swift.org]
```

Because not all strings can be turned into `URL` types, `URL.init` returns an optional `URL`. Then `compactMap` filters out these `nil` values. For instance, you can't turn `"OMG SHOES"` into a `URL`, so `compactMap` filters out this `nil` for you. The result is that you end up with proper URLs where none are optional.

If a *for* loop is more your cup of tea, you can use one to filter an optional array as well via a case let expression, as in listing 10.34. This expression allows you to pattern match on an enum's case, such as optionals (because optionals are enums). For instance, you can obtain an array with optional URL types and loop over them, filtering any nils, and end up with an unwrapped value inside the loop.

```
let optionalUrls: [URL?] = [
    URL(string: "https://www.duckduckgo.com"),
    URL(string: "Bananaphone"),
    URL(string: "https://www.twitter.com"),
    URL(string: "https://www.swift.org")
]
for case let url? in optionalUrls {
    print("The url is \(url)") // url is unwrapped here
}

// Output:
// The url is https://www.duckduckgo.com
// The url is https://www.twitter.com
// The url is https://www.swift.org
```

As mentioned before, with *for* loops you get the benefit of using break, continue, or return to break loops halfway.

10.6.4 *Nesting or chaining*

A nice trick with flatMap and compactMap is that it doesn't matter whether you nest or chain flatMap or compactMap operations. For instance, you could flatMap over an Optional twice in a row. Alternatively, you can nest two flatMap operations. Either way, you end up with the same result:

```
let value = Optional(40)
let lhs = value.flatMap(half).flatMap(half)
let rhs = value.flatMap { int in half(int).flatMap(half) }
lhs == rhs // true
print(rhs) // Optional(10)
```

Another benefit of the nested flatMap or compactMap approach is that you can refer to encapsulated values inside a nested closure.

For instance, you can both flatMap and compactMap over the same String. First, each element inside the string is bound to a inside a flatMap operation; then you compactMap over the same string again, but you'll bind each element to b. You end up with a way to combine a and b to build a new list.

Using this technique as shown next, you build up an array of unique tuples from the characters in the same string.

Listing 10.35   Combining characters from a `string`

```
let string = "abc"
let results = string.flatMap { a -> [(Character, Character)] in
    string.compactMap { b -> (Character, Character)? in
        if a == b {
            return nil
        } else {
            return (a, b)
        }
    }
}
print(results) // [("a", "b"), ("a", "c"), ("b", "a"), ("b", "c"), ("c", "a"),
    ("c", "b")]
```

flatMap over a string.

Nest a compactMap operation, again over the same string.

Because of nesting, you can refer to both a and b constants from this inner compactMap operation.

If a and b are the same, you return a nil, so that you end up with unique combinations only.

The result is a unique combination of characters, filtered and flattened thanks to nested operations.

It's a small trick, but knowing that `flatMap` and `compactMap` can be chained or nested can help you refactor your code in different ways for similar results.

10.6.5 *Exercises*

6   Create a function that turns an array of integers into an array with a value subtracted and added for each integer—for instance, [20, 30, 40] is turned into [19, 20, 21, 29, 30, 31, 39, 40, 41]. Try to solve it with the help of `map` or `flatMap`.

7   Generate values from 0 to 100, with only even numbers. But be sure to skip every factor of 10, such as 10, 20, and so on. You should end up with [2, 4, 6, 8, 12, 14, 16, 18, 22 …]. See if you can solve it with the help of `map` or `flatMap`.

8   Create a function that removes all vowels from a `string`. Again, see if you can solve it with `map` or `flatMap`.

9   Given an array of tuples, create an array with tuples of all possible tuple pairs of these values—for example, [1, 2] gets turned into [(1, 1), (1, 2), (2, 1), (2, 2)]. Again, see if you can do it with the help from `map` and/or `flatMap` and make sure that there are no duplicates.

10 Write a function that duplicates each value inside an array—for example, [1, 2, 3] turns into [1, 1, 2, 2, 3, 3] and [["a", "b"],["c", "d"]], turns into [["a", "b"], ["a", "b"], ["c", "d"], ["c", "d"]]. See if you can use `map` or `flatMap` for this.

10.7   *Closing thoughts*

Depending on your background, a functional style of programming can feel a bit foreign. Luckily, you don't need functional programming to create spectacular applications. But by adding `map` and `flatMap` to your toolbelt, you can harness their powers and add powerful immutable abstractions to your code in a succinct manner.

Whether you prefer an imperative style or a functional style to programming, I hope you feel confident picking an approach that creates a delicate balance between readability, robustness, and speed.

Summary

- The `map` and `flatMap` methods are concepts taken from the functional programming world.
- The `map` method is an abstraction called a *functor*.
- A functor represents a container—or context—of which you can transform its value with `map`.
- The `map` method is defined on many types, including `Array`, `Dictionary`, `Sequence`, and `Collections` protocol, and `Optional`.
- The `map` method is a crucial element when transforming data inside a pipeline.
- Imperative-style programming is a fine alternative to functional, style programming.
- Imperative-style programming can be more performant. In contrast, functional-style programming can involve immutable transformations and can sometimes be more readable and show clearer intent.
- The `flatMap` method is a flatten operation after a `map` operation.
- With `flatMap` you can flatten a nested optional to a single optional.
- With `flatMap` you can sequence operations on an optional in an immutable way.
- Once an optional is nil, `map` and `flatMap` ignores any chained operations.
- If you return `nil` from a `flatMap`, you can short-circuit operations.
- With `flatMap` you can transform arrays and sequences in powerful ways with very little code.
- With `compactMap` you can filter `nils` out of arrays and sequences of optionals.
- You can also filter `nils` with an imperative style by using a *for* loop.
- You can nest `flatMap` and `compactMap` operations for the same results.
- On collections and sequences, you can combine `flatMap` with `map` to combine all their values.

Answers

1 Create a function that turns an array into a nested array, make sure to use the map function:

```
func makeSubArrays<T>(_ arr: [T]) -> [[T]] {
    return arr.map { [$0] }
}

makeSubArrays(["a","b","c"]) // [[a], [b], [c]]
makeSubArrays([100,50,1]) // [[100], [50], [1]]
```

2 Create a function that transforms the values inside a dictionary for movies. Each rating, from 1 to 5, needs to be turned into a human readable format:

```
// E.g.
// A rating of 1.2 is "Very low", a rating of 3 is "Average", a rating
⮕ of 4.5 is "Excellent".
```

```swift
func transformRating<T>(_ dict: [T: Float]) -> [T: String] {
    return dict.mapValues { (rating) -> String in
        switch rating {
        case ..<1: return "Very weak"
        case ..<2: return "Weak"
        case ..<3: return "Average"
        case ..<4: return "Good"
        case ..<5: return "Excellent"
        default: fatalError("Unknown rating")
        }
    }
}

let moviesAndRatings: [String : Float] = ["Home Alone 4" : 1.2,
➥ "Who framed Roger Rabbit?" : 4.6, "Star Wars: The Phantom Menace"
➥ : 2.2, "The Shawshank Redemption" : 4.9]
let moviesHumanRadable = transformRating(moviesAndRatings)
```

3 Still looking at the movies and ratings, convert the dictionary into a single description per movie with the rating appended to the title:

```swift
let movies: [String : Float] = ["Home Alone 4" : 1.2, "Who framed Roger
➥ Rabbit?" : 4.6, "Star Wars: The Phantom Menace" : 2.2, "The Shawshank
➥ Redemption" : 4.9]

func convertRating(_ rating: Float) -> String {
    switch rating {
    case ..<1: return "Very weak"
    case ..<2: return "Weak"
    case ..<3: return "Average"
    case ..<4: return "Good"
    case ..<5: return "Excellent"
    default: fatalError("Unknown rating")
    }
}

let movieDescriptions = movies.map { (tuple) in
    return "\(tuple.key) (\(convertRating(tuple.value)))"
}

print(movieDescriptions) // ["Home Alone 4 (Weak)", "Star Wars: The
➥ Phantom Menace (Average)", "Who framed Roger Rabbit? (Excellent)",
➥ "The Shawshank Redemption (Excellent)"]
```

4 Generate an array of the letters "a", "b", "c" 10 times. The end result should be ["a", "b", "c", "a", "b", "c", "a" …]. The array should be 30 elements long. See if you can solve this with a map operation on some kind of iterator:

```swift
let values = (0..<30).map { (int: Int) -> String in
    switch int % 3 {
    case 0: return "a"
    case 1: return "b"
    case 2: return "c"
```

```
            default: fatalError("Not allowed to come here")
            }
    }

    print(values)
```

5 Given a contact data dictionary, the following code gets the street and city from the data and cleans up the strings. See if you can reduce the boilerplate. Be sure to use map somewhere:

```
let someStreet = contact["address"]?["street"].map(capitalizedAndTrimmed)
let someCity = contact["address"]?["city"].map(capitalizedAndTrimmed)
```

6 Create a function that turns an array of integers into an array with a value subtracted and added for each integer. For instance, [20, 30, 40] will be turned into [19, 20, 21, 29, 30, 31, 39, 40, 41]. Try to solve it with the help of map or flatMap:

```
func buildList(_ values: [Int]) -> [Int] {
    return values.flatMap {
        [$0 - 1, $0, $0 + 1]
    }
}
```

7 Generate values from 0 to 100, with only even numbers. But be sure to skip every factor of 10, such as 10, 20, and so on. You would end up with [2, 4, 6, 8, 12, 14, 16, 18, 22 ...]. See if you can solve it with the help of map or flatMap:

```
let strideSequence = stride(from: 0, through: 30, by: 2).flatMap { int in
    return int % 10 == 0 ? nil : int
}
```

8 Create a function that removes all vowels from a string. Again, see if you can solve it with map or flatMap:

```
func removeVowels(_ string: String) -> String {
    let characters = string.flatMap { char -> Character? in
        switch char {
        case "e", "u", "i", "o", "a": return nil
        default: return char
        }
    }

    return String(characters)
}

removeVowels("Hi there!") // H thr!
```

9 Given an array of tuples, create an array with tuples of all possible tuple pairs of these values—for example, [1, 2] gets turned into [(1, 1), (1, 2), (2, 1), (2, 2)]. Again, see if you can do it with the help from map and/or flatMap:

```
func pairValues(_ values: [Int]) -> [(Int, Int)] {
    return values.flatMap { lhs in
        values.map { rhs -> (Int, Int) in
            return (lhs, rhs)
        }
    }
}
```

10 Write a function that duplicates each value inside an array—for example, [1, 2, 3] turns into [1, 1, 2, 2, 3, 3], and [["a", "b"],["c", "d"]] turns into [["a", "b"], ["a", "b"], ["c", "d"], ["c", "d"]]. See if you can use map or flatMap for this:

```
func double<T>(_ values: [T]) -> [T] {
    return values.flatMap { [$0, $0] }
}

print(double([1,2,3]))
print(double([["a", "b"], ["c", "d"]]))
```

11

Asynchronous error handling with Result

This chapter covers

- Learning about the problems with Cocoa style error handling
- Getting an introduction to Apple's `Result` type
- Seeing how `Result` provides compile-time safety
- Preventing bugs involving forgotten callbacks
- Transforming data robustly with `map`, `mapError`, and `flatMap`
- Focusing on the happy path when handling errors
- Mixing throwing functions with `Result`
- Learning how `AnyError` makes `Result` less restrictive
- How to show intent with the `Never` type

You've covered a lot of Swift's error handling mechanics, and you may have noticed in chapter 6 that you were throwing errors synchronously. This chapter focuses on handling errors from asynchronous processes, which is, unfortunately, an entirely different idiom in Swift.

Asynchronous actions could be some code running in the background while a current method is running. For instance, you could perform an asynchronous API call to fetch JSON data from a server. When the call finishes, it triggers a callback giving you the data or an error.

Swift doesn't yet offer an official solution to asynchronous error handling. According to rumor, Swift won't offer one until the async/await pattern gets introduced somewhere around Swift version 7 or 8. Luckily, the community seems to favor asynchronous error handling with the `Result` type (which is reinforced by Apple's inclusion of an unofficial `Result` type in the Swift Package Manager). You may already have worked with the `Result` type and even implemented it in projects. In this chapter, you'll use one offered by Apple, which may be a bit more advanced than most examples found online. To get the most out of `Result`, you'll go deep into the rabbit hole and look at propagation, so-called monadic error handling, and its related `AnyError` type. The `Result` type is an enum like `Optional`, with some differences, so if you're comfortable with `Optional`, then `Result` should not be too big of a jump.

You'll start off by exploring the `Result` type's benefits and how you can add it to your projects. You'll create a networking API, and then keep improving it in the following sections. Then you'll start rewriting the API, but you'll use the `Result` type to reap its benefits.

Next, you'll see how to propagate asynchronous errors and how you can keep your code clean while focusing on the happy path. You do this via the use of `map`, `mapError`, and `flatMap`.

Sooner or later you'll use regular throwing functions again to transform your asynchronous data. You'll see how to mix the two error handling idioms by working with throwing functions in combination with `Result`.

After building a solid API, you'll look at a unique `AnyError` type that Apple also offers in combination with `Result`. This type gives you the option to store multiple types of errors inside a `Result`. The benefit is that you can loosen up the error handling strictness without needing to look back to Objective-C by using `NSError`. You'll try out plenty of convenience functions to keep the code concise.

You'll then take a look at the `Never` type to indicate that your code can never fail or succeed. It's a little theoretical but a nice finisher. Consider it a bonus section.

By the end of the chapter, you'll feel comfortable applying powerful transformations to your asynchronous code while dealing with all the errors that can come with it. You'll also be able to avoid the dreaded pyramid of doom and focus on the happy path. But the significant benefit is that your code will be safe and succinct while elegantly handling errors—so let's begin!

11.1 Why use the Result type?

> **JOIN ME!**   It's more educational and fun if you can check out the code and follow along with the chapter. You can download the source code at http://mng .bz/5YP1.

Swift's error handling mechanism doesn't translate well to asynchronous error handling. At the time of writing, Swift's asynchronous error handling is still not fleshed out. Generally speaking, developers tend to use Cocoa's style of error handling—coming from the good ol' Objective-C days—where a network call returns multiple values. For instance, you could fetch some JSON data from an API, and the callback gives you both a value *and* an error where you'd have to check for nil on both of them.

Unfortunately, the Cocoa Touch way has some problems—which you'll uncover in a moment—and the `Result` type solves them. The `Result` type, inspired by Rust's `Result` type and the `Either` type in Haskell and Scala, is a functional programming idiom that has been taken on by the Swift community, making it a non-official standard of error handling.

At the time of writing, developers repeatedly reimagine the `Result` type because no official standard exists yet. Even though Swift doesn't officially offer the `Result` type, the Swift Package Manager offers it unofficially. So Apple (indirectly) offers a `Result` type, which justifies implementing it in your codebases. You'll power up `Result` with useful custom functionality as well.

11.1.1 *Getting your hands on Result*

You can find the `Result` type inside this chapter's playgrounds file. But you can also directly pluck it from the Swift Package Manager—also known as SwiftPM—on GitHub found at http://mng.bz/6GPD.

You can also retrieve `Result` via dependencies of the SwiftPM. This chapter doesn't provide a full guide on how to create a Swift command-line tool via the SwiftPM, but these following commands should get you started.

First, run the following to set up a folder and a Swift executable project. Open the command line and enter the following:

```
mkdir ResultFun
cd ResultFun
swift package init --type executable
```

Next, open Package.swift and change it to the following:

```
// swift-tools-version:4.2
// The swift-tools-
    version declares the minimum version of Swift the required to build this
    package.

import PackageDescription

let package = Package(
    name: "ResultFun",
    dependencies: [
        .package(url: "https://github.com/apple/swift-package-manager",
        from: "0.2.1")
    ],
```

You link to the SwiftPM project from the SwiftPM itself.

```
        targets: [
            .target(                                    You need to depend on the
                name: "ResultFun",                      Utility package to get
                dependencies: ["Utility"]),   ◁──┐      required source files.
        ]
)
```

Inside your project folder, open `Sources/ResultFun/main.swift` and change it to the following:

```
import Basic        ◁──┐  The Basic package is
                        offered by the SwiftPM.
```

```
let result = Result<String, AnyError>("It's working, hooray!")   ◁──┐
print(result)
```

AnyError is covered   **Create a Result type to make sure**
later in this chapter.   **the import worked correctly.**

Type `swift run`, and you'll see `Result(It's working, hooray!)`. Ready? Let's continue.

11.1.2 *Result is like Optional, with a twist*

`Result` is a *lot* like `Optional`, which is great because if you're comfortable with optionals (see chapter 4), you'll feel right at home with the `Result` type.

Swift's `Result` type is an enum with two cases: namely, a success case and a failure case. But don't let that fool you. `Optional` is also "just" an enum with two cases, but it's powerful, and so is `Result`.

In its simplest form, the `Result` type looks as follows.

Listing 11.1   The `Result` type

```
public enum Result<Value, ErrorType: Swift.Error> {        ◁──┐   The Result type
    /// Indicates success with value in the associated object.    requires two
    case success(Value)                                    ◁──┘   generic values.

    /// Indicates failure with error inside the associated object.   In the success
    case failure(ErrorType)        ◁──┐                              case, a Value is
                                       The ErrorType                 bound.
    // ... The rest is left out for later   generic is bound in
}                                           the failure case.
```

The difference with `Optional` is that instead of a value being present (`some` case) or nil (`none` case), `Result` states that it either has a value (`success` case) or it has an error (`failure` case). In essence, the `Result` type indicates possible failure instead of nil. In other words, with `Result` you can give context for why an operation failed, instead of missing a value.

`Result` contains a value for each case, whereas with `Optional`, only the `some` case has a value. Also the `ErrorType` generic is constrained to Swift's `Error` protocol, which means that only `Error` types can fit inside the `failure` case of `Result`. The constraint comes in handy for some convenience functions, which you'll discover in a later section. Note that the `success` case can fit any type because it isn't constrained.

You haven't seen the full `Result` type, which has plenty of methods, but this code is enough to get you started. Soon enough you'll get to see more methods, such as bridging to and from throwing functions and transforming values and errors inside `Result` in an immutable way.

Let's quickly move on to the *raison d'être* of `Result`: error handling.

11.1.3 Understanding the benefits of Result

To better understand the benefits of the `Result` type in asynchronous calls, let's first look at the downsides of Cocoa Touch–style asynchronous APIs before you see how `Result` is an improvement. Throughout the chapter, you'll keep updating this API with improvements.

Let's look at `URLSession` inside the `Foundation` framework. You'll use `URLSession` to perform a network call, as shown in listing 11.2, and you're interested in the data and error of the response. The iTunes app isn't known for its "popular" desktop application, so you'll create an API for searching the iTunes Store without a desktop app.

To start, you'll use a hardcoded string to search for "iron man"—which you percent encode manually at first—and make use of a function `callURL` to perform a network call.

Listing 11.2 Performing a network call

The @escaping keyword is required in this situation; it indicates that the completionHandler closure can potentially be stored and retain memory.

The callURL function has a completionHandler handler that is called when the URLSession.dataTask finishes.

```
func callURL(with url: URL, completionHandler: @escaping (Data?, Error?)
    -> Void) {
    let task = URLSession.shared.dataTask(with: url, completionHandler:
    { (data, response, error) -> Void in
        completionHandler(data, error)     ⬅  You get the data from a
    })                                         URL, and you pass the data
                                               and error back to the caller.
    task.resume()
}

let url = URL(string: "https://itunes.apple.com/search?term=iron%20man")!

callURL(with: url) { (data, error) in        ⬅  You call the callURL function to get the
    if let error = error {                      data and error, which are returned at
        print(error)                            some point in time (asynchronously).
    } else if let data = data {
        let value = String(data: data, encoding: .utf8)   ⬅  You turn the data to
        print(value)                                         String to read the
    } else {                                                 raw value.
        // What goes here?     ⬅  Here's the problem: If
    }                             both error and data are
}                                 nil, what do you do then?
```

As soon as the callback is called, any error is unwrapped.

If there is data, you can work with the response.

But the problem is that you have to check whether an error and/or the data is nil. Also, what happens if both values are nil? The URLSession documentation (http://mng.bz/oVxr) states that either data or error has a value; yet in code this isn't reflected, and you still have to check against all values.

When returning multiple values from an asynchronous call from URLSession, a success and failure value are not mutually exclusive. In theory, you could have received both response data and a failure error or neither. Or you can have one or the other, but falsely assume that if there is no error, the call must have succeeded. Either way, you don't have a compile-time guarantee to enforce safe handling of the returned data. But you're going to change that and see how Result will give you these compile-time guarantees.

11.1.4 Creating an API using Result

Let's get back to the API call. With a Result type, you can enforce at compile time that a response is either a success (with a value) or a failure (with an error). As an example, let's update the asynchronous call so that it passes a Result.

You're going to introduce a NetworkError and make the callURL function use the Result type.

Listing 11.3   A response with Result

```
enum NetworkError: Error {
    case fetchFailed(Error)
}
```
◁── Define a custom error to pass around inside Result. You can store a lower-level error from URLSession inside the fetchFailed case to help with troubleshooting.

```
func callURL(with url: URL, completionHandler: @escaping (Result<Data,
    NetworkError>) -> Void) {
    let task = URLSession.shared.dataTask(with: url, completionHandler: {
    (data, response, error) -> Void in
        // ... details will be filled in shortly
    })

    task.resume()
}
```
◁── This time, callURL passes a Result type containing either a Data or NetworkError.

```
let url = URL(string: "https://itunes.apple.com/search?term=iron%20man")!

callURL(with: url) { (result: Result<Data, NetworkError>) in
    switch result {
    case .success(let data):
        let value = String(data: data, encoding: .utf8)
        print(value)
    case .failure(let error):
        print(error)
    }
}
```
◁── Call callURL to get the Result back via a closure.

Pattern match on the success case to get the value out of a Result.

◁── Pattern match on the failure case to catch any error.

As you can see, you receive a `Result<Data, NetworkError>` type when you call `callURL()`. But this time, instead of matching on both `error` and `data`, the values are now mutually exclusive. If you want the value out of `Result`, you *must* handle both cases, giving you compile-time safety in return and removing any awkward situations where both `data` and `error` can be nil or filled at the same time. Also, a big benefit is that you know beforehand that the error inside the `failure` case is of type `NetworkError`, as opposed to throwing functions where you only know the error type at runtime.

You may also use an error handling system where a data type contains an `onSuccess` or `onFailure` closure. But I want to emphasize that with `Result`, if you want the value out, you *must* do something with the error.

AVOIDING ERROR HANDLING

Granted, you can't fully enforce handling an error inside of `Result` if you match on a single case of an enum with the `if case let` statement. Alternatively, you can ignore the error with the infamous `// TODO` handle error comment, but then you'd be consciously going out of your way to avoid handling an error. Generally speaking, if you want to get the value out of `Result`, the compiler tells you to handle the error, too.

As another option, if you're not interested in the reason for failure, yet still want a value out of `Result`, you can get the value out by using the `dematerialize` method. This function either returns the value or throws the error inside `Result`. If you use the `try?` keyword, as shown in the following listing, you can instantly convert the `Result` to an `Optional`.

Listing 11.4 Dematerializing `Result`

```
let value: Data? = try? result.dematerialize()
```

11.1.5 Bridging from Cocoa Touch to Result

Moving on, the response from `URLSession`'s `dataTask` returns three values: `data`, `response`, and `error`.

Listing 11.5 The `URLSession`'s response

```
URLSession.shared.dataTask(with: url, completionHandler: { (data, response,
    error) -> Void in ... }
```

But if you want to work with `Result`, you'll have to convert the values from `URLSession`'s completion handler to a `Result` yourself. Let's take this opportunity to flesh out the `callURL` function so that you can bridge Cocoa Touch–style error handling to a `Result`-style error handling.

One way to convert a value and error to `Result` is to add a custom initializer to `Result` that performs the conversion for you, as shown in the next listing. You can pass this initializer the data and error, and then use that to make a new `Result`. In your `callURL` function, you can then return a `Result` via the closure.

Listing 11.6 Converting a response and error into a `Result`

```
public enum Result<Value, ErrorType> {
    // ... snip

    init(value: Value?, error: ErrorType?) {
        if let error = error {
            self = .failure(error)
        } else if let value = value {
            self = .success(value)
        } else {
            fatalError("Could not create Result")
        }
    }
}
```

Create an initializer that accepts an optional value and optional error.

If both a value and error are nil, you end up in a bad state and crash, because you can be confident that URLSession returns either a value or error.

```
func callURL(with url: URL, completionHandler: @escaping (Result<Data,
➥ NetworkError>) -> Void) {
    let task = URLSession.shared.dataTask(with: url, completionHandler:
➥ { (data, response, error) -> Void in
        let dataTaskError = error.map { NetworkError.fetchFailed($0) }
        let result = Result<Data, NetworkError>(value: data, error:
➥ dataTaskError)
        completionHandler(result)
    })

    task.resume()
}
```

Create a Result from the data and error values.

Pass the Result back to the completionHandler closure.

Turn the current error into a higher-level NetworkError and pass the lower-level error from URLSession to its fetchFailed case to help with troubleshooting.

IF AN API DOESN'T RETURN A VALUE Not all APIs return a value, but you can still use `Result` with a so-called *unit type* represented by `Void` or `()`. You can use `Void` or `()` as the value for a `Result`, such as `Result<(), MyError>`.

11.2 *Propagating Result*

Let's make your API a bit higher-level so that instead of manually creating URLs, you can search for items in the iTunes Store by passing strings. Also, instead of dealing with lower-level errors, let's work with a higher-level `SearchResultError`, which better matches the new search abstraction you're creating. This section is a good opportunity to see how you can propagate and transform any `Result` types.

The API that you'll create allows you to enter a search term, and you'll get JSON results back in the shape of `[String: Any]`.

Listing 11.7 Calling the search API

The invalidTerm case is used when an URL can't be created.

The underlyingError case carries the lower-level NetworkError for troubleshooting or to help recover from an error.

```
enum SearchResultError: Error {
    case invalidTerm(String)
    case underlyingError(NetworkError)
    case invalidData
}
```

The invalidData case is for when the raw data could not be parsed to JSON.

```
search(term: "Iron man") { result: Result<[String: Any], SearchResultError> in  ◁─┐
    print(result)
}
```

> **Search for a term, and you retrieve a Result via a closure.**

11.2.1 Typealiasing for convenience

Before creating the `search` implementation, you create a few typealiases for convenience, which come in handy when repeatedly working with the same `Result` over and over again.

For instance, if you work with many functions that return a `Result<Value, SearchResultError>`, you can define a typealias for the `Result` containing a `SearchResultError`. This typealias is to make sure that `Result` requires only a single generic instead of two by pinning the error generic.

> **Listing 11.8 Creating a typealias**

> **A generic typealias is defined that pins the Error generic to SearchResultError.**

```
typealias SearchResult<Value> = Result<Value, SearchResultError>  ◁─┘

let searchResult = SearchResult("Tony Stark")  ◁─┐
print(searchResult) // success("Tony Stark")
```

> **Result offers a convenience initializer to create a Result from a value, if it can deduce the error.**

PARTIAL TYPEALIAS The typealias still has a `Value` generic for `Result`, which means that the defined `SearchResult` is pinned to `SearchResultError`, but its value could be anything, such as a `[String: Any]`, `Int`, and so on.

You can create this `SearchResult` by only passing it a value. But its true type is `Result<Value, SearchResultError>`.

Another typealias you can introduce is for the JSON type, namely a dictionary of type `[String: Any]`. This second typealias helps you to make your code more readable, so that you work with `SearchResult<JSON>` in place of the verbose `SearchResult<[String: Any]>` type.

> **Listing 11.9 The JSON typealias**

```
typealias JSON = [String: Any]
```

With these two typealiases in place, you'll be working with the `SearchResult<JSON>` type.

11.2.2 The search function

The new search function makes use of the `callURL` function, but it performs two extra tasks: it parses the data to JSON, and it translates the lower-level `NetworkError` to a `SearchResultError`, which makes the function a bit more high-level to use, as shown in the following listing.

Listing 11.10 The `search` function implementation

The function makes use of the JSON and SearchResult typealiases.

The function transforms the search term into a URL-encoded format. Note that encodedString is an optional.

```
func search(term: String, completionHandler: @escaping (SearchResult<JSON>)
    -> Void) {
    let encodedString = term.addingPercentEncoding(withAllowedCharacters:
    .urlHostAllowed)
    let path = encodedString.map { "https://itunes.apple.com/search?term="
    + $0 }

    guard let url = path.flatMap(URL.init) else {
        completionHandler(SearchResult(.invalidTerm(term)))
        return
    }

    callURL(with: url) { result in
        switch result {
        case .success(let data):
            if
                let json = try? JSONSerialization.jsonObject(with: data,
    options: []),
                let jsonDictionary = json as? JSON {
                let result = SearchResult<JSON>(jsonDictionary)
                completionHandler(result)
            } else {
                let result = SearchResult<JSON>(.invalidData)
                completionHandler(result)
            }
        case .failure(let error):
            let result = SearchResult<JSON>(.underlyingError(error))
            completionHandler(result)
        }
    }
}
```

Append the encoded string to the iTunes API path. You use map for this to delay unwrapping.

Transform the complete path into a URL via a flatMap. The guard performs the unwrapping action.

You make sure that an URL is created; on failure, you short-circuit the function by calling the closure early.

On the success case, the function tries to convert the data to a JSON format [String: Any].

The original callURL is called to get raw data.

If the data successfully converts to JSON, you can pass it to the completion handler.

If conversion to JSON format fails, you pass a SearchResultError, wrapped in a Result. You can omit SearchResultError because Swift can infer the error type for you.

On failure of callURL, you translate the lower-level NetworkError to a higher-level SearchResultError, passing the original NetworkError to a SearchResultError for troubleshooting.

Thanks to the search function, you end up with a higher-level function to search the iTunes API. But, it's still a little bit clunky because you're manually creating multiple result types and calling the completionHandler in multiple places. It's quite the boilerplate, and you could possibly forget to call the completionHandler in larger functions. Let's clean that up with map, mapError, and flatMap so that you'll transform and propagate a single Result type and you'll only need to call completionHandler once.

11.3   *Transforming values inside Result*

Similar to how you can weave optionals through an application and map over them (which delays the unwrapping), you can also weave a Result through your functions and methods while programming the happy path of your application. In essence, after you obtained a Result, you can pass it around, transform it, and only switch on it when you'd like to extract its value or handle its error.

One way to transform a Result is via map, similar to mapping over Optional. Remember how you could map over an optional and transform its inner value if present? Same with Result: you transform its success value if present. Via mapping, in this case, you'd turn Result<Data, NetworkError> into Result<JSON, NetworkError>.

Related to how map ignores nil values on optionals, map also ignores errors on Result (see figure 11.1).

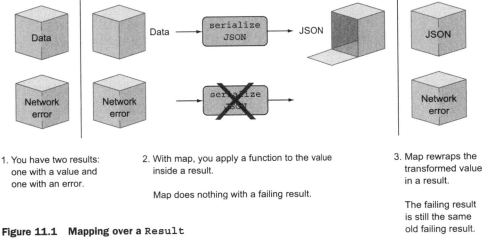

1. You have two results: one with a value and one with an error.

2. With map, you apply a function to the value inside a result.

   Map does nothing with a failing result.

3. Map rewraps the transformed value in a result.

   The failing result is still the same old failing result.

Figure 11.1   Mapping over a Result

As a special addition, you can *also* map over an error instead of a value inside Result. Having mapError is convenient because you translate a NetworkError inside Result to a SearchResultError.

With mapError, you'd therefore turn Result<JSON, NetworkError> into Result<JSON, SearchResultError>, which matches the type you pass to the completion-Handler (see figure 11.2).

With the power of both map and mapError combined, you can turn a Result<Data, NetworkError> into a Result<JSON, SearchResultError>, aka SearchResult<JSON>, without having to switch on a result once (see figure 11.3). The listing 11.11 gives an example of mapping over an error and value.

Applying mapError and map help you remove some boilerplate from earlier in the search function.

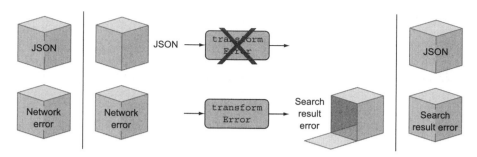

1. You have two results:
   one with a value and
   one with an error.

2. mapError does nothing with a successful result.

   With mapError, you apply a function to the error
   inside a result.

3. The successful result
   is still the same.

   mapError rewraps
   the transformed error
   in a result.

Figure 11.2   Mapping over an error inside `Result`

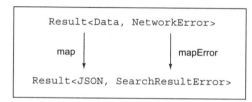

**Figure 11.3   Mapping over
both the value and error**

Listing 11.11   Mapping over an error and value

```
func search(term: String, completionHandler: @escaping (SearchResult<JSON>)
   -> Void) {
   // ... snip

   callURL(with: url) { result in

      let convertedResult: SearchResult<JSON> =
          result
              // Transform Data to JSON
             .map { (data: Data) -> JSON in
                  guard
                      let json = try? JSONSerialization.jsonObject(with:
   data, options: []),
                      let jsonDictionary = json as? JSON else {
                          return [:]
                  }

                  return jsonDictionary
              }
              // Transform NetworkError to SearchResultError
             .mapError { (networkError: NetworkError) ->
   SearchResultError in
```

This result is of type
Result<Data, NetworkError>.

On success, you map
the data to a JSON.

On failure, you now end up with
an empty JSON instead of an
error, which you'll solve with
flatMap in a moment.

You map the error so that the error
type matches SearchResultError.

```
                        return SearchResultError.underlyingError(networkError)
➡ // Handle error from lower layer
     }
                                                          You pass the SearchResult<JSON>
         completionHandler(convertedResult)  ⟵┤         type to the completionHandler after
    }                                                     all is done.
}
```

Now, instead of manually unwrapping result types and passing them to the `completionHandler` in multiple flows, you transform the `Result` to a `SearchResult`, and pass it to the `completionHandler` only once. Just like with optionals, you delay any error handling until you want to get the value out.

Unfortunately, `mapError` is not part of the `Result` type offered by Apple. You have to define the method yourself (see the upcoming exercise), but you can also look inside the relevant playgrounds file.

As the next step for improvement, let's improve failure, because currently you're returning an empty dictionary instead of throwing an error. You'll improve this with `flatMap`.

11.3.1 Exercise

1 By looking at the `map` function on `Result`, see if you can create `mapError`.

11.3.2 *flatMapping over Result*

One missing piece from your search function is that when the data can't be converted to JSON format, you'd need to obtain an error. You could throw, but throwing is somewhat awkward because you would be mixing Swift's throwing idiom with the `Result` idiom. You'll take a look at that in the next section.

To stay in the `Result` way of thinking, let's return another `Result` from inside `map`. But you may have guessed that returning a `Result` from a mapping operation leaves you with a nested `Result`, such as `SearchResult<SearchResult<JSON>>`. You can make use of `flatMap`—that is defined on `Result`—to get rid of one extra layer of nesting.

Exactly like how you can use `flatMap` to turn `Optional<Optional<JSON>>` into `Optional<JSON>`, you can also turn `SearchResult<SearchResult<JSON>>` into `SearchResult<JSON>` (see figure 11.4).

By replacing `map` with `flatMap` when parsing `Data` to `JSON`, you can return an error `Result` from inside the `flatMap` operation when parsing fails, as shown in listing 11.12.

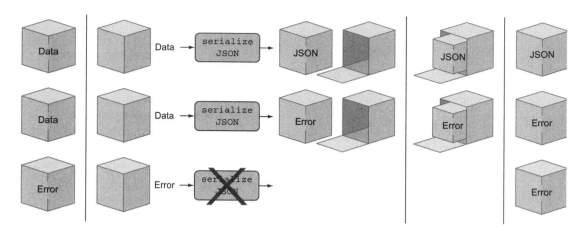

1. You start with a sucessful result containing Data (x2) and with one result containing an error.

2. With flatMap, you apply a function to the value inside the result. This function will itself return a new result. This new result could be successful and carry a value, or be a failure result containing an error.

   But if you start with a result containing an error, any flatMap action is ignored.

3. You end up with a nested result.

   If you start with an error, then nothing is transformed or nested.

4. The nested result is flattened to a regular result.

   If you start with an error, nothing happened and the result remains the same.

Figure 11.4　How `flatMap` works on `Result`

Listing 11.12　`flatMaping` over `Result`

```
func search(term: String, completionHandler: @escaping (SearchResult<JSON>)
➥ -> Void) {
    // ... snip

    callURL(with: url) { result in

        let convertedResult: SearchResult<JSON> =
            result
                // Transform error type to SearchResultError
                .mapError { (networkError: NetworkError) ->
➥ SearchResultError in
                    return SearchResultError.underlyingError(networkError)
                }
                // Parse Data to JSON, or return SearchResultError
                .flatMap { (data: Data) -> SearchResult<JSON> in
                    guard
                        let json = try? JSONSerialization.jsonObject(with:
➥ data, options: []),
                        let jsonDictionary = json as? JSON else {
                            return SearchResult(.invalidData)
                    }

                    return SearchResult(jsonDictionary)
        }
```

mapError is moved higher up the chain, so that the error type is SearchResultError before you flatMap over the value. This helps the flatMap so that it can also return SearchResultError instead of NetworkError.

The map operation is replaced by flatMap.

Now you can return a Result from inside a flatMap operation.

```
        completionHandler(convertedResult)
    }
}
```

FLATMAP DOESN'T CHANGE THE ERROR TYPE A flatMap operation on Result doesn't change an error type from one to another. For instance, you can't turn Result<Value, SearchResultError> to a Result<Value, NetworkError> via a flatMap operation. This is something to keep in mind and why mapError is moved up the chain.

11.3.3 Exercises

2 Using the techniques you've learned, try to connect to a real API. See if you can implement the FourSquare API (http://mng.bz/nxVg) and obtain the venues JSON. You can register to receive free developer credentials.

Be sure to use Result to return any venues that you can get from the API.

To allow for asynchronous calls inside playgrounds, add the following:

```
import PlaygroundSupport
PlaygroundPage.current.needsIndefiniteExecution = true
```

3 See if you can use map, mapError, and even flatMap to transform the result so that you call the completion handler only once.

4 The server can return an error, even if the call succeeds. For example, if you pass a latitude and longitude of 0, you get an errorType and errorDetail value in the meta key in the JSON, like so:

```
{"meta":{"code":400,"errorType":"param_error","errorDetail":"Must
➥  provide parameters (ll and radius) or (sw and ne) or (near and
➥  radius)","requestId":"5a9c09ba9fb6b70cfe3f2e12"},"response":{}}
```

Try to make sure that this error is reflected in the Result type.

11.4 Mixing Result with throwing functions

Earlier, you avoided throwing an error inside a Result's mapping or flatmapping operation so that you could focus on one idiom at a time.

Let's up the ante. Once you start working with returned data, you'll most likely be using synchronous "regular" functions for processing data, such as parsing or storing data or validating values. In other words, you'll be applying throwing functions to a value inside Result. In essence, you're mixing two idioms of error handling.

11.4.1 From throwing to a Result type

Previously, you were parsing data to JSON from inside the flatMap operation. To mimic a real-world scenario, let's rewrite the flatMap operation so that this time you'll be converting Data to JSON using a throwing function called parseData. To make it more realistic, parseData comes with an error called ParsingError, which deviates from the SearchResultError you've been using.

Listing 11.13   The `parseData` function

```
enum ParsingError: Error {          ← A specific error used
    case couldNotParseJSON            for parsing data
}
                                              The parseData function
func parseData(_ data: Data) throws -> JSON {    ← turns Data into JSON and
    guard                                          can throw a ParsingError.
        let json = try? JSONSerialization.jsonObject(with: data, options: []),
        let jsonDictionary = json as? JSON else {
            throw ParsingError.couldNotParseJSON
    }
    return jsonDictionary
}
```

You can turn this throwing function into a `Result` via an initializer on `Result`. The initializer accepts a closure that may throw; then the `Result` initializer catches any errors thrown from the closure and creates a `Result` out of it. This `Result` can be successful or failing (if an error has been thrown).

It works as follows: you pass a throwing function to `Result` and, in this case, have it convert to Result<JSON, SearchResultError>.

Listing 11.14   Converting a throwing function to `Result`

```
let searchResult: Result<JSON, SearchResultError> = Result(try parseData(data))
```

You're almost there, but one thing is missing. You try to convert `parseData` to a `Result` with a `SearchResultError` via an initializer. Yet, `parseData` doesn't throw a `SearchResultError`. You can look in the body of `parseData` to confirm. But Swift only knows at runtime what error `parseData` throws.

If during conversion any error slips out that is not `SearchResultError`, the initializer on `Result` throws the error from `parseData`, which means that you need to catch that error, too. Moreover, this is why the initializer on `Result` is throwing, because it throws any errors that it can't convert. This awkwardness is a bit of the pain you have when turning a runtime-known error into a compile-time-known error.

To complete the conversion, you need to add a *do catch* statement; you remain in the do block on success or when `Result` receives a `SearchResultError`. But as soon as `parseData` throws a `ParsingError`, as shown in the following example, you end up in the `catch` block, which is an opportunity to fall back to a default error.

Listing 11.15   Passing a throwing function to `Result`

```
do {
  let searchResult: Result<JSON, SearchResultError> = Result(try
parseData(data))
  } catch {                                    ← You call parseData();
  print(error) // ParsingError.couldNotParseData    if it succeeds you have
                                                     a searchResult.
```

```
let searchResult: Result<JSON, SearchResultError> =
    Result(.invalidData(data))     ◀──
}
```
If conversion fails, you end up in the catch statement, where you default back to returning a SearchResult with default error.

11.4.2 Converting a throwing function inside flatMap

Now that you know how to convert a throwing function to Result, you can start mixing these in with your pipeline via flatMap.

Inside the flatMap method from earlier, create a Result from the throwing parseData function.

Listing 11.16 Creating a Result from parseData

```
func search(term: String, completionHandler: @escaping (SearchResult<JSON>)
➥ -> Void) {
    // ... snip

    callURL(with: url) { result in                      You're entering a
        let convertedResult: SearchResult<JSON> =        flatMap operation.
            result
                .mapError { SearchResultError.underlyingError($0) }
                .flatMap { (data: Data) -> SearchResult<JSON> in    ◀──┘
                    do {
                        // Catch if the parseData method throws a ParsingError.
                        let searchResult: SearchResultError<JSON> =
➥ Result(try parseData(data))            ◀──┐
                        return searchResult          The parseData function is
                    } catch {                        passed to the initializer.
                        // You ignore any errors that parseData throws and
➥ revert to SearchResultError.
                        return SearchResult(.invalidData(data))    ◀────────
                    }
                }                                    If the parseData conversion fails,
        }                                           you end up in the catch statement
                                                          and default back to
        completionHandler(convertedResult)          SearchResultError.invalidData.
    }
}
```

11.4.3 Weaving errors through a pipeline

By composing Result with functions via mapping and flatmapping, you're performing so-called *monadic* error handling. Don't let the term scare you—flatMap is based on *monad* laws from functional programming. The beauty is that you can focus on the happy path of transforming your data.

As with optionals, flatMap isn't called if Result doesn't contain a value. You can work with the real value (whether Result is erroneous or not) while carrying an error context and propagate the Result higher—all the way to where some code can pattern match on it, such as the caller of a function.

As an example, if you were to continue the data transformations, you could end up with multiple chained operations. In this pipeline, map would always keep you on the happy path, and with `flatMap` you could short-circuit and move to either the happy path or error path.

For instance, let's say you want to add more steps, such as validating data, filtering it, and storing it inside a database (perhaps a cache). You would have multiple steps where `flatMap` could take you to an error path. In contrast, `map` always keeps you on the happy path (see figure 11.5).

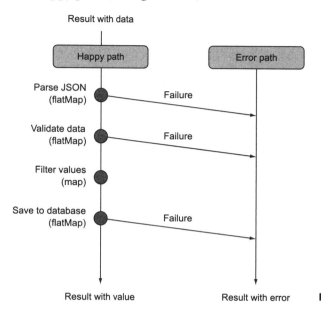

Figure 11.5   Happy path programming

For the sake of brevity, you aren't going to implement all these methods, but the point is that you can build a sophisticated pipeline, as shown in the following listing, weave the error through it, and only call the completion handler once.

Listing 11.17   A longer pipeline

```
func search(term: String, completionHandler: @escaping (SearchResult<JSON>)
    -> Void) {
  // ... snip

  callURL(with: url) { result in

    let convertedResult: SearchResult<JSON> =
        result
            // Transform error type to SearchResultError
            .mapError { (networkError: NetworkError) ->
    SearchResultError in
              // code omitted
            }
            // Parse Data to JSON, or return SearchResultError
            .flatMap { (data: Data) -> SearchResult<JSON> in
              // code omitted
            }
```

```
                   // validate Data
                   .flatMap { (json: JSON) -> SearchResult<JSON> in
                     // code omitted
                   }
                   // filter values
                   .map { (json: JSON) -> [JSON] in
                     // code omitted
                   }
                   // Save to database
                   .flatMap { (mediaItems: [JSON]) -> SearchResult<JSON> in
                     // code omitted
                     database.store(mediaItems)
              }

       completionHandler(convertedResult)
    }
}
```

SHORT-CIRCUITING A CHAINING OPERATION Note that map and flatMap are ignored if Result contains an error. If any flatMap operation returns a Result containing an error, any subsequent flatMap and map operations are ignored as well.

With flatMap you can short-circuit operations, just like with flatMap on Optional.

11.4.4 *Finishing up*

It may not look like much, but your API packs quite the punch. It handles network errors and parsing errors, and it's easy to read and to extend. And still you avoid having an ugly pyramid of doom, and your code focuses on the happy path. On top of that, calling search means that you only need to switch on the Result.

Receiving a simple Result enum looks a little underwhelming after all that work. But clean APIs tend to appear simple from time to time.

11.4.5 *Exercise*

5 Given the following throwing functions, see if you can use them to transform Result in your FourSquare API:

```
func parseData(_ data: Data) throws -> JSON {
    guard
        let json = try? JSONSerialization.jsonObject(with: data,
    options: []),
        let jsonDictionary = json as? JSON else {
            throw FourSquareError.couldNotParseData
    }
    return jsonDictionary
}

func validateResponse(json: JSON) throws -> JSON {
    if
        let meta = json["meta"] as? JSON,
```

```
            let errorType = meta["errorType"] as? String,
            let errorDetail = meta["errorDetail"] as? String {
            throw FourSquareError.serverError(errorType: errorType,
    errorDetail: errorDetail)
      }

        return json
   }

   func extractVenues(json: JSON) throws -> [JSON] {
        guard
            let response = json["response"] as? JSON,
            let venues = response["venues"] as? [JSON]
            else {
                throw FourSquareError.couldNotParseData
        }
        return venues
   }
```

11.5 *Multiple errors inside of Result*

Working with `Result` may feel constricting at times when multiple actions can fail.
Previously, you were translating each failure into a `Result` holding a single error
type—`SearchResultError` in the examples. Translating errors to a single error type is
a good practice to follow. But it may get burdensome moving forward if you're dealing
with many different errors, especially when you're beginning a new project and you
need to glue together all kinds of throwing methods. Translating every error to the
correct type may slow you down.

Not to worry; if you want to move fast and keep errors known at runtime, you can
use a generic type called `AnyError`—also offered by the Swift Package Manager.

11.5.1 *Introducing AnyError*

`AnyError` represents any error that could be inside `Result`, allowing you to mix and
match all types of errors in the same `Result` type. With `AnyError`, you avoid having to
figure out each error at compile time.

`AnyError` wraps around an `Error` and stores the error inside; then a `Result` can
have `AnyError` as its error type, such as `Result<String, AnyError>`. You can manually create an `AnyError`, but you can also create a `Result` of type `Result<String,
AnyError>` in multiple ways.

Notice how `Result` has two initializers specialized to `AnyError`: one converts a regular error to `AnyError`, the other accepts a throwing function in which the error converts to `AnyError`.

> **Listing 11.18   Creating a `Result` with `AnyError`**

```
enum PaymentError: Error {
    case amountTooLow
    case insufficientFunds
}
```

You can pass an error to the AnyError type yourself.

You can also pass an error to Result directly, which automatically converts an error to AnyError because the Result is of type Result<String, AnyError>.

```
let error: AnyError = AnyError(PaymentError.amountTooLow)

let result: Result<String, AnyError> = Result(PaymentError.amountTooLow)

let otherResult: Result<String, AnyError> = Result(anyError: { () throws ->
    String in
    throw PaymentError.insufficientFunds
})
```

You can even pass throwing functions to Result; because AnyError represents all possible errors, the conversion always succeeds.

Functions returning a Result with AnyError are similar to a throwing function where you only know the error type at runtime.

Having AnyError makes sense when you're developing an API and don't want to focus too much on the proper errors yet. Imagine that you're creating a function to transfer money, called processPayment. You can return different types of errors in each step, which relieves you of the burden of translating different errors to one specific type. Notice how you also get a special mapAny method.

Listing 11.19 Returning different errors

```
func processPayment(fromAccount: Account, toAccount: Account, amountInCents:
    Int, completion: @escaping (Result<String, AnyError>) -> Void) {

    guard amountInCents > 0 else {                          Return a
        completion(Result(PaymentError.amountTooLow))       PaymentError
        return                                              here.
    }

    guard isValid(toAccount) && isValid(fromAccount) else {
        completion(Result(AccountError.invalidAccount))     But you can return a
        return                                              different error here,
    }                                                       of type AccountError.

    // Process payment

    moneyAPI.transfer(amountInCents, from: fromAccount, to: toAccount) {
    (result: Result<Data, AnyError>) in
        let response = result.mapAny(parseResponse)         Utilize a special
        completion(response)                                mapAny method.
    }

}
```

An interesting thing to note is that if Result has AnyError as its type, you gain a special mapAny method for free. The mapAny method works similarly to map, except that it can accept any throwing function. If a function inside mapAny throws, mapAny automatically wraps this error inside an AnyError. This technique allows you to pass throwing functions to map without requiring you to catch any errors.

Also, a big difference with `flatMap` is that you could not change the `ErrorType` from within the operations. With `flatMap`, you would have to create and return a new `Result` manually. With `mapAny`, you can pass a regular throwing function and let `mapAny` handle the catching and wrapping into `AnyError`. Applying `mapAny` allows you to map over the value and even change the error inside `Result`.

HOW TO CHOOSE BETWEEN MAP OR MAPANY The difference between `map` and `mapAny` is that `map` works on all `Result` types, but it doesn't catch errors from throwing functions. In contrast, `mapAny` works on both throwing and non-throwing functions, but it's available only on `Result` types containing `AnyError`. Try to use `map` when you can; it communicates that a function cannot throw. Also, if you ever refactor `AnyError` back to a regular `Error` inside `Result`, then `map` is still available.

MATCHING WITH ANYERROR

To get the error out when dealing with `AnyError`, you can use the `underlyingError` property of `AnyError` to match on the actual error inside of it.

Listing 11.20 Matching on `AnyError`

```
processPayment(fromAccount: from, toAccount: to, amountInCents: 100) {
    (result: Result<String, AnyError>) in
    switch result {
    case .success(let value): print(value)
    case .failure(let error) where error.underlyingError is AccountError:
        print("Account error")
    case .failure(let error):
        print(error)
    }
}
```

`AnyError` is a useful placeholder to let you handle "proper" error handling at a later time. When time permits and your code solidifies, you can start replacing the general errors with stricter error translations for extra compile-time benefits.

Working with `AnyError` gives you a lot more flexibility. But you suffer somewhat from code erosion because you lose a big benefit of `Result`, which is being able to see which errors you can expect before even running your code. You may also consider `NSError` instead of `AnyError` because `NSError` is also flexible. But then you'll be looking back to Objective-C, and you also lose the benefits of using Swift errors, such as strong pattern matching on enum-type errors. Before going the `NSError` route, you may want to reconsider and see if you get to keep using Swift errors in combination with `AnyError`.

11.6 *Impossible failure and Result*

Sometimes you may need to conform to a protocol that wants you to use a `Result` type. But the type that implements the protocol may never fail. Let's see how you can improve your code in this scenario with a unique tidbit. This section is a bit esoteric and theoretical, but it proves useful when you run into a similar situation.

11.6.1 *When a protocol defines a Result*

Imagine that you have a `Service` protocol representing a type that loads some data for you. This `Service` protocol determines that data is to be loaded asynchronously, and it makes use of a `Result`.

You have multiple types of errors and data that can be loaded, so `Service` defines them as associated types.

> **Listing 11.21 The `Service` protocol**

```
protocol Service {
    associatedtype Value          The Value
    associatedtype Err: Error     that the
    func load(complete: @escaping (Result<Value, Err>) -> Void)
}
```

The Value that the Service loads

This is the Error the Service can give. Note how your associated type is called Err, and it's constrained to the Error protocol.

The load method returns a Result containing a Value and Err, passed by a completion closure.

Now you want to implement this `Service` by a type called `SubscriptionsLoader`, which loads a customer's subscriptions for magazines. This is shown in listing 11.22. Note that loading subscriptions *always* succeeds, which you can guarantee because they are loaded from memory. But the `Service` type declares that you use `Result`, which needs an error, so you do need to declare what error a `SubscriptionsLoader` throws. `SubscriptionsLoader` doesn't have errors to throw. To remedy this problem, let's create an empty enum—conforming to `Error`—called `BogusError` so that `SubscriptionsLoader` can conform to `Service` protocol. Notice that `BogusError` has no cases, meaning that nothing can actually create this enum.

> **Listing 11.22 Implementing the `Service` protocol**

```
struct Subscription {         The Subscription is the type of data
    // ... details omitted     retrieved from SubscriptionsLoader.
}

                              You create a dummy error type so
enum BogusError: Error {}      that you can define it on the Result
                               type, in order to please Service.
final class SubscriptionsLoader: Service {
    func load(complete: @escaping (Result<[Subscription], BogusError>) ->
      Void) {
        // ... load data. Always succeeds
        let subscriptions = [Subscription(), Subscription()]
        complete(Result(subscriptions))
    }
}
```

The load method now returns a Result returning an array of subscriptions. Notice how you defined the uninhabitable BogusError type to please the protocol.

You made an empty enum that conforms to `Error` merely to please the compiler. But because `BogusError` has no cases, you can't instantiate it, and Swift knows this. Once you call `load` on `SubscriptionsLoader` and retrieve the `Result`, you can match *only* on the success case, and Swift is smart enough to understand that you can *never* have a failure case. To emphasize, a BogusError can *never* be created, so you don't need to match on this, as the following example shows.

Listing 11.23 Matching only on the success case

```
let subscriptionsLoader = SubscriptionsLoader()
subscriptionsLoader.load { (result: Result<[Subscription], BogusError>) in
    switch result {
    case .success(let subscriptions): print(subscriptions)
        // You don't need .failure
    }
}
```

> Swift lets you get away with this. Normally you'd get a compiler error!

This technique gives you compile-time elimination of cases to match on and can clean up your APIs and show clearer intent. But an official solution—the Never type—lets you get rid of BogusError.

THE NEVER TYPE

To please the compiler, you made a bogus error type that can't be instantiated. Actually, such a type already exists in Swift and is called the Never type.

The Never type is a so-called *bottom type*; it tells the compiler that a certain code path can't be reached. You may also find this mechanism in other programming languages, such as the Nothing type in Scala, or when a function in Rust returns an exclamation mark (!).

Never is a hidden type used by Swift to indicate impossible paths. For example, when a function calls a fatalError, it can return a Never type, indicating that returning something is an impossible path.

Listing 11.24 From the Swift source

```
func crashAndBurn() -> Never {
    fatalError("Something very, very bad happened")
}
```

> The Never type is returned, but the code guarantees it never returns.

If you look inside the Swift source, you can see that Never is nothing but an empty enum.

Listing 11.25 The Never type

```
public enum Never {}
```

In your situation, you can replace your BogusError with Never and get the same result. You do, however, need to make sure that Never implements Error.

```
┌──────────────────────────────────────────────────────────────┐
│ Listing 11.26  Implementing Never                              │
└──────────────────────────────────────────────────────────────┘
extension Never: Error {}                    ◄──────┐   You extend Never to make it
                                                     │   conform to the Error protocol.
final class SubscriptionsLoader: Service {
    func load(complete: @escaping (Result<[Subscription], Never>) -> Void) {   ◄─┐
        // ... load data. Always succeeds                                         │
        let subscriptions = [Subscription(), Subscription()]     You now use the Never
        complete(Result(subscriptions))                          type to indicate that your
    }                                                            SubscriptionsLoader
}                                                                never fails.
```

NOTE   From Swift 5 on, Never conforms to some protocols, like Error.

Notice that Never can also indicate that a service never succeeds. For instance, you can put the Never as the success case of a Result.

11.7 Closing thoughts

I hope that you can see the benefits of error handling with Result. You've seen how Result can give you compile-time insights into which error to expect. Along the way you took your map and flatMap knowledge and wrote code that pretended to be error-free, yet was carrying an error-context. Now you know how to apply monadic error handling.

Here's a controversial thought: you can use the Result type for *all* the error handling in your project. You get more compile-time benefits, but at the price of more difficult programming. Error handling is more rigid with Result, but your code will be safer and stricter as a reward. And if you want to speed up your work a little, you can always create a Result type containing AnyError and take it from there.

Summary

- Using the default way of URLSession's data tasks is an error-prone way of error handling.
- Result is offered by the Swift Package Manager and is a good way to handle asynchronous error handling.
- Result has two generics and is a lot like Optional, but has a context of why something failed.
- Result is a compile-time safe way of error handling, and you can see which error to expect before running a program.
- By using map and flatMap and mapError, you can cleanly chain transformations of your data while carrying an error context.
- Throwing functions can be converted to a Result via a special throwing initializer. This initializer allows you to mix and match two error throwing idioms.
- You can postpone strict error handling with the use of AnyError.
- With AnyError, multiple errors can live inside Result.
- If you're working with many types of errors, working with AnyError can be faster, at the expense of not knowing which errors to expect at compile time.

- AnyError can be a good alternative to NSError so that you reap the benefits of Swift error types.
- You can use the Never type to indicate that a Result can't have a failure case, or a success case.

Answers

1 By looking at the map function on Result, see if you can create mapError:

```
extension Result {

    public func mapError<E: Error>(_ transform: (ErrorType) throws
    -> E) rethrows -> Result<Value, E> {
        switch self {
        case .success(let value):
            return Result<Value, E>(value)
        case .failure(let error):
            return Result<Value, E>(try transform(error))
        }
    }

}
```

The following part is the answer to exercises 2 and 3:

2 Using the techniques you've learned, try to connect to a real API. See if you can implement the FourSquare API (http://mng.bz/nxVg) and obtain the venues JSON. You can register to receive free developer credentials.

3 See if you can use map, mapError, and even flatMap to transform the result, so that you call the completion handler only once.

4 The server can return an error, even if the call succeeds. For example, if you pass a latitude and longitude of 0, you get an errorType and errorDetail value in the meta key in the JSON. Try to make sure that this error is reflected in the Result type:

```
// You need an error
enum FourSquareError: Error {
    case couldNotCreateURL
    case networkError(Error)
    case serverError(errorType: String, errorDetail: String)
    case couldNotParseData
}

let clientId = ENTER_YOUR_ID
let clientSecret = ENTER_YOUR_SECRET
let apiVersion = "20180403"

// A helper function to create a URL
func createURL(endpoint: String, parameters: [String: String]) -> URL? {
    let baseURL = "https://api.foursquare.com/v2/"
```

```
    // You convert the parameters dictionary in an array of URLQueryItems
    var queryItems = parameters.map { pair -> URLQueryItem in
        return URLQueryItem(name: pair.key, value: pair.value)
    }

    // Add default parameters to query
    queryItems.append(URLQueryItem(name: "v", value: apiVersion))
    queryItems.append(URLQueryItem(name: "client_id", value: clientId))
    queryItems.append(URLQueryItem(name: "client_secret", value:
clientSecret))

    var components = URLComponents(string: baseURL + endpoint)
    components?.queryItems = queryItems
    return components?.url
}

// The getvenues call
func getVenues(latitude: Double, longitude: Double, completion:
⮕ @escaping (Result<[JSON], FourSquareError>) -> Void) {
    let parameters = [
        "ll": "\(latitude),\(longitude)",
        "intent": "browse",
        "radius": "250"
    ]

    guard let url = createURL(endpoint: "venues/search", parameters:
parameters)
        else {
            completion(Result(.couldNotCreateURL))
            return
    }

    let task = URLSession.shared.dataTask(with: url) { data, response,
error in
        let translatedError = error.map { FourSquareError.networkError(
$0) }
        // Convert optional data and optional to Result
        let result = Result<Data, FourSquareError>(value: data, error:
translatedError)
            // Parsing Data to JSON
            .flatMap { data in
                guard
                    let rawJson = try?
JSONSerialization.jsonObject(with: data, options: []),
                    let json = rawJson as? JSON
                    else {
                        return Result(.couldNotParseData)
                }
                return Result(json)
            }
            // Check for server errors
            .flatMap { (json: JSON) -> Result<JSON, FourSquareError> in
                if
                    let meta = json["meta"] as? JSON,
                    let errorType = meta["errorType"] as? String,
```

```
                let errorDetail = meta["errorDetail"] as? String {
                    return Result(.serverError(errorType: errorType,
        errorDetail: errorDetail))
                }

                return Result(json)
            }
            // Extract venues
            .flatMap { (json: JSON) -
    > Result<[JSON], FourSquareError> in
                guard
                    let response = json["response"] as? JSON,
                    let venues = response["venues"] as? [JSON]
                    else {
                        return Result(.couldNotParseData)
                }
                return Result(venues)
        }

        completion(result)
    }

    task.resume()
}


// Times square
let latitude = 40.758896
let longitude = -73.985130

// Calling getVenues

getVenues(latitude: latitude, longitude: longitude) { (result:
    Result<[JSON], FourSquareError>) in
    switch result {
    case .success(let categories): print(categories)
    case .failure(let error): print(error)
    }
}
```

5 Given the throwing functions, see if you can use them to transform Result in
   your FourSquare API:

```
enum FourSquareError: Error {
    // ... snip
    case unexpectedError(Error) // Adding new error for when conversion
    to Result fails
}

func getVenues(latitude: Double, longitude: Double, completion:
➥ @escaping (Result<[JSON], FourSquareError>) -> Void) {
    // ... snip
    let result = Result<Data, FourSquareError>(value: data, error:
    translatedError)
            // Parsing Data to JSON
```

```
        .flatMap { data in
            do {
                return Result(try parseData(data))
            } catch {
                return Result(.unexpectedError(error))
            }
        }
        // Check for server errors
        .flatMap { (json: JSON) -> Result<JSON, FourSquareError> in
            do {
                return Result(try validateResponse(json: json))
            } catch {
                return Result(.unexpectedError(error))
            }
        }
        // Extract venues
        .flatMap { (json: JSON) -> Result<[JSON], FourSquareError> in
            do {
                return Result(try extractVenues(json: json))
            } catch {
                return Result(.unexpectedError(error))
            }
        }
}
```

Protocol extensions 12

This chapter covers

- Flexibly modeling data with protocols instead of subclasses
- Adding default behavior with protocol extensions
- Extending regular types with protocols
- Working with protocol inheritance and default implementations
- Applying protocol composition for highly flexible code
- Showing how Swift prioritizes method calls
- Extending types containing associated types
- Extending vital protocols, such as `Sequence` and `Collection`

Previous chapters have shown how to work with protocols, associated types, and generics. To improve your abstract protocol game, this chapter sheds some light on protocol extensions. To some, being able to extend a protocol is the most significant feature of Swift, as you'll see later in this chapter.

Besides declaring a method signature, with protocols you can supply full implementations. Extending a protocol means that you can offer default implementations to a protocol so that types don't have to implement certain methods. The benefits are profound. You can elegantly bypass rigid subclassing structures and end up with highly reusable, flexible code in your applications.

In its purest form, a protocol extension sounds simple. Offer a default implementation and be on your merry way. Moreover, protocol extensions can be easy to grasp if you stay at the surface. But as you progress through this chapter, you'll discover many different use cases, pitfalls, best practices, and tricks related to correctly extending protocols.

You'll see that it takes more than merely getting your code to compile. You also have the problem that code can be too decoupled, and understanding which methods you're calling can be hard; even more so when you mix protocols with protocol inheritance while overriding methods. You'll see how protocols are not always easy to comprehend. But when applied correctly, protocols enable you to create highly flexible code. At first, you're going to see how protocols enable you to model your data *horizontally* instead of *vertically*, such as with subclassing. You'll also take a look at how protocol extensions work and how you can override them.

Then you'll model a mailing API in two ways and consider their trade-offs. First, you'll use protocol inheritance to deliver a default implementation that is more specialized. Then, you'll model the same API via a signature feature called *protocol composition*. You'll see the benefits and downsides of both approaches side by side.

Then, it's time for some theory for a better understanding of which methods are called when. You'll look at overriding methods, inheriting from protocols, and the calling priorities of Swift. It's a little theoretical if you're into that.

As a next step, you'll see how you can extend types in multiple directions. You'll discover the trade-offs between extending a type to conform to a protocol, and to extend a protocol constrained to a type. It's a subtle but important distinction.

Going further down the rabbit hole, you'll see how to extend types with associated types. Then you'll find out how to extend the `Collection` protocol and how Swift prioritizes methods that rely on a constrained associated type.

As the finishing touch, you get to go lower-level and see how Swift extends `Sequence`. You'll apply this knowledge to create highly reusable extensions. You're going to create a `take(while:)` method that is the opposite of `drop(while:)`. You'll also create the `inspect` method, which helps you to debug iterators. A brief look at higher-order functions comes next, along with the esoteric `ContiguousArray` to write these lower-level extensions.

After you have finished this chapter, you may catch yourself writing more highly decoupled code, so let's get started.

12.1 *Class inheritance vs. Protocol inheritance*

In the world of object-oriented programming, the typical way to achieve inheritance was via subclassing. Subclassing is a legit way to achieve polymorphism and offer sane defaults for subclasses. But as you've seen throughout this book, inheritance can be a rigid form of modeling data. As one alternative to class-based inheritance, Swift offers protocol-inheritance, branded as *protocol-oriented programming*, which wowed many developers watching Apple's World Wide Developers Conference (WWDC) presentations. Via the power of protocol extensions, you can slap a method with a complete implementation on (existing) types without the need for subclassing hierarchies, while offering high reusability.

In this section, you're going to see how modeling works horizontally rather than vertically when you make use of protocols.

12.1.1 *Modeling data horizontally instead of vertically*

> **JOIN ME!**   It's more educational and fun if you can check out the code and follow along with the chapter. You can download the source code at http://mng.bz/vOvJ.

You can think of subclassing as a vertical way to model data. You have a superclass, and you can subclass it and override methods and behavior to add new functionality, and then you can go even lower and subclass again. Imagine that you're creating a `RequestBuilder`, which creates `URLRequest` types for a network call. A subclass could expand functionality by adding default headers, and another subclass can encrypt the data inside the request. Via subclassing, you end up with a type that can build encrypted network requests for you (see figure 12.1).

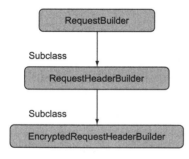

Figure 12.1   Class-based inheritance

Protocols, on the other hand, can be imagined as a horizontal way of modeling data. You take a type and add extra functionality to it by making it adhere to protocols, like adding building blocks to your structure. Instead of creating a superclass, you create separate protocols with a default implementation for building requests and headers and for encryption (see figure 12.2).

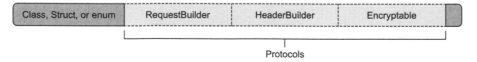

Figure 12.2   Implementing protocols

The concept of decoupling functionality from a type gives you a ton of flexibility and code reuse. You are not constrained to a single superclass anymore. As long as a type conforms to a RequestBuilder, it gets its default functionality for free. Any type could be a RequestBuilder—an enum, a struct, a class, a subclass—it doesn't matter.

12.1.2 Creating a protocol extension

Creating a protocol extension is painless. Let's continue with the RequestBuilder example. First, you define a protocol, and then you extend the protocol where you can add a default implementation for each type that conforms to this protocol.

Listing 12.1   A protocol extension

```
protocol RequestBuilder {                          Define a RequestBuilder protocol
    var baseURL: URL { get }    ◁─────             with a baseURL property.
    func makeRequest(path: String) -> URLRequest   ◁───    Also define the
}                                                          makeRequest
                                                           method. A method on
                                                           a protocol definition
                                                           can't have a body.
extension RequestBuilder {                    ◁─
    func makeRequest(path: String) -> URLRequest {    ◁──┐    Extend
       let url = baseURL.appendingPathComponent(path)       RequestBuilder,
The extension                                                because methods
makes use of    var request = URLRequest(url: url)          inside extensions
the baseURL     request.httpShouldHandleCookies = false     can have bodies.
property.       request.timeoutInterval = 30
                return request              Offer a default
    }                                       implementation of the
}                                           makeRequest method.
```

> **NOTE** A default implementation on a protocol is always added via an extension.

To get the implementation of makeRequest for free, you merely have to conform to the RequestBuilder protocol. You conform to RequestBuilder by making sure to store the baseURL property. For instance, imagine having an app for a startup that lists thrilling bike trips. The application needs to make requests to retrieve data. For that to happen, the BikeRequestBuilder type conforms to the RequestBuilder protocol, and you make sure to implement the baseURL property. As a result, it gets makeRequest for free.

Listing 12.2   Implementing a protocol with default implementation

```
A BikeRequestBuilder type conforms to the
RequestBuilder  protocol and implements the      The BikeRequestBuilder type gets the
baseURL property requirement.                    makeRequest method for free because
                                                 of the default implementation.
    struct BikeRequestBuilder: RequestBuilder {
        let baseURL: URL = URL(string: "https://www.biketriptracker.com")!
    }

let bikeRequestBuilder = BikeRequestBuilder()
let request = bikeRequestBuilder.makeRequest(path: "/trips/all")    ◁──
print(request) // https://www.biketriptracker.com/trips/all     ◁──┐
                  Confirm that a successful request has been made.
```

12.1.3 *Multiple extensions*

A type is free to conform to multiple protocols. Imagine having a `BikeAPI` that both builds requests and handles the response. It can conform to two protocols: `Request-Builder` from before, and a new one, `ResponseHandler`, as in the following example. `BikeAPI` is now free to conform to both protocols and gain multiple methods for free.

Listing 12.3 `ResponseHandler`

```
enum ResponseError: Error {          Introduce
    case invalidResponse             another
}                                    protocol.
protocol ResponseHandler {     ◁─┘
    func validate(response: URLResponse) throws
}

extension ResponseHandler {
    func validate(response: URLResponse) throws {
        guard let httpresponse = response as? HTTPURLResponse else {
            throw ResponseError.invalidResponse
        }                                        The BikeAPI class
    }                                            can adhere to two
}                                                protocols.
class BikeAPI: RequestBuilder, ResponseHandler {   ◁─┘
    let baseURL: URL = URL(string: "https://www.biketriptracker.com")!
}
```

12.2 *Protocol inheritance vs. Protocol composition*

You've seen before how you can offer default implementations via a protocol extension. You can model data with extensions several other ways, namely via *protocol inheritance* and *protocol composition*.

You're going to build a hypothetical framework that can send emails via SMTP. You'll focus on the API and omit the implementation. You'll start by taking the protocol inheritance approach, and then you'll create a more flexible approach via the use of composing protocols. This way, you can see the process and trade-offs in both approaches.

12.2.1 *Builder a mailer*

First, as shown in the following listing, you define an `Email` type, which uses a `MailAddress` struct to define its email properties. A `MailAddress` shows more intent than simply using a `String`. You also define the `Mailer` protocol with a default implementation via a protocol extension (implementation omitted).

Listing 12.4 The `Email` and `Mailer` types

```
struct MailAddress {     ◁─┐  MailAddress represents
    let value: String       │  an email address.
}
```

```
struct Email {                          Email contains the values
    let subject: String                 to send an email.
    let body: String
    let to: [MailAddress]
    let from: MailAddress
}

protocol Mailer {                       The Mailer protocol
    func send(email: Email)             can send emails.
}

extension Mailer {
    func send(email: Email) {           By default, the Mailer protocol
        // Omitted: Connect to server   will be able to send an email
        // Omitted: Submit email        (implementation omitted).
        print("Email is sent!")
    }
}
```

You're off to a good start. Now, imagine that you want to add a default implementation for a Mailer that *also* validates the Email before sending. But not all mailers validate the email. Perhaps a mailer is based on UNIX sendmail or a different service that doesn't validate an email per sé. Not all mailers validate, so you can't assume that Mailer validates an email by default.

12.2.2 Protocol inheritance

If you do want to offer a default implementation that allows for sending validated emails, you can take at least two approaches. You'll start with a protocol inheritance approach and then switch to a composition approach to see both pros and cons.

With protocol inheritance, you can expand on a protocol to add extra requirements. You do this by making a subprotocol that inherits from a superprotocol, similar to how Hashable inherits from Equatable.

As a next step, you start by creating a ValidatingMailer that inherits from Mailer. ValidatingMailer overrides the send(email:) method by making it throwing. ValidatingMailer also introduces a new method called validate(email:) (see figure 12.3).

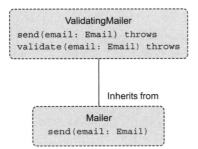

Figure 12.3 ValidatingMailer inheriting from Mailer

To make life easier for implementers of `ValidatingMailer`, you extend `Validating-Mailer` and offer a default `send(email:)` method, which uses the `validate(email:)` method before sending. Again, to focus on the API, implementations are omitted, as shown in this listing.

Listing 12.5 `ValidatingMailer`

```
protocol ValidatingMailer: Mailer {
    func send(email: Email) throws // Send is now throwing
    func validate(email: Email) throws
}

extension ValidatingMailer {
    func send(email: Email) throws {
        try validate(email: email)
        // Connect to server
        // Submit email
        print("Email validated and sent.")
    }

    func validate(email: Email) throws {
        // Check email address, and whether subject is missing.
    }
}
```

> Redeclare `send(email:)` so that you can make it a throwing method.

> The send(email:) method uses the validate(email:) method to validate an email before sending.

Now, `SMTPClient` implements `ValidatingMailer` and automatically get's a validated `send(email:)` method.

Listing 12.6 `SMTPClient`

```
struct SMTPClient: ValidatingMailer {
    // Implementation omitted.
}

let client = SMTPClient()
try? client.send(email: Email(subject: "Learn Swift",
                              body: "Lorem ipsum",
                              to: [MailAdress(value: "john@appleseed.com")],
                              from: MailAdress(value: "stranger@somewhere.com")))
```

A downside of protocol inheritance is that you don't separate functionality and semantics. For instance, because of protocol inheritance, anything that validates emails automatically has to be a `Mailer`. You can loosen this restriction by applying protocol composition—let's do that now.

12.2.3 *The composition approach*

For the composition approach, you keep the `Mailer` protocol. But instead of a `ValidatingMailer` that inherits from `Mailer`, you offer a standalone `MailValidator` protocol that doesn't inherit from anything. The `MailValidator` protocol also offers a default implementation via an extension, which you omit for brevity as shown here.

Listing 12.7 The `MailValidator` protocol

```
protocol MailValidator {
    func validate(email: Email) throws
}

extension MailValidator {
    func validate(email: Email) throws {
        // Omitted: Check email address, and whether subject is missing.
    }
}
```

Now you can compose. You make SMTPClient conform to both separate protocols. Mailer does not know about MailValidator, and vice versa (see figure 12.4).

SMTPClient	Mailer send(email: Email)	MailValidator validate(email: Email) throws

Figure 12.4 **SMTPClient implementing `Mailer` and `MailValidator`**

With the two protocols in place, you can create an extension that only works on a protocol intersection. Extending on an intersection means that types adhering to both Mailer and MailValidator get a specific implementation or even bonus method implementations. Inside the intersection, send(email:) combines functionality from both Mailer and MailValidator (see figure 12.5).

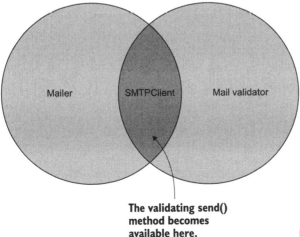

The validating send() method becomes available here.

Figure 12.5 **Intersecting extension**

To create an extension with an intersection, you extend one protocol that conforms to the other via the Self keyword.

Listing 12.8   Intersecting `Mailer` and `MailValidator`

```
extension MailValidator where Self: Mailer {          ◁——   You can define an intersection
                                                             via a Self clause.
    func send(email: Email) throws {          ◁——
        try validate(email: email)                   You can offer a default implementation
        // Connect to server                         when both the send(email:) and
        // Submit email                              validate(email:) methods are implemented.
        print("Email validated and sent.")           Notice how send(email:) is throwing here.
    }

}
```

> **NOTE** Whether you extend `MailValidator` or `Mailer` doesn't matter—either direction is fine.

Another benefit of this approach is that you can come up with new methods such as `send(email:, at:)`, which allows for a mail to be validated and queued. You validate the email so that the queue has the confidence that the mail can be sent. You can define new methods on a protocol intersection.

Listing 12.9   Adding bonus methods

```
extension MailValidator where Self: Mailer {
    // ... snip

    func send(email: Email, at: Date) throws {          ◁——   In the intersection,
        try validate(email: email)                             you can introduce
        // Connect to server                                   new methods.
        // Add email to delayed queue.
        print("Email validated and stored.")
    }
}
```

12.2.4 Unlocking the powers of an intersection

Now, you're going to make `SMTPClient` adhere to both the `Mailer` and `MailValidator` protocols, which unlocks the code inside the protocol intersection. In other words, `SMTPClient` gets the validating `send(email:)` and `send(email:, at:)` methods for free.

Listing 12.10   Implementing two protocols to get a free method

```
struct SMTPClient: Mailer, MailValidator {}          ◁——   SMTPClient conforms
                                                            to both protocols, which
let client = SMTPClient()                                   unlocks the intersection
let email = Email(subject: "Learn Swift",                   methods.
    body: "Lorem ipsum",
    to: [MailAdress(value: "john@appleseed.com")],
    from: MailAdress(value: "stranger@somewhere.com"))
```

```
try? client.send(email: email) // Email validated and sent.        ◀─┐
try? client.send(email: email, at: Date(timeIntervalSinceNow: 3600))
➥ // Email validated and queued.   ◀─┐
```

A bonus method is unlocked for use, too.

The intersection send(email:) method is used.

Another way to see the benefits is via a generic function, as in listing 12.11. When you constrain to both protocols, the intersection implementation becomes available. Notice how you define the generic `T` and constrain it to both protocols. By doing so, the delayed `send(email:, at:)` method becomes available.

Listing 12.11 Generic with an intersection

```
func submitEmail<T>(sender: T, email: Email) where T: Mailer, T: MailValidator {
    try? sender.send(email: email, at: Date(timeIntervalSinceNow: 3600))
}
```

Taking a composition approach decouples your code significantly. In fact, it may even become *too* decoupled. Implementers may not know precisely which method implementation is used under the hood; they may also be unable to decipher when bonus methods are unlocked. Another downside is that a type such as `SMTPClient` has to implement multiple protocols. But the benefits are profound. When used carefully, you can have elegant, highly reusable, highly decoupled code by using compositions.

A second way to think of intersecting protocols is to offer free benefits, under the guise of "Because you conform to both A and B, you might as well offer C for free."

With protocol inheritance, `SMTPClient` has to implement only a single protocol, and it's more rigid. Knowing what an implementer gets is also a little more straightforward. When you're working with protocols, trying to find the best abstraction can be a tough balancing act.

12.2.5 Exercise

1 Create an extension that enables the `explode()` function, but only on types that conform to the `Mentos` and `Coke` protocols:

```
protocol Mentos {}
protocol Coke {}

func mix<T>(concoction: T) where T: Mentos, T: Coke {
//    concoction.explode() // make this work, but only if T conforms
➥ to both protocols, not just one
}
```

12.3 Overriding priorities

When implementing protocols, you need to follow a few rules. As a palate cleanser, you'll move away from `Mailer` from the previous section and get a bit more conceptual.

12.3.1 *Overriding a default implementation*

To see how protocol inheritance works, imagine having a protocol `Tree` with a method called `grow()`. This protocol offers a default implementation via a protocol extension. Meanwhile, an `Oak` struct implements `Tree` *and* also implements `grow()` (see figure 12.6).

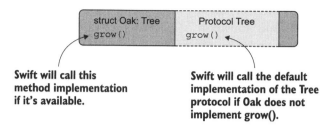

Swift will call this method implementation if it's available.

Swift will call the default implementation of the Tree protocol if Oak does not implement grow().

Figure 12.6 Overriding a protocol

Swift picks the most specific method it can find. If a type implements the same method as the one on a protocol extension, Swift ignores the protocol extension's method. In other words, Swift calls the `grow()` on `Oak`, and *not* the one on `Tree`. This allows you to override methods that are defined on a protocol extension.

Keep in mind that a protocol extension can't override methods from actual types, such as trying to give an existing type a new implementation via a protocol. Also, at the time of writing, no special syntax exists that lets you know if a type overrides a protocol method. When a type—such as a class, struct, or enum—implements a protocol and implements the same method as the protocol extension, seeing which method Swift is calling under the hood is opaque.

12.3.2 *Overriding with protocol inheritance*

To make things a bit more challenging, you'll introduce protocol inheritance. This time you'll introduce another protocol called `Plant`. `Tree` inherits from `Plant`. `Oak` still implements `Tree`. `Plant` also offers a default implementation of `grow()`, which `Tree` overrides.

Swift again calls the most specialized implementation of `grow()` (see figure 12.7). Swift calls `grow()` on `Oak`, if available; otherwise, it calls `grow()` on `Tree`, if available. If all else fails, Swift calls `grow()` on `Plant`. If nothing offers a `grow()` implementation, the compiler throws an error.

You can see the overrides happening with a code example. In the next listing, you're going to define a `growPlant` function; notice how it accepts a `Plant`, not a `Tree` or `Oak`. Swift picks the most specialized implementation either way.

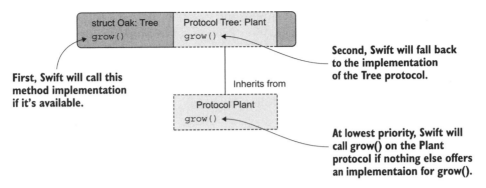

First, Swift will call this method implementation if it's available.

Second, Swift will fall back to the implementation of the Tree protocol.

Inherits from

At lowest priority, Swift will call grow() on the Plant protocol if nothing else offers an implementaion for grow().

Figure 12.7 Overrides with protocol inheritance

Listing 12.12 Overrides in action

```
func growPlant<P: Plant>(_ plant: P) {
    plant.grow()
}

protocol Plant {
    func grow()
}

extension Plant {
    func grow() {
        print("Growing a plant")
    }
}

protocol Tree: Plant {}

extension Tree {
    func grow() {
        print("Growing a tree")
    }
}

struct Oak: Tree {
    func grow() {
        print("The mighty oak is growing")
    }
}

struct CherryTree: Tree {}

struct KiwiPlant: Plant {}

growPlant(Oak()) // The mighty oak is growing
growPlant(CherryTree()) // Growing a tree
growPlant(KiwiPlant()) // Growing a plant
```

A growPlant function is defined. Notice how it accepts Plant.

The Plant protocol offers a default method for grow.

The Tree protocol inherits from Plant and offers its own implementation for grow().

The Oak struct overrides the grow() method by implementing its own version.

The CherryTree struct does not override grow().

The KiwiPlant also does not override grow().

Despite growPlant accepting Plant types, Swift calls the most specialized version of the methods.

With protocol inheritance, an interesting detail is that you get overriding behavior, similar to classes and subclasses. With protocols this behavior is available to not only classes but also to structs and enums.

12.3.3 Exercise

2 What is the output of the following code?

```
protocol Transaction {
    var description: String { get }
}
extension Transaction {
    var description: String { return "Transaction" }
}

protocol RefundableTransaction: Transaction {}

extension RefundableTransaction {
    var description: String { return "RefundableTransaction" }
}

struct CreditcardTransaction: RefundableTransaction {}

func printDescription(transaction: Transaction) {
    print(transaction.description)
}

printDescription(transaction: CreditcardTransaction())
```

12.4 Extending in two directions

Generally speaking, the urge to subclass becomes less needed with these protocol extensions, with a few exceptions. Subclassing can be a fair approach from time to time, such as when bridging to Objective-C and subclassing NSObject, or dealing with specific frameworks like UIKit, which offer views and subviews amongst other things. Even though this book normally doesn't venture into frameworks, let's make a small exception for a real practical use case related to extensions, UI, and subclassing.

A typical use of protocols in combination with subclasses involves UIKit's UIView-Controller, which represents a (piece of) screen that is rendered on an iPhone, iPad, or AppleTV. UIViewController is meant to be subclassed and makes for a good use case in this section.

12.4.1 Opting in to extensions

Imagine that you have an AnalyticsProtocol protocol that helps track analytic events for user metrics. You could implement AnalyticsProtocol on UIViewController, which offers a default implementation. This adds the functionality of Analytics-Protocol to all UIViewController types and its subclasses.

But assuming that *all* viewcontrollers need to conform to this protocol is probably not safe. If you're delivering a framework with this extension, a developer implementing this framework gets this extension automatically, whether they like it or not. Even worse, the extension from a framework could clash with an existing extension in an application if they share the same name!

One way to avoid these issues is to flip the extension. Flipping the extension means that instead of extending a UIViewController with a protocol, you can extend a protocol constrained to a UIViewController, as follows.

Listing 12.13 Flipping extension directions

```
protocol AnalyticsProtocol {
    func track(event: String, parameters: [String: Any])
}

// Not like this:
extension UIViewController: AnalyticsProtocol {
    func track(event: String, parameters: [String: Any]) { // ... snip }
}

// But as follows:
extension AnalyticsProtocol where Self: UIViewController {
    func track(event: String, parameters: [String: Any]) { // ... snip }
}
```

Now if a UIViewController explicitly adheres to this protocol, it opts in for the benefits of the protocol—for example, a NewsViewController can explicitly adhere to AnalyticsProtocol and reap its free methods. This way, you prevent *all* viewcontrollers from adhering to a protocol by default.

Listing 12.14 Opting in for benefits

```
extension NewsViewController: UIViewController, AnalyticsProtocol {
    // ... snip

    override func viewDidAppear(_ animated: Bool) {
        super.viewDidAppear(animated)
        track("News.appear", params: [:])
    }
}
```

This technique becomes even more critical when you're offering a framework. Extensions are not namespaced, so be careful with adding public extensions inside a framework, because implementers may not want their classes to adhere to a protocol by default.

12.4.2 Exercise

3 What is the difference between these two extensions?

```
extension UIViewController: MyProtocol {}

extension MyProtocol where Self: UIViewController {}
```

12.5 *Extending with associated types*

Let's see how Swift prioritizes method calls on protocols, especially protocols with associated types.

You start by looking at Array. It implements the Collection protocol, which has an associated type of Element, representing an element inside a collection. If you extend Array with a special function—such as unique(), which removes all duplicates—you can do so by referring to Element as its inner value.

Listing 12.15 Applying unique () **to** Array

```
[3, 2, 1, 1, 2, 3].unique() // [3, 2, 1]
```

Let's extend Array. To be able to check each element for equality, you need to make sure that an Element is Equatable, which you can express via a constraint. Constraining Element to Equatable means that unique() is only available on arrays with Equatable elements.

Listing 12.16 Extending Array

```
extension Array where Element: Equatable {
    func unique() -> [Element] {
        var uniqueValues = [Element]()
        for element in self {
            if !uniqueValues.contains(element) {
                uniqueValues.append(element)
            }
        }
        return uniqueValues
    }
}
```

> You need to constrain Element so that you can compare elements.

> The unique method returns an array without duplicate elements.

> You can pass Equatable elements to the contains method.

Extending Array is a good start. But it probably makes more sense to give this extension to many types of collections, not only Array but perhaps also the values of a dictionary or even strings. You can go a bit lower-level and decide to extend the Collection protocol instead, as shown here, so that multiple types can benefit from this method. Shortly after, you'll discover a shortcoming of this approach.

Listing 12.17 Extending Collection **protocol**

```
// This time we're extending Collection instead of Array
extension Collection where Element: Equatable {
    func unique() -> [Element] {
        var uniqueValues = [Element]()
        for element in self {
            if !uniqueValues.contains(element) {
                uniqueValues.append(element)
            }
        }
```

```
        return uniqueValues
    }
}
```

Now, every type adhering to the `Collection` protocol inherits the `unique()` method. Let's try it out.

Listing 12.18 Testing out the `unique()` method

```
// Array still has unique()
[3, 2, 1, 1, 2, 3].unique() // [3, 2, 1]

// Strings can be unique() now, too
"aaaaaaabcdef".unique() // ["a", "b", "c", "d", "e", "f"]

// Or a Dictionary's values
let uniqueValues = [1: "Waffle",
 2: "Banana",
 3: "Pancake",
 4: "Pancake",
 5: "Pancake"
].values.unique()

print(uniqueValues) // ["Banana", "Pancake", "Waffle"]
```

Extending `Collection` instead of `Array` benefits more than one type, which is the benefit of extending a protocol versus a concrete type.

12.5.1 A specialized extension

One thing remains. The `unique()` method is not very performant. For every value inside the collection, you need to check if this value already exists in a new unique array, which means that for each element, you need to loop through (possibly) the whole `uniqueValues` array. You would have more control if `Element` were `Hashable` instead. Then you could check for uniqueness via a hash value via a `Set`, which is much faster than an array lookup because a `Set` doesn't keep its elements in a specific order.

To support lookups via a `Set`, you create another `unique()` extension on `Collection` where its elements are `Hashable`. `Hashable` is a subprotocol of `Equatable`, which means that Swift picks an extension with `Hashable` over an extension with `Equatable`, if possible (see figure 12.8). For instance, if an array has `Hashable` types inside it, Swift

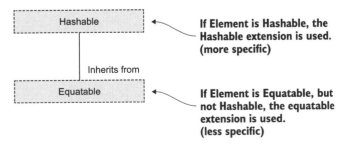

Figure 12.8 Specializing an associated type

uses the fast `unique()` method; but if elements are `Equatable` instead, Swift uses the slower version.

In your second extension—also called `unique()`—you can put each element in a `Set` for a speed improvement.

Listing 12.19   Extending `Collection` with a `Hashable` constraint on `Element`

```
// This extension is an addition, it is NOT replacing the other extension.
extension Collection where Element: Hashable {          ◁
    func unique() -> [Element] {
        var set = Set<Element>()                        ◁
        var uniqueValues = [Element]()
        for element in self {
            if !set.contains(element) {                 ◁
                uniqueValues.append(element)
                set.insert(element)
            }
        }
        return uniqueValues
    }
}
```

You extend Collection only for elements that are Hashable.

You create a Set for very fast (unordered) lookup of elements.

You check if an element already exists inside the set; if it doesn't, you can add it to the uniqueValues array.

Now you have two extensions on `Collection`. One constrains `Element` to `Equatable`, and another constrains `Element` to `Hashable`. Swift picks the most specialized one.

12.5.2   A wart in the extension

Picking an abstraction can be tricky from time to time. In fact, there's a wart in this API. At the moment, `Set` by its nature is unique already, and yet it gains the `unique` method because `Set` conforms to `Collection`. You can put a bandage on this wart and on `Set` override the method for a quick conversion to `Array`.

Listing 12.20   `unique` on `Set`

```
extension Set {
    func unique() -> [Element] {
        return Array(self)
    }
}
```

The `unique` method on `Set` does not add real value, but at least you have a quick way to convert a `Set` to `Array` now. The point is, finding the balance between extending the lowest common denominator without weakening the API of concrete types is a bit of an art.

Warts aside, what's interesting is that Swift again picks the most concrete implementation. Swift picks `Equatable` as the lowest denominator, `Hashable` if elements are `Hashable`, and with `Set`, Swift uses use its concrete implementation, ignoring any same-name method extensions on `Collection`.

12.6 *Extending with concrete constraints*

You can also constrain associated types to a concrete type instead of constraining to a protocol. As an example, let's say you have an `Article` struct with a `viewCount` property, which tracks the number of times that people viewed an `Article`.

Listing 12.21 An `Article` struct

```
struct Article: Hashable {
    let viewCount: Int
}
```

You can extend `Collection` to get the total number of view counts inside a collection. But this time you constrain an `Element` to `Article`, as shown in the following. Since you're constraining to a concrete type, you can use the `==` operator.

Listing 12.22 Extending `Collection`

```
// Not like this
extension Collection where Element: Article { ... }

// But like this
extension Collection where Element == Article {
    var totalViewCount: Int {
        var count = 0
        for article in self {
            count += article.viewCount
        }
        return count
    }
}
```

With this constraint in place, you can get the total view count whenever you have a collection with articles in it, whether that's an `Array`, a `Set`, or something else altogether.

Listing 12.23 Extension in action

```
let articleOne = Article(viewCount: 30)
let articleTwo = Article(viewCount: 200)

// Getting the total count on an Array.
let articlesArray = [articleOne, articleTwo]
articlesArray.totalViewCount // 230

// Getting the total count on a Set.
let articlesSet: Set<Article> = [articleOne, articleTwo]
articlesSet.totalViewCount // 230
```

Whenever you make an extension, deciding how low-level you need to go can be tricky. A concrete extension on `Array` is enough for 80% of the cases, in which case you don't need to go to `Collection`. If you notice that you need the same implementation on other types, you may want to strap in and go lower-level where you'll extend `Collection`. In doing so, you'll be working with more abstract types. If you need to go even lower-level, you can end up at `Sequence`, so that you can offer extensions to even more types. To see how you can go super low-level, let's try to extend `Sequence` to offer useful extensions for many types.

12.7 Extending Sequence

A very interesting protocol to extend is `Sequence`. By extending `Sequence` you can power up many types at once, such as `Set`, `Array`, `Dictionary`, your collections—you name it.

When you're comfortable with `Sequence`, it lowers the barrier for creating your extensions for methods you'd like to see. You can wait for Swift updates, but if you're a little impatient or have special requirements, you can create your own. Extending `Sequence` as opposed to a concrete type—such as `Array`—means that you can power up many types at once.

Swift loves borrowing concepts from the Rust programming language; the two languages are quite similar in many respects. How about you shamelessly do the same and add some useful methods to the `Sequence` vocabulary? Extending `Sequence` won't merely be a programming exercise, because these methods are helpful utilities you can use in your projects.

12.7.1 Looking under the hood of filter

Before extending `Sequence`, let's take a closer look at a few interesting things regarding how Swift does it. First, `filter` accepts a function. This function is the closure you pass to `filter`.

Listing 12.24   A small `filter` method

```
let moreThanOne = [1,2,3].filter { (int: Int) in
  int > 1
}
print(moreThanOne) // [2, 3]
```

Looking at the signature of `filter`, you can see that it accepts a function, which makes `filter` a higher-order function. A higher-order function is a ten-dollar concept for a one-dollar name, indicating that a function can accept or return another function. This function is the closure you pass to `filter`.

Also note that `filter` has the `rethrows` keyword as showing in listing 12.25. If a function or method `rethrows`, any errors thrown from a closure are propagated back to the caller. Having a method with `rethrows` is similar to regular error propagation, except `rethrows` is reserved for higher-order functions, such as `filter`. The benefit of this is that `filter` accepts both nonthrowing and throwing functions; it's the caller that has to handle any errors.

Listing 12.25 Looking at `filter`'s signature

```
public func filter(
    _ isIncluded: (Element) throws -> Bool
) rethrows -> [Element] {
    // ... snip
}
```

The filter method accepts another function called isIncluded, which represents the closure you pass.

The rethrows keyword is defined on filter.

Now, let's look at the body. You can see that `filter` creates a `results` array, which is of the obscure type called `ContiguousArray`—more on that in a minute—and iterates through each element via the low-level, no-overhead `makeIterator` method. For each element, `filter` calls the `isIncluded` method, which is the closure you pass to `filter`. If `isIncluded`—also known as the *passed closure*—returns `true`, then `filter` appends the element to the `results` array.

Finally, `filter` converts the `ContiguousArray` back to a regular `Array`.

Listing 12.26 Looking at `filter`

The filter method accepts another function to check against each element.

```
public func filter(
    _ isIncluded: (Element) throws -> Bool
) rethrows -> [Element] {
    var result = ContiguousArray<Element>()

    var iterator = self.makeIterator()

    while let element = iterator.next() {
        if try isIncluded(element) {
            result.append(element)
        }
    }

    return Array(result)
}
```

Inside the body, the filtered results are stored in a result of type ContiguousArray.

The method uses the low-level iterating mechanism without overhead.

Each element is matched against the isIncluded function.

If isIncluded returns true for an element, the element is added to result.

The result with filtered elements is converted to a regular Array and returned.

NOTE In the Swift source, the `filter` method forwards the call to another `_filter` method which does the work. For example purposes, we kept referring to the method as `filter`.

CONTIGUOUSARRAY

Seeing `ContiguousArray` there instead of `Array` may feel out of place. The `filter` method uses `ContiguousArray` for extra performance, which makes sense for such a low-level, highly reused method.

`ContiguousArray` can potentially deliver performance benefits when containing classes or an Objective-C protocol; otherwise, the performance is the same as a regular `Array`. But `ContiguousArray` does not bridge to Objective-C.

When `filter` did its work, it returns a regular `Array`. Regular arrays can bridge to `NSArray` if needed for Objective-C, whereas `ContiguousArray` cannot. So using

ContiguousArray can help squeeze out the last drops of performance, which matters on low-level methods such as filter.

Now that you've seen how to create an extension on Sequence, let's make a custom extension.

12.7.2 *Creating the take(while:) method*

Complimentary to the drop(while:) method, which drops the first number of elements, you can offer an opposite method called take(while:).

As a quick refresher, drop(while:) is useful to drop the first amount of unusable data, such as empty lines. You pass a closure to the drop method, which keeps ignoring—or dropping—the lines until you find some text. At that point, drop stops dropping and returns the rest of the sequence, as shown here.

Listing 12.27 drop(while:)

```
let silenceLines =
    """

    The silence is finally over.
    """.components(separatedBy: "\n")

let lastParts = silenceLines.drop(while: { (line) -> Bool in
    line.isEmpty
})

print(lastParts) // ["The silence is finally over."]
```

For your custom take(while:) method, you have a different use case. You might want the strings *until* you run into an empty line. It's the opposite of drop(while:) and complementary to it. Before you create your take(while:) method, let's see how it works. Notice how the iteration keeps going until it breaks off at the empty line.

Listing 12.28 Get the first lines

```
let lines =
    """
    We start with text...
    ... and then some more

    This is ignored because it came after empty space
    and more text
    """.components(separatedBy: "\n")

let firstParts = lines.take(while: { (line) -> Bool in
    !line.isEmpty
})

print(firstParts) // ["We start with text...", "... and then some more"]
```

In the implementation, you mimic the internals of filter where you make use of ContiguousArray and makeIterator.

Listing 12.29 Extending Sequence with take(while:)

```
extension Sequence {
    public func take(
        while predicate: (Element) throws -> Bool
    ) rethrows -> [Element] {

        var iterator = makeIterator()

        var result = ContiguousArray<Element>()

        while let element = iterator.next() {
            if try predicate(element) {
                result.append(element)
            } else {
                break
            }
        }

        return Array(result)
    }
}
```

The take(while:) method also accepts a closure to check against each element.

You can also use makeIterator.

You can also use a ContiguousArray.

Iterate through each element.

If an element matches the predicate, you keep going.

As soon as the closure returns false, you stop iterating and return your result.

12.7.3 Creating the Inspect method

Another useful method you may want to add to your library is inspect. It is *very* similar to forEach, with one difference: it returns the sequence. The inspect method is especially useful for debugging a pipeline where you chain operations.

You can squeeze inspect in the middle of a chained pipeline operation, do something with the values, such as logging them, and continue with the pipeline as if nothing happened, whereas forEach would end the iteration, as shown here.

Listing 12.30 The inspect method in action

```
["C", "B", "A", "D"]
    .sorted()
    .inspect { (string) in
        print("Inspecting: \(string)")
    }.filter { (string) -> Bool in
        string < "C"
    }.forEach {
        print("Result: \($0)")
    }

// Output:
// Inspecting: A
// Inspecting: B
// Inspecting: C
```

```
// Inspecting: D
// Result: A
// Result: B
```

To add inspect to your codebase, you can take the following code. Notice how you don't have to use makeIterator if you don't want to.

> **Listing 12.31   Extending Sequence with inspect**

```
extension Sequence {
    public func inspect(                          The inspect method also
        _ body: (Element) throws -> Void          accepts a function.
    ) rethrows  -> Self {
        for element in self {                You call the body function
            try body(element)               with each element.
        }
        return self        You return the same type again
    }                      so that you can keep chaining.
}
```

Extending Sequence means that you go quite low-level. Not only does Array gain extra methods, but so does Set, Range, zip, String, and others. You're only scratching the surface. Apple uses many optimization tricks and particular sequences for further optimizations. The approach in this section should cover many cases, however.

Extending Sequence with methods you feel are missing is a good and useful exercise. What other extensions can you create?

12.7.4 Exercise

4 Up for a challenge? Create a "scan" extension on Sequence. The scan method is like reduce, but besides returning the end value it also returns intermediary results, all as one array, which is very useful for debugging a reduce method! Be sure to use makeIterator and ContiguousArray for extra speed:

```
let results = (0..<5).scan(initialResult: "") { (result: String, int:
➥ Int) -> String in
        return "\(result)\(int)"
}
print(results) // ["0", "01", "012", "0123", "01234"]

let lowercased = ["S", "W", "I", "F", "T"].scan(initialResult: "") {
➥ (result: String, string: String) -> String in
        return "\(result)\(string.lowercased())"
}

print(lowercased) // ["s", "sw", "swi", "swif", "swift"]
```

12.8   *Closing thoughts*

The lure of using extensions and protocols is strong. Keep in mind that sometimes a concrete type is the right way to go before diving into clever abstractions. Extending protocols is one of the most powerful—if not *the* most powerful—feature of Swift. It allows you to write highly decoupled, highly reusable code. Finding a suitable abstraction to solve a problem is a tough balancing act. Now that you've read this chapter, I hope that you know to extend horizontally and vertically in clever ways that will help you deliver concise and clean code.

Summary

- Protocols can deliver a default implementation via protocol extensions.
- With extensions, you can think of modeling data horizontally, whereas with subclassing, you're modeling data in a more rigid vertical way.
- You can override a default implementation by delivering an implementation on a concrete type.
- Protocol extensions cannot override a concrete type.
- Via protocol inheritance, you can override a protocol's default implementation.
- Swift always picks the most concrete implementation.
- You can create a protocol extension that only unlocks when a type implements two protocols, called a protocol intersection.
- A protocol intersection is more flexible than protocol inheritance, but it's also more abstract to understand.
- When mixing subclasses with protocol extensions, extending a protocol and constraining it to a class is a good heuristic (as opposed to extending a class to adhere to a protocol). This way, an implementer can pick and choose a protocol implementation.
- For associated types, such as `Element` on the `Collection` protocol, Swift picks the most specialized abstraction, such as `Hashable` over `Equatable` elements.
- Extending a low-level protocol—such as `Sequence`—means you offer new methods to many types at once.
- Swift uses a special `ContiguousArray` when extending `Sequence` for extra performance.

Answers

1 Create an extension that enables the `explode()` function, but only on types that conform to `Mentos` and `Coke` protocols:

```
extension Mentos where Self: Coke {
    func explode() {
        print("BOOM!")
    }
}
```

2 What is the output of the following code?

```
"RefundableTransaction"
```

3 What is the difference between these two extensions?

```
extension UIViewController: MyProtocol {}

extension MyProtocol where Self: UIViewController {}
```

The first line makes all viewcontrollers and their subclasses conform to MyProtocol. The second line makes a viewcontroller only adhere to a protocol on an as-needed basis.

4 Create a "scan" extension on Sequence. Be sure to use makeIterator and ContiguousArray for extra speed:

```
extension Sequence {
    func scan<Result>(
        initialResult: Result,
        _ nextPartialResult: (Result, Element) throws -> Result
    ) rethrows -> [Result] {
        var iterator = makeIterator()

        var results = ContiguousArray<Result>()
        var accumulated: Result = initialResult
        while let element = iterator.next() {
            accumulated = try nextPartialResult(accumulated, element)
            results.append(accumulated)
        }

        return Array(results)
    }
}
```

Swift patterns

In this chapter, you're going to see some useful patterns that you can apply in your Swift programming. I made sure that these patterns were more Swift-focused, as opposed to a more-traditional OOP focus. We're focusing on Swift patterns, so protocols and generics take center stage.

First, you're going to mock existing types with protocols. You'll see how to replace a networking API with a fake offline one, and also replace this networking API with one that's focused on testing. I throw in a little trick related to associated types that will help you mock types, including ones from other frameworks.

Conditional conformance is a powerful feature that allows you to extend types with a protocol, but only under certain conditions. You'll see how to extend existing types with conditional conformance, even if these types have associated types. Then, you'll go a bit further and create a generic type, which you'll power up as well by using conditional conformance.

Then the chapter takes a look at the shortcomings that come with protocols with associated types and Self requirements, which you can unofficially consider compile-time protocols. You'll see how to best deal with these shortcomings. You'll first consider an approach involving enums, and then a more complex, but also more flexible, approach involving *type erasure*.

As an alternative to protocols, you'll see how to create a generic struct that can replace a protocol with associated types. This type will be highly flexible and an excellent tool to have.

This chapter aims to give you new approaches to existing problems and to help you understand protocols and generics on a deeper level. Let's get started by seeing how to mock types, which is a technique you can apply across numerous projects.

13.1   *Dependency injection*

In chapter 8, you saw how protocols are used as an interface or type, where you could pass different types to a method, as long as these types adhere to the same protocol.

You can take this mechanic a bit further and perform *inversion of control*, or *dependency injection*, which are fancy words to say that you pass an implementation to a type. Think of supplying an engine to a motorcycle.

The goal of this exercise is to end up with an interchangeable implementation where you can switch between three network layers: a real network layer, an offline network layer, and a testing layer.

The real network layer is for when you ship an application for production. The fake network layer loads prepared files, which is useful for working with fixed responses where you control all the data, such as when the backend server is not finished yet, or when you need to demo your application without a network connection. The testing layer makes writing unit tests easier.

> **JOIN ME!**   It's more educational and fun if you can check out the code and follow along with the chapter. You can download the source code at http://mng .bz/4vPa.

13.1.1   *Swapping an implementation*

You're going to create a class called WeatherAPI that retrieves the latest weather status. To create network calls, WeatherAPI would use a URLSession from the Foundation framework. But you're going to do it differently. WeatherAPI accepts a type conforming to a Session protocol, because a protocol allows you to pass a custom implementation. This way, WeatherAPI calls network methods on the protocol without knowing about which concrete implementation it received. You're mocking URLSession as a challenge because if you know how to mock a type you don't own, it will be even easier for types that you *do* own.

First, let's define a protocol called Session representing URLSession but also other sessions, such as an offline session. This way you're able to run an app in demo mode without a network connection, but also a testing session that enables you to verify that your API calls the methods when expected (see figure 13.1).

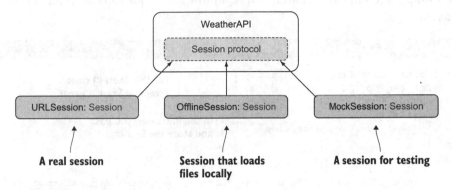

Figure 13.1   Mocking

WeatherAPI calls methods on Session. Let's mirror a common method on URLSession: creating a dataTask that can be run to fetch data.

In the dataTask method of URLSession, you would normally receive a URLSession-DataTask type. But you'll apply a little trick.

Instead of returning URLSessionDataTask or another protocol, you return an associated type. The reason is that an associated type resolves to a concrete type at compile time. It can represent a URLSessionDataTask, but also other types that each implementer can choose to return. Let's call this associated type Task.

Listing 13.1   A Session protocol

```
protocol Session {
    associatedtype Task          ⊲──┤ Define a Task that the
                                      dataTask method returns.

    func dataTask(with url: URL, completionHandler: @escaping (Data?,
    URLResponse?, Error?) -> Void) -> Task          ⊲──┐
}                                                        The dataTask method mirrors
                                                         the method on URLSession.
```

Because Session mirrors URLSession, you merely have to conform URLSession to Session without writing any implementation code. Let's extend URLSession now and make it conform to Session.

> **Listing 13.2   Conforming** `URLSession` **to** `Session`

```
extension URLSession: Session {}
```

13.1.2 *Passing a custom Session*

Now you can create the `WeatherAPI` class and define a generic called `Session` to allow for a swappable implementation. You're almost there, but you can't call resume yet on `Session.Task`.

> **Listing 13.3   The** `WeatherAPI` **class**

```
final class WeatherAPI<S: Session> {                    The WeatherAPI class
    let session: S                                      accepts a Session generic.

    init(session: S) {                     In the initializer, you pass
        self.session = session             and store the Session.
    }

    func run() {
        guard let url = URL(string: "https://www.someweatherstartup.com")
        else {
            fatalError("Could not create url")
        }
        let task = session.dataTask(with: url) { (data, response, error) in
            // Work with retrieved data.
        }
        task.resume() // Doesn't work, task is of type S.Task
    }

}

let weatherAPI = WeatherAPI(session: URLSession.shared)
weatherAPI.run()
```

You store the Session in a property.

You can call the dataTask method on session.

Unfortunately, you can't call the resume() method yet on Task.

You pass URLSession to WeatherAPI via the initializer.

You try to run a `task`, but you can't. The associated type `Task` that `dataTask(with: completionHandler:)` returns is of type `Session.Task`, which doesn't have any methods. Let's fix that now.

13.1.3 *Constraining an associated type*

`URLSessionDataTask` has a `resume()` method, but `Session.Task` does not. To fix this, you introduce a new protocol called `DataTask`, which contains the `resume()` method. Then you constrain `Session.Task` to `DataTask`.

To finalize the implementation, you'll make `URLSessionDataTask` conform to the `DataTask` protocol as well (see figure 13.2).

In code, let's create the `DataTask` protocol and constrain `Session.Task` to it.

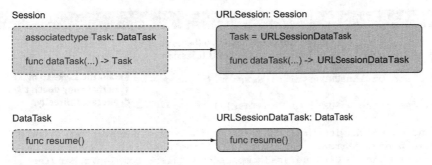

Figure 13.2 Mirroring `URLSession`

Listing 13.4 Creating a `DataTask` **protocol**

```
protocol DataTask {          ⟵  Introduce a new protocol
    func resume()            ⟵  called DataTask.
}                                The DataTask can now resume(),
                                 just like URLSession.

protocol Session {
    associatedtype Task: DataTask          ⟵  The associated type is now
                                                conforming to DataTask, so that
                                                dataTask(with:completionHandler:)
                                                returns a task you can resume.

    func dataTask(with url: URL, completionHandler: @escaping (Data?,
➥  URLResponse?, Error?) -> Void) -> Task
}
```

To complete your adjustment, you make `URLSessionDataTask` conform to your `DataTask` protocol so that everything compiles again.

Listing 13.5 Implementing `DataTask`

```
extension URLSessionDataTask: DataTask {}     ⟵  URLSessionDataTask now
                                                  conforms to DataTask.
```

All is well again. Now, `URLSession` returns a type conforming to `DataTask`. At this stage, all the code compiles. You can call your API with a real `URLSession` to perform a request.

13.1.4 Swapping an implementation

You can pass `URLSession` to your `WeatherAPI`, but the real power lies in the capability to swap out an implementation. Here's a fake `URLSession` that you'll name `Offline-URLSession`, which loads local files instead of making a real network connection. This way, you're not dependent on a backend to play around with the `WeatherAPI` class. Every time that the `dataTask(with url:)` method is called, the `OfflineURLSession` creates an `OfflineTask` that loads the local file, as shown in the following listing.

Listing 13.6   An offline task

The **OfflineURLSession** adheres to
Session and mimics URLSession.

```
final class OfflineURLSession: Session {          ◁      Retain the tasks to make
                                                         sure that they doesn't get
    var sessions = [URL: OfflineTask]()     ◁            deallocated directly.

    func dataTask(with url: URL, completionHandler: @escaping (Data?,
➥   URLResponse?, Error?) -> Void) -> OfflineTask {
        let task = OfflineTask(completionHandler: completionHandler)    ◁
        sessions[url] = task
        return task                                 The OfflineURLSession
    }                                               creates and returns
}                                                   OfflineTask types.
                              You need an error to
enum ApiError: Error {    ◁   return. You could also
    case couldNotLoadData     choose to mimic
}                             URLSession's error           For convenience, you
                              completely.                  define a typealias
struct OfflineTask: DataTask {                             to mimic the
                                                           Completion closure.
    typealias Completion = (Data?, URLResponse?, Error?) -> Void    ◁
    let completionHandler: Completion
                                                      The completion closure
    init(completionHandler: @escaping Completion) {   ◁   from OfflineURLSession
        self.completionHandler = completionHandler        is passed and stored by
    }                                                     the OfflineTask.

    func resume() {
        let url = URL(fileURLWithPath: "prepared_response.json")
        let data = try! Data(contentsOf: url)
        completionHandler(data, nil, nil)
    }
}
```

Once OfflineTask runs, it loads local JSON
data and calls the completionHandler that
was originally passed to OfflineURLSession.

NOTE   A more mature implementation would also deallocate tasks and allow
for more configuration of loading files.

Now that you have multiple implementations adhering to Session, you can start swapping them without having to touch the rest of your code. You can choose to create a production WeatherAPI or an offline WeatherAPI.

Listing 13.7   Swapping out implementations

```
let productionAPI = WeatherAPI(session: URLSession.shared)
let offlineApi = WeatherAPI(session: OfflineURLSession())
```

With protocols you can swap out an implementation, such as feeding different sessions to WeatherAPI. If you use an associated type, you can make it represent another type inside the protocol, which can make it easier to mimic a concrete type. You don't always have to use associated types, but it helps when you can't instantiate certain types, such as when you want to mock code from third-party frameworks.

That's all it took. Now WeatherAPI works with a production layer or a fake offline layer, which gives you much flexibility. With this setup, testing can be made easy as well. Let's move on to creating the testing layer so that you can properly test WeatherAPI.

13.1.5 Unit testing and Mocking with associated types

With a swappable implementation in place, you can pass an implementation that helps you with testing. You can create a particular type conforming to Session, loaded up with testing expectations. As an example, you can create a MockSession and MockTask that see if specific URLs are called.

Listing 13.8 Creating a MockTask and MockSession

```
class MockSession: Session {                      ◁── The MockSession also
                                                       adheres to Session.
    let expectedURLs: [URL]
    let expectation: XCTestExpectation

    init(expectation: XCTestExpectation, expectedURLs: [URL]) {
        self.expectation = expectation
        self.expectedURLs = expectedURLs
    }

    func dataTask(with url: URL, completionHandler: @escaping (Data?,
    URLResponse?, Error?) -> Void) -> MockTask {
        return MockTask(expectedURLs: expectedURLs, url: url, expectation:
    expectation)
    }                      ◁── The MockSession
}                               returns a MockTask.

struct MockTask: DataTask {                        The MockTask holds a
    let expectedURLs: [URL]                         testing expectation that
    let url: URL                                    should be fulfilled with
    let expectation: XCTestExpectation    ◁──       your test.

    func resume() {
        guard expectedURLs.contains(url) else {
            return
        }

        self.expectation.fulfill()
    }
}
```

Now, if you want to test your API, you can test that the expected URLs are called.

Listing 13.9   Testing the API

```swift
class APITestCase: XCTestCase {

    var api: API<MockSession>!

    func testAPI() {
        let expectation = XCTestExpectation(description: "Expected
someweatherstartup.com")
        let session = MockSession(expectation: expectation, expectedURLs:
[URL(string: "www.someweatherstartup.com")!])
        api = API(session: session)
        api.run()
        wait(for: [expectation], timeout: 1)
    }
}

let testcase = APITestCase()
testcase.testAPI()
```

You create an API and define it as having a MockSession.

You create an expectation that needs to be fulfilled.

The session is created containing the expectation.

You check if the expectation is fulfilled, with a waiting time of one second.

Once the API runs, the expectation is hopefully fulfilled.

13.1.6 *Using the Result type*

Because you're using a protocol, you can offer a default implementation to all sessions via the use of a protocol extension. You may have noticed how you used Session's regular way of handling errors. But you have the powerful Result type available to you from the Swift Package Manager, as covered in chapter 11. You can extend Session and offer a variant that uses Result instead, as shown in the following listing. This way, all types adhering to Session will be able to return a Result.

Listing 13.10   Extending `Session` with a `Result` type

```swift
protocol Session {
    associatedtype Task: DataTask

    func dataTask(with url: URL, completionHandler: @escaping (Data?,
URLResponse?, Error?) -> Void) -> Task
    func dataTask(with url: URL, completionHandler: @escaping (Result<Data,
AnyError>) -> Void) -> Task
}

extension Session {
    func dataTask(with url: URL, completionHandler: @escaping (Result<Data,
AnyError>) -> Void) -> Task {
        return dataTask(with: url, completionHandler: { (data, response,
error) in
            if let error = error {
                let anyError = AnyError(error)
                completionHandler(Result.failure(anyError))
            } else if let data = data {
                completionHandler(Result.success(data))
            } else {
                fatalError()
            }
        }
    }
}
```

Add a new method to the Session protocol.

The implementation still calls the regular dataTask method for you, but it converts the response to a Result type.

You can give a default implementation to Session that uses Result.

```
         })
     }
 }
```

Now, implementers of `Session`, including Apple's `URLSession`, can return a `Result` type.

Listing 13.11 Multiple sessions retrieving a `Result`

```
URLSession.shared.dataTask(with: url) { (result: Result<Data, AnyError>) in
    // ...
}

OfflineURLSession().dataTask(with: url) { (result: Result<Data, AnyError>) in
    // ...
}
```

With the power of protocols, you have the ability to swap between multiple implementations between production, debugging, and testing use. With the help of extensions, you can use `Result` as well.

13.1.7 Exercise

1 Given these types, see if you can make `WaffleHouse` testable to verify that a `Waffle` has been served:

```
struct Waffle {}

class Chef {
    func serve() -> Waffle {
        return Waffle()
    }
}

struct WaffleHouse {

    let chef = Chef()

    func serve() -> Waffle {
        return chef.serve()
    }

}

let waffleHouse = WaffleHouse()
let waffle = waffleHouse.serve()
```

13.2 Conditional conformance

Conditional conformance is a compelling feature introduced in Swift 4.1. With conditional conformance, you can make a type adhere to a protocol but only under certain conditions. Chapter 7 covered conditional conformance briefly, but let's take this opportunity to become more comfortable with it and see more-advanced use cases.

After this section, you'll know precisely when and how to apply conditional conformance—let's get to it!

13.2.1   *Free functionality*

The easiest way to see conditional conformance in action is to create a struct, implement Equatable or Hashable, and without implementing any of the protocol's method, you get equatability or hashability for free.

The following is a Movie struct. Notice how you can already compare movies by merely making Movie adhere to the Equatable protocol, without implementing the required == function; this is the same technique you applied to Pair in chapter 7.

Listing 13.12   Auto Equatable

```
struct Movie: Equatable {
    let title: String
    let rating: Float
}

let movie = Movie(title: "The princess bride", rating: 9.7)

movie == movie // true. You can already compare without implementing Equatable
```

MANUALLY OVERRIDING   You can still implement the == function from Equatable if you want to supply your own logic.

Automatically having an Equatable type is possible because all the properties are Equatable. Swift synthesizes this for free on some protocols, such as Equatable and Hashable, but not every protocol. For instance, you don't get Comparable for free, or the ones that you introduce yourself.

WARNING   Unfortunately, Swift doesn't synthesize methods on classes.

13.2.2   *Conditional conformance on associated types*

Another approachable way to see conditional conformance in action is by looking at Array and its Element type, representing an element inside the array. Element is an associated type from Sequence, which Array uses, as covered in chapter 9.

Imagine that you have a Track protocol, representing a track used in audio software, such as a wave sample or a distortion effect. You can have an AudioTrack implement this protocol; it could play audio files at a specific URL.

Listing 13.13   The Track protocol

```
protocol Track {
    func play()
}

struct AudioTrack: Track {
    let file: URL
```

```
    func play() {
        print("playing audio at \(file)")
    }
}
```

If you have an array of tracks and want to play these tracks at the same time for a musical composition, you could naively extend Array only where Element conforms to Track, and then introduce a play() method here. This way, you can trigger play() for all Track elements inside an array. This approach has a shortcoming, however, which you'll solve in a bit.

Listing 13.14 Extending Array (with a shortcoming)

```
extension Array where Element: Track {
    func play() {
        for element in self {
            element.play()
        }
    }
}

let tracks = [
    AudioTrack(file: URL(fileURLWithPath: "1.mp3")),
    AudioTrack(file: URL(fileURLWithPath: "2.mp3"))
]
tracks.play() // You use the play() method
```

But this approach has a shortcoming. Array itself does not conform to Track; it merely implements a method with the same name as the one inside Track, namely the play() method.

Because Array doesn't conform to Track, you can't call play() anymore on a nested array. Alternatively, if you have a function accepting a Track, you also can't pass an Array with Track types.

Listing 13.15 Can't use Array as a Track type

```
let tracks = [
    AudioTrack(file: URL(fileURLWithPath: "1.mp3")),
    AudioTrack(file: URL(fileURLWithPath: "2.mp3"))
]

// If an Array is nested, you can't call play() any more.
[tracks, tracks].play() // error: type of expression is ambiguous without
    more context

// Or you can't pass an array if anything expects the Track protocol.
func playDelayed<T: Track>(_ track: T, delay: Double) {
  // ... snip
}

playDelayed(tracks, delay: 2.0) // argument type '[AudioTrack]' does not
    conform to expected type 'Track'
```

13.2.3 *Making Array conditionally conform to a custom protocol*

Since Swift 4.1, you can solve this problem where `Array` will conform to a custom protocol. You can make `Array` conform to `Track`, but *only* if its elements conform to `Track`. The only difference from before is that you add `: Track` after `Array`.

Listing 13.16   Making `Array` conform

```
// Before. Not conditionally conforming.
extension Array where Element: Track {
    // ... snip
}

// After. You have conditional conformance.
extension Array: Track where Element: Track {
    func play() {
        for element in self {
            element.play()
        }
    }
}
```

> **WARNING** If you're making a type conditionally conformant to a protocol with a constraint—such as `where Element: Track`—you need to supply the implementation yourself. Swift won't synthesize this for you.

Now `Array` is a true `Track` type. You can pass it to functions expecting a `Track`, or nest arrays with other data and you can still call `play()` on it, as shown here.

Listing 13.17   Conditional conformance in action

```
let nestedTracks = [
    [
        AudioTrack(file: URL(fileURLWithPath: "1.mp3")),
        AudioTrack(file: URL(fileURLWithPath: "2.mp3"))
    ],
    [
        AudioTrack(file: URL(fileURLWithPath: "3.mp3")),
        AudioTrack(file: URL(fileURLWithPath: "4.mp3"))
    ]
]

// Nesting works.
nestedTracks.play()

// And, you can pass this array to a function expecting a Track!
playDelayed(tracks, delay: 2.0)
```

13.2.4 *Conditional conformance and generics*

You've seen how you extend `Array` with a constraint on an associated type. What's pretty nifty is that you can also constrain on generic type parameters.

As an example, let's take `Optional`, because `Optional` only has a generic type called `Wrapped` and no associated types. You can make `Optional` implement `Track` with conditional conformance on its generic as follows.

Listing 13.18 Extending `Optional`

```
extension Optional: Track where Wrapped: Track {
    func play() {
        switch self {
        case .some(let track):          If there is a Track value inside the
            track.play()                Optional, you can call play on it.
        case nil:
            break // do nothing
        }
    }
}
```

Now `Optional` conforms to `Track`, but only if its inner value conforms to `Track`. Without conditional conformance you could already call `play()` on optionals conforming to `Track`.

Listing 13.19 Calling `play()` on an optional

```
let audio: AudioTrack? = AudioTrack(file: URL(fileURLWithPath: "1.mp3"))
audio?.play()          ◄──┐  Calling a method on an optional
```

But now `Optional` officially is a `Track` as well, allowing us to pass it to types and functions expecting a `Track`. In other words, with conditional conformance, you can pass an optional `AudioTrack?` to a method expecting a non-optional `Track`.

Listing 13.20 Passing an optional to `playDelayed`

```
let audio: AudioTrack? = AudioTrack(file: URL(fileURLWithPath: "1.mp3"))
playDelayed(audio, delay: 2.0)      ◄──┐  playDelayed expects a Track.
                                         Now accepts an optional.
```

13.2.5 *Conditional conformance on your types*

Conditional conformance shines when you work with generic types, such as `Array`, `Optional`, or your own. Conditional conformance becomes powerful when you have a generic type storing an inner type, and you want the generic type to mimic the behavior of the inner type inside (see figure 13.3). Earlier, you saw how an `Array` becomes a `Track` if its elements are a `Track`.

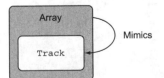

Figure 13.3 A type mimicking an inner type

Let's see how this works when creating a generic type yourself. One such type could be a `CachedValue` type. `CachedValue` is a class storing a value. Once a certain time limit has passed, the value is refreshed by a closure that `CachedValue` stores.

The benefit of `CachedValue` is that it can cache expensive calculations for a while before refreshing. It can help limit repeatedly loading large files or repetition of expensive computations.

You can, for instance, store a value with a time-to-live value of two seconds. If you were to ask for the value after three seconds or more, the stored closure would be called again to refresh the value, as shown here.

Listing 13.21   `CachedValue` in action

```
let simplecache = CachedValue(timeToLive: 2, load: { () -> String in
    print("I am being refreshed!")
    return "I am the value inside CachedValue"
})

// Prints: "I am being refreshed!"
simplecache.value // "I am the value inside CachedValue"
simplecache.value // "I am the value inside CachedValue"

sleep(3) // wait 3 seconds

// Prints: "I am being refreshed!"
simplecache.value // "I am the value inside CachedValue"
```

If the value is retrieved, you print a string for debugging.

You create a CachedValue and pass it a custom closure in the initializer. Notice how you set the timeToLive to two seconds.

The value is cached, you can ask for it, and you receive the string.

After two seconds, the closure is called again and gives a new string for CachedValue to store.

Let's look at the internals of `CachedValue` and see how it works; then you'll move on to conditional conformance.

Listing 13.22   Inside `CachedValue`

```
final class CachedValue<T> {
    private let load: () -> T
    private var lastLoaded: Date

    private var timeToLive: Double
    private var currentValue: T

    public var value: T {
        let needsRefresh = abs(lastLoaded.timeIntervalSinceNow) > timeToLive
        if needsRefresh {
            currentValue = load()
            lastLoaded = Date()
        }
        return currentValue
    }

    init(timeToLive: Double, load: @escaping (() -> T)) {
        self.timeToLive = timeToLive
        self.load = load
        self.currentValue = load()
```

CachedValue can store anything, represented as type T.

A load closure is stored, which is used to refresh the value inside.

Every time value is accessed, you check if a refresh is needed.

If you need to refresh, you refresh the value and set the lastLoaded date.

You return the value.

```
            self.lastLoaded = Date()
        }
    }
```

MAKING YOUR TYPE CONDITIONALLY CONFORMANT

Here comes the fun part. Now that you have a generic type, you can get in your starting positions and start adding conditional conformance. This way, `CachedValue` reflects the capabilities of its value inside. For instance, you can make `CachedValue` `Equatable` if its value inside is `Equatable`. You can make `CachedValue` `Hashable` if its value inside is `Hashable`, and you can make `CachedValue` `Comparable` if its value inside is `Comparable` (see figure 13.4).

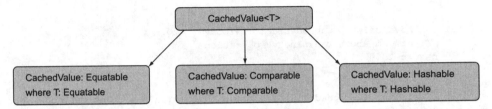

Figure 13.4   Making `CachedValue` **conditionally conform to** `Equatable`, `Hashable`, **and** `Comparable`.

You can add extensions for all the protocols you can imagine (if they make sense). Ready? Set? Go!

Listing 13.23   Conditional conformance on `CachedValue`

```
// Conforming to Equatable
extension CachedValue: Equatable where T: Equatable {
    static func == (lhs: CachedValue, rhs: CachedValue) -> Bool {
        return lhs.value == rhs.value
    }
}

// Conforming to Hashable
extension CachedValue: Hashable where T: Hashable {
    func hash(into hasher: inout Hasher) {
        hasher.combine(value)
    }
}

// Conforming to Comparable
extension CachedValue: Comparable where T: Comparable {
    static func <(lhs: CachedValue, rhs: CachedValue) -> Bool {
        return lhs.value < rhs.value
    }

    static func ==(lhs: CachedValue, rhs: CachedValue) -> Bool {
        return lhs.value == rhs.value
    }
}
```

This is just the beginning; you can use your custom protocols and many others that Swift offers.

Now with conditional conformance in place, CachedValue takes on the properties of its inner type. Let's try it out and see if CachedValue is properly Equatable, Hashable, and Comparable.

> **Listing 13.24   CachedValue is now Equatable, Comparable, and Hashable**

```
let cachedValueOne = CachedValue(timeToLive: 60) {
    // Perform expensive operation
    // E.g. Calculate the purpose of life
    return 42
}

let cachedValueTwo = CachedValue(timeToLive: 120) {
    // Perform another expensive operation
    return 1000
}

cachedValueOne == cachedValueTwo // Equatable: You can check for equality.
cachedValueOne > cachedValueTwo // Comparable: You can compare two cached values.

let set = Set(arrayLiteral: cachedValueOne, cachedValueTwo) // Hashable:
➥ You can store CachedValue in a set
```

You could keep going. For instance, you can make CachedValue implement Track or any other custom implementations.

Conditional conformance works best when storing the lowest common denominator inside the generic, meaning that you should aim to not add too many constraints on T in this case.

If a generic type by default is not constrained too much, then extending the type with conditional conformance is easier. In CachedValue's case, T is unconstrained, so all types fit, and then you add functionality with conditional conformance. This way, both simple and advanced types fit inside CachedValue. As an exaggeration, if you were to constrain T to 10 protocols, very few types would fit inside CachedValue, and then there would be little benefit to adding functionality with conditional conformance.

13.2.6 *Exercise*

2 What is the benefit of a generic having few constraints, when applying conditional conformance?

3 Make CachedValue conform to the custom Track protocol from this chapter.

13.3   *Dealing with protocol shortcomings*

Protocols are a recipe for a love-hate relationship. They're a fantastic tool, but then once in a while things that "should just work" simply aren't possible.

For instance, a common problem for Swift developers is wanting to store `Hashable` types. You'll quickly find out that it isn't as easy as it seems.

Imagine that you're modeling a game server for poker games. You have a Poker-Game protocol, and `StudPoker` and `TexasHoldem` adhere to this protocol. Notice in the following listing how `PokerGame` is `Hashable` so that you can store poker games inside sets and use them as dictionary keys.

Listing 13.25 `PokerGame`

```
protocol PokerGame: Hashable {
    func start()
}

struct StudPoker: PokerGame {
    func start() {
        print("Starting StudPoker")
    }
}
struct TexasHoldem: PokerGame {
    func start() {
        print("Starting Texas Holdem")
    }
}
```

You can store `StudPoker` and `TexasHoldem` types into arrays, sets, and dictionaries. But if you want to mix and match different types of `PokerGame` as keys in a dictionary or inside an array, you stumble upon a shortcoming.

For instance, let's say you want to store the number of active players for each game inside a dictionary, where `PokerGame` is the key.

Listing 13.26 `PokerGame` as a key throws an error

```
// This won't work!
var numberOfPlayers = [PokerGame: Int]()

// The error that the Swift compiler throws is:
error: using 'PokerGame' as a concrete type conforming to protocol 'Hashable'
    is not supported
var numberOfPlayers = [PokerGame: Int]()
```

It sounds plausible to store `Hashable` as a dictionary key. But the compiler throws this error because you can't use this protocol as a concrete type. `Hashable` is a subprotocol of `Equatable` and therefore has `Self` requirements, which prevents you from storing a `Hashable` at runtime. Swift wants `Hashable` resolved at compile time into a concrete type; a protocol, however, is not a concrete type.

You could store one type of `PokerGame` as a dictionary key, such as `[TexasHoldem: Int]`, but then you can't mix them.

You could also try generics, which resolve to a concrete type. But this also won't work.

Listing 13.27   Trying to mix games

```
func storeGames<T: PokerGame>(games: [T]) -> [T: Int] {
  /// ... snip
}
```

Unfortunately, this generic would resolve to a *single* type per function, such as the following.

Listing 13.28   A resolved generic

```
func storeGames(games: [TexasHoldem]) -> [TexasHoldem: Int] {
  /// ... snip
}

func storeGames(games: [StudPoker]) -> [StudPoker: Int] {
  /// ... snip
}
```

Again, you can't easily mix and match `PokerGame` types into a single container, such as a dictionary.

Let's take two different approaches to solve this problem. The first one involves an enum and the second one involves something called *type erasure*.

13.3.1 *Avoiding a protocol using an enum*

Instead of using a `PokerGame` protocol, consider using a concrete type. Creating a `PokerGame` superclass is tempting, but you've explored the downsides of class-based inheritance already. Let's use an enum instead.

As shown in listing 13.29, first, `PokerGame` becomes an enum, and stores `StudPoker` and `TexasHoldem` in each case as an associated value. Then, you make `StudPoker` and `TexasHoldem` conform to `Hashable` because `PokerGame` is not a protocol anymore. You also make `PokerGame` conform to `Hashable` so that you can store it inside a dictionary. This way, you have concrete types, and you can store poker games inside a dictionary.

Listing 13.29   `PokerGame`

```
enum PokerGame: Hashable {
    case studPoker(StudPoker)
    case texasHoldem(TexasHoldem)
}

struct StudPoker: Hashable {
    // ... Implementation omitted
}
struct TexasHoldem: Hashable {
    // ... Implementation omitted
}

// This now works
var numberOfPlayers = [PokerGame: Int]()
```

> **NOTE** Notice how Swift generates the `Hashable` implementation for you, saving you from writing the boilerplate.

13.3.2 *Type erasing a protocol*

Enums are a quick and painless solution to the problem where you can't use some protocols as a type. But enums don't scale well; maintaining a large number of cases is a hassle. Moreover, at the time of writing, you can't let others extend enums with new cases if you were to build a public API. On top of that, protocols are *the* way to achieve dependency injection, which is fantastic for testing.

If you want to stick to a protocol, you can also consider using a technique called *type erasure*, sometimes referred to as *boxing*. With type erasure, you can move a compile-time protocol to runtime by wrapping a type in a container type. This way, you can have protocols with `Self` requirements—such as `Hashable` or `Equatable` types—or protocols with associated types as dictionary keys.

Before you begin, I must warn you. Erasing a type in Swift is as fun as driving in Los Angeles rush hour. Type erasure is a display of how Swift's protocols aren't fully matured yet, so don't feel bad if it seems complicated. Type erasure is a workaround until the Swift engineers offer a native solution.

> **NOTE** Inside the Swift source, type erasure is also used. You're not the only ones running into this problem!

You'll introduce a new struct, called `AnyPokerGame`. This concrete type wraps a type conforming to `PokerGame` and hides the inner type. Then `AnyPokerGame` conforms to `PokerGame` and forwards the methods to the stored type (see figure 13.5).

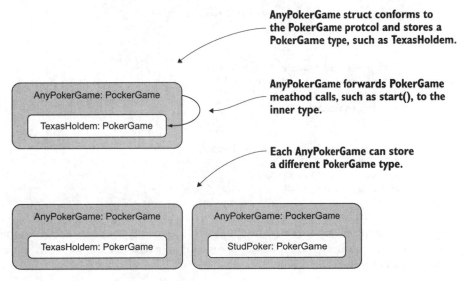

Figure 13.5 Type-erasing `PokerGame`

Because `AnyPokerGame` is a concrete type—namely, a struct—you can use `AnyPoker-Game` to store different poker games inside a single array, set, or dictionaries, and other places (see figure 13.6).

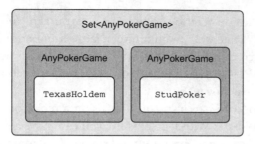

Figure 13.6   Storing `AnyPokerGame` inside a `Set`

In code, you can see how `AnyPokerGame` wraps the `PokerGame`. Notice how you wrap both a `StudPoker` and `TexasHoldem` game in a single `Array` and `Set`, and also as `Dictionary` keys. Problem solved!

Listing 13.30   `AnyPokerGame` in action

```
let studPoker = StudPoker()
let holdEm = TexasHoldem()

// You can mix multiple poker games inside an array.
let games: [AnyPokerGame] = [
    AnyPokerGame(studPoker),
    AnyPokerGame(holdEm)
]

games.forEach { (pokerGame: AnyPokerGame) in
    pokerGame.start()
}

// You can store them inside a Set, too
let setOfGames: Set<AnyPokerGame> = [
    AnyPokerGame(studPoker),
    AnyPokerGame(holdEm)
]

// You can even use poker games as keys!
var numberOfPlayers = [
    AnyPokerGame(studPoker): 300,
    AnyPokerGame(holdEm): 400
]
```

NOTE Remember `AnyError` from chapter 11? It also type-erases `Error` so that you can mix error types. Also, `AnyIterator` is a type-erased iterator, which you saw in chapter 9.

CREATING ANYPOKERGAME

Now that you've seen AnyPokerGame in action, it's time to create it. You start by introducing AnyPokerGame, which adheres to PokerGame. In the initializer, you pass a
PokerGame type constrained by a generic. Then, you store the start method from the
passed PokerGame inside a private property called _start. Once start() is called on
AnyPokerGame, you forward it to the stored _start() method.

Listing 13.31   Introducing AnyPokerGame

```
struct AnyPokerGame: PokerGame {              You introduce AnyPokerGame,
                                              conforming to the PokerGame protocol.
    init<Game: PokerGame>(_ pokerGame: Game)  {    You accept a
        _start = pokerGame.start                   PokerGame generic.
    }
                                              You store the start method
                                              into the _start property.
    private let _start: () -> Void            The _start property
                                              is defined here.
    func start() {
        _start()         Whenever start() is called,
    }                    you call the internal
}                        _start() property.
```

To erase a type, you tediously have to mirror every method from the protocol and
store them in their functions as properties. But you're in luck, because PokerGame
only has a single method.

You're almost done. Because PokerGame is also Hashable, you need to make Any-
PokerGame adhere to Hashable. In this case, Swift can't synthesize the Hashable implementation for you because you're storing a closure. Like a class, a closure is a
reference type, which Swift won't synthesize; so you have to implement Hashable yourself. Luckily, Swift offers the AnyHashable type, which is a type-erased Hashable type.
You can store the poker game inside AnyHashable and forward the Hashable methods
to the AnyHashable type.

Let's take a look at the complete implementation of AnyPokerGame.

Listing 13.32   Implementing Hashable

```
struct AnyPokerGame: PokerGame {
                                          The hashable
    private let _start: () -> Void        property stores the
    private let _hashable: AnyHashable    AnyHashable type.

    init<Game: PokerGame>(_ pokerGame: Game) {
        _start = pokerGame.start
        _hashable = AnyHashable(pokerGame)    You store the poker
    }                                         game inside _hashable.

    func start() {
        _start()
```

```
        }
    }
    extension AnyPokerGame: Hashable {
```

AnyPokerGame
adheres to Hashable.

You forward
the required
methods to the
AnyHashable
methods.

```
        func hash(into hasher: inout Hasher) {
            _hashable.hash(into: &hasher)
        }

        static func ==(lhs: AnyPokerGame, rhs: AnyPokerGame) -> Bool {
            return lhs._hashable == rhs._hashable
        }
    }
```

NOTE AnyPokerGame is extended as a style choice to separate the code to conform to Hashable.

Congratulations, you've erased a type! AnyPokerGame wraps any PokerGame type, and now you're now free to use AnyPokerGame inside collections. With this technique, you can use protocols with Self requirements—or associated types—*and* work with them at runtime!

Unfortunately, the solution covered here is just the tip of the iceberg. The more complex your protocol is, the more complicated your type-erased protocol turns out. But it could be worth the trade-off; the consumers of your code benefit if you hide these internal complexities from them.

13.3.3 *Exercise*

4 Are you up for an advanced challenge? You're building a small Publisher/Subscriber (also known as Pub/Sub) framework, where a publisher can notify all its listed subscribers of an event:

```
// First, you introduce the PublisherProtocol.
protocol PublisherProtocol {
    // Message defaults to String, but can be something else too.
    // This saves you a typealias declaration.
    associatedtype Message = String

    // PublisherProtocol has a Subscriber, constrained to the
➡ SubscriberProtocol.
    // They share the same message type.
    associatedtype Subscriber: SubscriberProtocol
        where Subscriber.Message == Message

    func subscribe(subscriber: Subscriber)
}

// Second, you introduce the SubscriberProtocol, resembling a
➡ subscriber that reacts to events from a publisher.
protocol SubscriberProtocol {
    // Message defaults to String, but can be something else too.
    // This saves you a typealias declaration.
```

```
            associatedtype Message = String
            func update(message: Message)
      }

      // You create a Publisher that stores a single type of Subscriber. But
    ⇒ it can't mix and match subscribers.
      final class Publisher<S: SubscriberProtocol>: PublisherProtocol where
    ⇒ S.Message == String {

          var subscribers = [S]()
          func subscribe(subscriber: S) {
              subscribers.append(subscriber)
          }

          func sendEventToSubscribers() {
              subscribers.forEach { subscriber in
                  subscriber.update(message: "Here's an event!")
              }
          }
      }
```

Currently, `Publisher` can maintain an array of a single type of subscriber. Can you type-erase `SubscriberProtocol` so that `Publisher` can store different types of subscribers?

Hint: because `SubscriberProtocol` has an associated type, you can make a generic `AnySubscriber<Msg>` where `Msg` represents the `Message` associated type.

13.4 *An alternative to protocols*

You have seen many use-cases when dealing with protocols. With protocols, you may be tempted to make most of the code protocol-based. Protocols are compelling if you have a complex API; then your consumers only need to adhere to a protocol to reap the benefits, while you as a producer can hide the underlying complexities of a system.

However, a common trap is starting with a protocol before knowing that you need one. Once you hold a hammer—and a shiny one at that—things can start looking like nails. Apple advocates starting with a protocol in their WWDC videos. But protocols can be a pitfall, too. If you religiously follow the protocol-first paradigm, but aren't sure yet if you need them, you may end up with unneeded complexity. You've also seen in the previous section how protocols have shortcomings that can make coming up with a fitting solution difficult.

Let's use this section to consider another alternative.

13.4.1 *With great power comes great unreadability*

First, consider if you truly need a protocol. Sometimes a little duplication is not that bad. With protocols, you pay the price of abstraction. Walking the line between over-abstractions and rigid code is a fine art.

A straightforward approach is sticking with concrete types when you're not sure if you need a protocol; for instance, it's easier to reason about a `String` than a complex generic constraint with three *where* clauses.

Let's consider another alternative for when you think you need a protocol, but perhaps you can avoid it.

One protocol that is a common occurrence in one shape or another is a `Validator` protocol, representing some piece of data that can be validated, such as in forms. Before being shown an alternative, you'll model the `Validator` with a protocol, as follows.

Listing 13.33 `Validator`

```
protocol Validator {                                    A type of value that
    associatedtype Value                                can be validated
     func validate(_ value: Value) -> Bool
}                                                        A Boolean indicating if
                                                        validation succeeded or failed
```

Then, you can use this `Validator`, for instance, to check whether a `String` has a minimal amount of characters.

Listing 13.34 Implementing the `Validator` protocol

```
struct MinimalCountValidator: Validator {
    let minimalChars: Int

    func validate(_ value: String) -> Bool {
        guard minimalChars > 0 else { return true }
        guard !value.isEmpty else { return false } // isEmpty is faster than
    count check
        return value.count >= minimalChars
    }
}

let validator = MinimalCountValidator(minimalChars: 5)
validator.validate("1234567890") // true
```

Now, for each different implementation, you have to introduce a new type conforming to `Validator` type, which is a fine approach but requires more boilerplate. Let's consider an alternative to prove that you don't always need protocols.

13.4.2 *Creating a generic struct*

With generics, you make a type—such as a struct—work with many other types, but the implementation stays the same. If you add a higher-order function into the mix, you can swap out implementations, too. Instead of creating a `Validator` protocol and many `Validator` types, you can offer a generic `Validator` struct instead. Now, instead of having a protocol and multiple implementations, you can have one generic struct.

Let's start by creating the generic `Validator` struct. Notice how it stores a closure, which allows you to swap out an implementation.

Listing 13.35 Introducing `Validator`

```
struct Validator<T> {

    let validate: (T) -> Bool

    init(validate: @escaping (T) -> Bool) {
        self.validate = validate
    }
}

let notEmpty = Validator<String>(validate: { string -> Bool in
    return !string.isEmpty
})

notEmpty.validate("") // false
notEmpty.validate("Still reading this book huh? That's cool!") // true
```

You end up with a type that can have different implementations *and* that works on many types. With minimal effort, you can seriously power up `Validator`. You can compose little validators into a smart validator via a `combine` method.

Listing 13.36 Combining validators

> On Validator, you declare a method that accepts two validators and returns a new one. Notice how you don't define a generic; the T from Validator<T> in the type definition is reused.

```
extension Validator {
    func combine(_ other: Validator<T>) -> Validator<T> {
        let combinedValidator = Validator<T>(validate: { (value: T) ->
        Bool in
            let ownResult = self.validate(value)
            let otherResult = other.validate(value)
            return ownResult && otherResult
        })

        return combinedValidator
    }
}

let notEmpty = Validator<String>(validate: { string -> Bool in
    return !string.isEmpty
})

let maxTenChars = Validator<String>(validate: { string -> Bool in
    return string.count <= 10
})

let combinedValidator: Validator<String> = notEmpty.combine(maxTenChars)
combinedValidator.validate("") // false
combinedValidator.validate("Hi") // true
combinedValidator.validate("This one is way too long") // false
```

> You pass a closure to a new combined-Validator.

> Inside the validation closure of the combinedValidator, you run both validations and return the result.

> You return the new combined validator.

> To showcase your new functionality, you create a new validator that wants maximally ten characters for string.

> You can now easily combine two validators into one.

You combined two validators. Because `combine` returns a new `Validator`, you can keep chaining, such as by combining a regular expression validator with a not-empty-string validator and so on. Also, because `Validator` is generic, it works on any type, such as `Int` validators and others. It's one example of how you get flexibility without using protocols.

13.4.3 Rules of thumb for polymorphism

Here are some heuristics to keep in mind when reasoning about polymorphism in Swift.

Requirements	Suggested approach
Light-weight polymorphism	Use enums.
A type that needs to work with multiple types	Make a generic type.
A type that needs a single configurable implementation	Store a closure.
A type that works on multiple types *and* has a single configurable implementation	Use a generic struct or class that stores a closure.
When you need advanced polymorphism, default extensions, and other advanced use cases	Use protocols.

13.5 Closing thoughts

You're armed and ready to make code testable, apply Swift's conditional conformance, type-erase generic types, and know when to use enums versus generic structs versus protocols!

This chapter laid out some tough sections, but you're persistent and reached the end. It's time to pat yourself on the back! The hardest part is over, and you've earned your Swift badge for covering the tough theory in this book.

Summary

- You can use protocols as an interface to swap out implementations, for testing, or for other use cases.
- An associated type can resolve to a type that you don't own.
- With conditional conformance, a type can adhere to a protocol, as long as its generic type or associated type adheres to this protocol.
- Conditional conformance works well when you have a generic type with very few constraints.
- A protocol with associated types or `Self` requirements can't be used as a concrete type.
- Sometimes, you can replace a protocol with an enum, and use that as a concrete type.

- You can use a protocol with associated types or Self requirements at runtime via *type erasure.*
- Often a generic struct is an excellent alternative to a protocol.
- Combining a higher-order function with a generic struct enables you to create highly flexible types.

Answers

1 Make WaffleHouse testable to verify that a Waffle has been served.

One way is to make Chef a protocol, and then you can swap out the implementation of Chef inside WaffleHouse. Then you can pass a testing chef to WaffleHouse:

```
struct Waffle {}

protocol Chef {
    func serve() -> Waffle
}

class TestingChef: Chef {
    var servedCounter: Int = 0
    func serve() -> Waffle {
        servedCounter += 1
        return Waffle()
    }
}

struct WaffleHouse<C: Chef> {

    let chef: C
    init(chef: C) {
        self.chef = chef
    }

    func serve() -> Waffle {
        return chef.serve()
    }

}

let testingChef = TestingChef()
let waffleHouse = WaffleHouse(chef: testingChef)
waffleHouse.serve()
testingChef.servedCounter == 1 // true
```

2 What is the benefit of a generic having few constraints when applying conditional conformance?

You have more flexibility in having a base working with many types, and you still have the option to get benefits when a type does conform to a protocol.

3 Make `CachedValue` conform to the custom `Track` protocol from this chapter:

```
extension CachedValue: Track where T: Track {
    func play() {
        currentValue.play()
    }
}
```

4 Build a small Publisher/Subscriber (also known as Pub/Sub) framework, where a publisher can notify all its listed subscribers of an event.

You solve it by creating `AnySubscriber`. Notice how you need to make `AnySubscriber` generic, because of the `Message` associated type from `Subscriber`. In this case, `Publisher` stores `AnySubscriber` of type `AnySubscriber<String>`:

```
struct AnySubscriber<Msg>: SubscriberProtocol {

    private let _update: (_ message: Msg) -> Void

    typealias Message = Msg

    init<S: SubscriberProtocol>(_ subscriber: S) where S.Message == Msg {
        _update = subscriber.update
    }

    func update(message: Msg) {
        _update(message)
    }
}
```

Publisher isn't generic anymore. Now it can mix and match subscribers:

```
final class Publisher: PublisherProtocol {

    // Publisher makes use of AnySubscriber<String> types. Basically,
    it pins down the Message associated type to String.
    var subscribers = [AnySubscriber<String>]()
    func subscribe(subscriber: AnySubscriber<String>) {
        subscribers.append(subscriber)
    }

    func sendEventToSubscribers() {
        subscribers.forEach { subscriber in
            subscriber.update(message: "Here's an event!")
        }
    }
}
```

14

Delivering quality Swift code

This chapter covers

- Documenting code via Quick Help
- Writing good comments that don't distract
- How style isn't too important
- Getting consistency and fewer bugs with SwiftLint
- Splitting up large classes in a Swifty way
- Reasoning about making types generic

Writing Swift code is fun, but in larger projects the ratio between writing and maintaining code shifts toward maintenance. Mature projects are where proper naming, code reusability, and documentation play an essential role. This chapter addresses these points to make programmers' lives more comfortable when looking at code from a maintenance perspective.

This is the least code-centric chapter in this book, but one of the more important ones when working on projects in teams or when trying to pass a code assignment for a new job. It also covers some refactoring approaches to make your code more generic and reusable.

It starts with documentation—who doesn't love to write it? I know I don't. But you can really help other programmers get up to speed when you supply them with good examples, descriptions, reasoning, and requirements. You'll see how to add documentation to code via the use of Quick Help.

Next, you're going to handle when and how to add comments to your code and see how you can add, not distract, by surgically placing valuable comments. Comments aren't Swift-centric, but they're still an influential part of daily (Swift) programming.

Swift offers a lot of different ways to write your code. But you'll see how style isn't too important and how consistency is more valuable to teams. You'll see how to install and configure SwiftLint to keep consistency in a codebase so that everyone, beginner or expert, can write code as if a single developer is writing it.

Then you'll discover how you can think differently about oversized classes. Generally, these tend to be "Manager" classes. Apple's source and examples include plenty of these manager classes, and following suit can be tempting. But more often than not, manager classes have many responsibilities that can harm maintainability. You'll discover how you can split up large classes and pave the road to making generic types.

Finding a fitting name is hard. You'll find out how types can get overspecified names and how suitable names are more future-proof and can prepare you for making types generic.

14.1   API documentation

Writing documentation can be tedious; you know it, I know it, you all know it. But even adding a little documentation to your properties and types can help a coworker get up to speed quickly.

Documentation is handy for internal types across a project. But it becomes especially important when offering elements that are marked as `public`, such as public functions, variables, and classes. Code marked as `public` is accessible when provided via a framework that can be reused across projects, which is all the more reason to provide complete documentation.

In this section, you'll see how you can add useful notations to accompany your code and to guide your readers via the use of doc comments, which are presented in Xcode via Quick Help.

Then, at the end, you'll see how to generate a documentation website based on Quick Help, via the help of a tool called Jazzy.

14.1.1   How Quick Help works

Quick Help documentation is a short markdown notation that accompanies types, properties, functions, enum cases, and others. Xcode can show tooltips after Quick Help documentation is added.

Imagine you're creating a turn-based, online game. You'll use a small enum to represent each turn a player can take, such as skipping a turn, attacking a location, or healing.

Xcode can display Quick Help tips in two ways. The pop-up, shown in figure 14.1, is activated by hovering over a word and pressing the Option key (Mac).

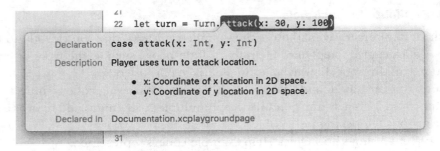

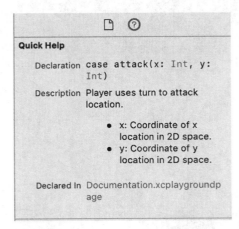

Figure 14.1   Quick Help pop-up

Quick Help is also available in Xcode's sidebar (see figure 14.2).

Figure 14.2   Quick Help in the sidebar

The enum in the Quick Help notation is formatted as follows.

Listing 14.1   The turn with Quick Help notations

```
/// A player's turn in a turn-based online game.
enum Turn {
    /// Player skips turn, will receive gold.
    case skip
    /// Player uses turn to attack location.
    /// - x: Coordinate of x location in 2D space.
    /// - y: Coordinate of y location in 2D space.
    case attack(x: Int, y: Int)
    /// Player uses round to heal, will not receive gold.
    case heal
}
```

By using a /// notation, you can add Quick Help notations to your types. By adding Quick Help documentation, you can add more information to the code you write.

14.1.2 Adding callouts to Quick Help

Quick Help offers many markup options—called *callouts*—that you can add to Quick Help. Callouts give your Quick Help tips a little boost, such as the types of errors a function can throw or showing an example usage of your code.

Let's go over how to add example code and error-throwing code by introducing a new function. This new function will accept multiple `Turn` enums and returns a string of the actions happening inside of it.

Figure 14.3 shows how Quick Help example code is represented.

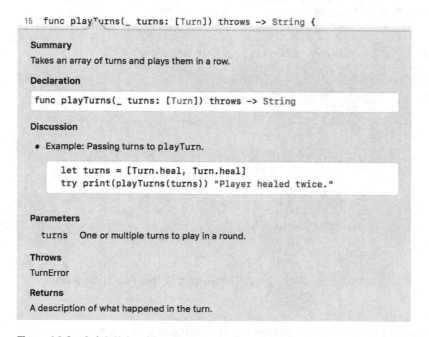

```
15  func playTurns(_ turns: [Turn]) throws -> String {
```

Summary
Takes an array of turns and plays them in a row.

Declaration
```
func playTurns(_ turns: [Turn]) throws -> String
```

Discussion
- Example: Passing turns to `playTurn`.

```
let turns = [Turn.heal, Turn.heal]
try print(playTurns(turns)) "Player healed twice."
```

Parameters
turns   One or multiple turns to play in a round.

Throws
TurnError

Returns
A description of what happened in the turn.

Figure 14.3 Quick Help with callouts

To create an example inside Quick Help, you need to tab text inside a Quick Help notation, as shown here.

Listing 14.2 Adding callouts

```
/// Takes an array of turns and plays them in a row.
///
/// - Parameter turns: One or multiple turns to play in a round.
/// - Returns: A description of what happened in the turn.
/// - Throws: TurnError
/// - Example: Passing turns to `playTurn`.
///
///         let turns = [Turn.heal, Turn.heal]
///         try print(playTurns(turns)) "Player healed twice."
func playTurns(_ turns: [Turn]) throws -> String {
```

Swift can tell you at compile time that a function can throw, but the thrown errors are only known at runtime. Adding a `Throws` callout can at least give the reader more information about which errors to expect.

You can even include more callouts, such as *Attention, Author, Authors, Bug, Complexity, Copyright, Date, Note, Precondition, Requires, See AlsoVersion, Warning,* and a few others.

For a full list of all the callout options, see Xcode's markup guidelines (http://mng.bz/Qgow).

14.1.3 *Documentation as HTML with Jazzy*

When you accompany your code with Quick Help documentation, you can get a rich documentation website that accompanies your project.

Jazzy (https://github.com/realm/jazzy) is a great tool to convert your Quick Help notations into an Apple-like documentation website. For instance, imagine that you're offering an Analytics framework. You can have Jazzy generate documentation for you, based on the public types and quick help information that's available (see figure 14.4).

Jazzy is a command-line tool and is installed as a Ruby gem. To install and run Jazzy, use these commands from the terminal:

```
gem install jazzy
jazzy
```

You'll see the following output:

```
Running xcodebuild
building site
building search index
downloading coverage badge
jam out to your fresh new docs in `docs`
```

Now you'll find a docs folder with your source code nicely documented. You can apply Jazzy to any project where you'd like to generate a website with documentation.

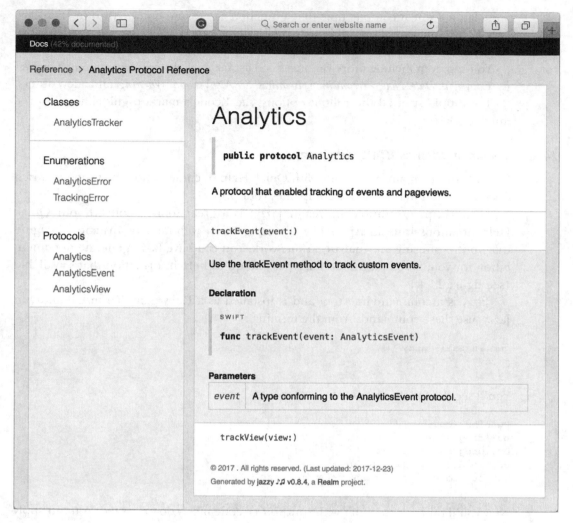

Figure 14.4   Jazzy documentation

14.2   *Comments*

Even though comments aren't related to Swift only, delivering code that is pleasing to read and quick to understand is still valuable.

Comments, or explicitly knowing when to add value with comments, are a vital component of day-to-day programming. Unfortunately, comments can muddy up your code if you're not careful. This section will show you how to write helpful comments.

14.2.1   *Explain the "why"*

A simple rule to follow is that a comment tells the reader "why" this element is there. In contrast, code tells the reader "what" it's doing.

Imagine a `Message` struct that allows a user to message another user privately. You can see in this example that when comments are focused on the "what," comments don't add much.

Listing 14.3   A struct with "what" comments

```
struct Message {
  // The id of the message
  let id: String

  // The date of the message
  let date: Date

  // The contents of the message
  let contents: String
}
```

These comments are redundant and muddy up the code. You can infer the meaning of these variables from the property names and, on top of that, they don't add anything to Quick Help.

Instead, try to explain the "why" with a comment, as shown here.

Listing 14.4   Message with a "why" comment

```
struct Message {
  let id: String
  let date: Date
  let contents: String

  // Messages can get silently cut off by the server at 280 characters.
  let maxLength = 280
}
```

Here you explain why `maxLength` is there and why 280 isn't just an arbitrary number, which isn't something you can infer from the property name.

14.2.2   *Only explain obscure elements*

Not all "whys" need to be explained.

Readers of your code tend only to be interested in obscure deviations from standard code, such as why you're storing data in two places instead of one (perhaps for performance benefits), or why you're reversing names in a list before you search in it (maybe so you can search on `lastname` instead).

You don't need to add comments to code your peers already know. Still, feel free to use them at significant deviations. As a rule of thumb, though, stay stingy with comments.

14.2.3   Code has the truth

No matter how many comments you write, the code has the truth. So when you refactor code, you'll have to refactor the comments that go with it. Out-of-date comments are garbage and noise in an otherwise pure environment.

14.2.4   Comments are no bandage for bad names

Comments can wrongfully be used as a bandage to compensate for bad function or variable names. Instead, explain yourself in code so that you won't need comments.

The next example shows comments added as a bandage, which you could omit by giving a Boolean check more context via code:

```
// Make sure user can access content.
if user.age > 18 && (user.isLoggedIn || user.registering) { ... }
```

Instead, give context via code so that a comment isn't needed:

```
let canUserAccessContent = user.age > 18 && (user.isLoggedIn ||
    user.registering)

if canUserAccessContent {
  ...
}
```

The code now gives context, and a comment isn't needed anymore.

14.2.5   Zombie code

Zombie code is commented-out code that doesn't do anything. It's dead but still haunts your workspace.

Zombie code is easily recognizable by commented-out chunks:

```
// func someThingUsefulButNotAnymore() {
//     user.save()
// }
```

Sometimes zombie code can linger inside codebases, probably because it's forgotten or because of a hunch that it may be needed again at some point.

Attachment issues aside, at some point you'll have to let go of old code. It will still live on in your memories, except those memories are called version control, such as git. If you need an old function again, you can use the version control of your choice to get it back while keeping your codebase clean.

14.3   Settling on a style

In this section, you'll see how to enforce style rules via a tool called SwiftLint.

It's rare to find a developer who doesn't have a strong preference for a style. John loves to use `forEach` wherever possible, whereas Carl wants to solve everything with for loops. Mary prefers her curly braces on the same line, and Geoff loves putting each function parameter on a new line so that git diffs are easier to read.

These style preferences can run deep, and they can cause plenty of debates inside teams.

But ultimately style isn't too important. If code looks sparkly-clean but is full of bugs, or no one uses it, then what is the point of good style? The goal of software isn't to look readable; it's to fill a need or solve a problem.

Of course, sometimes style does matter for making a codebase more pleasant to read and easier to understand. In the end, style is a means to an end and not the goal itself.

14.3.1 Consistency is key

When working in a team, more valuable than a style itself is style consistency. You save time when code is predictable and seemingly written by a single developer.

Having a general idea of what a Swift file looks like—before you even open it—is beneficial. You don't want to spend much time deciphering the code you're looking at, which lowers the cognitive load of you and your team members. Newcomers to a project are up to speed quicker and adopt stylistic choices when they recognize a clear style to conform to.

By removing style debates from the equation, you can focus on the important parts, which is making software that solves problems or fills needs.

14.3.2 Enforcing rules with a linter

You can increase codebase consistency and minimize style discussions by adding a linter to a project. A linter tries to detect problems, suspicious code, and style deviations before you compile or run your program. Using a linter to analyze your code ensures that you keep a consistent codebase across teams and projects.

With the help of a linter, both newcomers and veterans to a project can work on new *and* old code and maintain a consistent style enforced by the linter. A linter even helps you check for bad practices that may occur from time to time.

Realm offers a great tool called SwiftLint (https://github.com/realm/SwiftLint) to fulfill this linting role. You can use SwiftLint to enforce style guidelines that you configure. By default, it uses guidelines determined by the Swift community (https://github.com/github/swift-style-guide).

For example, the code in figure 14.5 violates some rules, such as force unwrapping and empty whitespace. SwiftLint lets you know via warnings and errors. You can consider SwiftLint to be a compiler extension.

It's not all about style, either. The empty count violation depicted in figure 14.5 alerts you to use `isEmpty` instead of `.count == 0`, because `isEmpty` performs better on large arrays.

Don't worry if you find some rules too strict; you can configure each rule to your liking. After a team settles on rules, everybody can move forward, and you can take style discussions out of the equation while reviewing code.

Read on to see how to install SwiftLint and configure its rules.

```
 9  import UIKit
10
11  class ViewController: UIViewController {
12      var lastLogin: Date?
13      var list: [Int] = []
14
15      override func viewDidLoad() {
16          super.viewDidLoad()
17
18          if list.count == 0 {          ❶ Empty Count Violation: Prefer checking `isEmpty` over comparing `count` to zero. (empty_count)
19              print(lastLogin!)         ⚠ Force Unwrapping Violation: Force unwrapping should be avoided. (force_unwrapping)
20          }
21                                        ⚠ Trailing Whitespace Violation: Lines should not have trailing whitespace. (trailing_whitespace)
22      } /
23
24                            ⚠ Vertical Whitespace Violation: Limit vertical whitespace to a single empty line. Currently 2. (vertical_whitespace)
25  }
26                        ⚠ Trailing Newline Violation: Files should have a single trailing newline. (trailing_newline)
27
```

Figure 14.5   SwiftLint in action

14.3.3 Installing SwiftLint

You can install SwiftLint using HomeBrew (https://brew.sh). In your command line, type the following:

```
brew install swiftlint
```

Alternatively, you can directly install the SwiftLint package from the Github repository (https://github.com/realm/Swiftlint/releases).

   SwiftLint is a command-line tool you can run with `swiftlint`. But chances are you're using Xcode. You'll configure it so that SwiftLint works there, too.

   In Xcode, locate the Build Phases tab (see figure 14.6). Click the plus button, and choose New Run Script Phase. Then add a new script and add the code shown in figure 14.7.

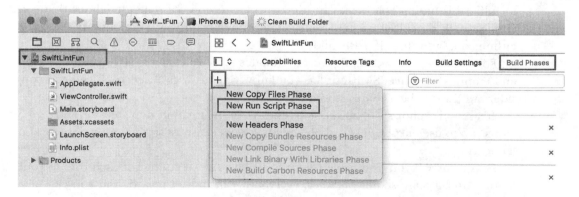

Figure 14.6   Xcode build phases

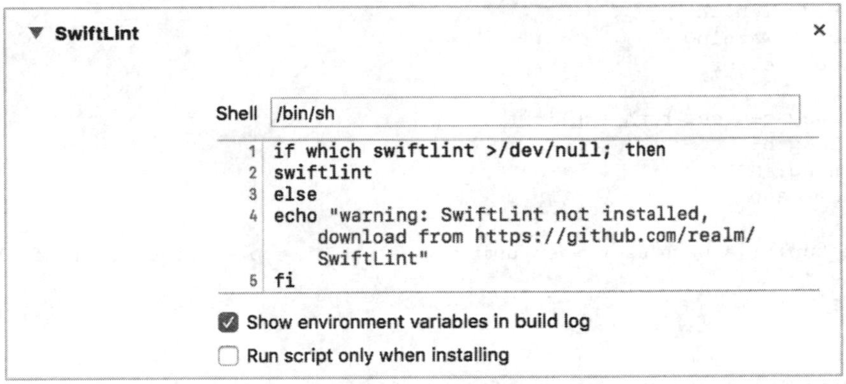

Figure 14.7 Xcode script

That's it! The next time you build your project, SwiftLint throws warnings and errors where applicable, based on a default configuration.

14.3.4 Configuring SwiftLint

Next, you'd probably like to configure SwiftLint to your liking. The configuration file is a yml—or yaml—file called .swiftlint.yml. This yaml file contains the rules you can enable and disable for your project.

Listing 14.5 SwiftLint configuration file

```
disabled_rules: # rule identifiers to exclude from running
  - variable_name
  - nesting
  - function_parameter_count
opt_in_rules: # some rules are only opt in
  - control_statement
  - empty_count
  - trailing_newline
  - colon
  - comma
included: # paths to include during linting. `--path` is ignored if present.
  - Project
  - ProjectTests
  - ProjectUITests
excluded: # paths to ignore during linting. Takes precedence over `included`.
  - Pods
  - Project/R.generated.swift

# configurable rules can be customized from this configuration file
# binary rules can set their severity level
force_cast: warning # implicitly. Give warning only for force casting

force_try:
  severity: warning # explicitly. Give warning only for force try
```

```
type_body_length:
  - 300 # warning
  - 400 # error

# or they can set both explicitly
file_length:
  warning: 500
  error: 800

large_tuple: # warn user when using 3 values in tuple, give error if there
  are 4
  - 3
  - 4

# naming rules can set warnings/errors for min_length and max_length
# additionally they can set excluded names
type_name:
  min_length: 4 # only warning

    error: 35
  excluded: iPhone # excluded via string
reporter: "xcode"
```

Alternatively, you can check all the rules that SwiftLint offers via the `swiftlint rules` command.

Move this .swiftlint.yml file to the root directory of your source code—such as where you can find the main.swift or AppDelegate.swift file. Now a whole team shares the same rules, and you can enable and disable them as your heart desires.

14.3.5 *Temporarily disabling SwiftLint rules*

Some rules are meant to be broken. For example, you may have force unwrapping set as a violation, but sometimes you might want it enabled. You can use SwiftLint modifiers to turn off specific rules for several lines in your code.

By applying specific comments in your code, you can disable SwiftLint rules at their respective lines. For example, you can disable and enable a rule in your code with the following:

```
// swiftlint:disable <rule1> [<rule> <rule>...]
// .. violating code here
// swiftlint:enable <rule1> [<rule> <rule>...]
```

You can modify these rules with the `:previous`, `:this`, or `:next` keywords.

For example, you can turn off the violating rules you had at the beginning of this section:

```
if list.count == 0 { // swiftlint:disable:this empty_count
    // swiftlint:disable:next force_unwrapping
    print(lastLogin!)
}
```

14.3.6 *Autocorrecting SwiftLint rules*

As soon as you add SwiftLint to an existing project, it will likely start raining SwiftLint warnings. Luckily, SwiftLint can fix warnings automatically via the following command you can run from the terminal:

```
swiftlint autocorrect
```

The autocorrect command adjusts the files for you and fixes warnings where it feels confident enough to do so.

Of course, it doesn't hurt to check the version control's diff file to see whether your code has been corrected properly.

14.3.7 *Keeping SwiftLint in sync*

If you use SwiftLint with multiple team members, chances are that one team member could have a different version of SwiftLint installed, especially when SwiftLint gets upgraded over time. You can add a small check so that Xcode gives a warning when you're on the wrong version.

This is another build phase you can add to Xcode. For example, the following command raises an Xcode warning when your SwiftLint isn't version 0.23.1:

```
EXPECTED_SWIFTLINT_VERSION="0.23.1"
if swiftlint version | grep -q ${EXPECTED_SWIFTLINT_VERSION}; then
echo "Correct version"
else
echo "warning: SwiftLint is not the right version
➥ ${EXPECTED_SWIFTLINT_VERSION}. Download from
➥ https://github.com/realm/SwiftLint"
```

Now, whenever a team member is falling behind with updates, Xcode throws a warning.

This section provided more than enough to get you started on SwiftLint. SwiftLint offers many more customizations and is regularly updated with new rules. Be sure to keep an eye on the project!

14.4   Kill the managers

Manager classes—recognized by the -Manager suffix—tend to pop up fairly often in the iOS and Swift community, most likely because Apple's code as an example offers manager types. But manager classes tend to have many (or too many) responsibilities. Challenge the "you've always done it this way" approach and see if you can improve code readability by tackling large manager classes.

You're going to see how you can reconsider a large class with many responsibilities by cutting it up into smaller reusable types. Working in a more modular way paves the road to a more modular and Swifty approach to architecture, including generic types.

Because manager classes tend to hold the crown of being oversized classes, they serve as a prime example in this section.

14.4.1 The value of managers

Managers tend to be classes with many responsibilities, such as the following examples:

- BluetoothManager—Checking connections, holding a list of devices, helping to reconnect, and offering a discovery service
- ApiRequestManager—Performing network calls, storing responses inside a cache, having a queue mechanism, and offering WebSocket support

Avoiding manager-like classes in the real world is easier said than done; it isn't 100% preventable. Also, manager types make sense when you compose them out of smaller types, versus classes containing many responsibilities.

If you have a large manager class, however, you can drop the Manager suffix, and the type's name tells the reader exactly as much as before. For example, rename BluetoothManager as Bluetooth and expose the same responsibilities. Alternatively, rename PhotosManager as Photos or Stack. Again, without the -Manager suffix, a type exposes the same amount of information of its tasks.

14.4.2 Attacking managers

Usually, when a type gains the -Manager suffix, it's an indicator that this class has a lot of essential responsibilities. Let's see how you can cut it up.

First, name these responsibilities explicitly so that a manager doesn't hide them. For example, an `ApiRequestManager` might be called `ApiRequestNetworkCache-QueueWebsockets`. That's a mouthful, but the truth has come out! Explicitly labeling responsibilities means that you uncovered all that the type does; it's now clear just how much responsibility the `ApiRequestManager` has.

As a next step, consider splitting up the responsibilities into smaller types, such as `ResponseCache`, `RequestQueue`, `Network`, and `Websockets` types (see figure 14.8). Also, you could now rename the `ApiRequestManager` to something more precise, such as `Network`.

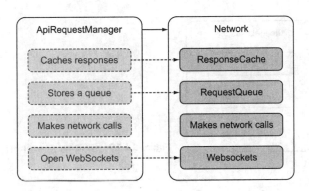

Figure 14.8 Refactoring `ApiRequestManager`

The `ApiRequestManager` is divided into precise pieces and is composed of these separated types you just extracted.

You can now reason about each type individually. Also, if a bug exists, such as in the caching mechanism, you don't need to look inside a giant `ApiRequestManager` class. You can most likely find the bug inside the `ResponseCache` type.

Not only are fewer managers great for getting work done faster—did I say that out loud?—you also gain clarity when writing software in smaller components.

14.4.3 Paving the road for generics

Now that the big `ApiRequestManager` has been cut up into smaller types, you can more easily decide which of these new types you can repurpose, so that they aren't limited to the network domain.

For example, the `ResponseCache` and `RequestQueue` types are focused explicitly on network-related functionality. But it's not a big leap to imagine that a cache and queue work on other types, too. If queueing and caching mechanisms are required in multiple parts of an application, you can decide to spend some effort to make `Response-Cache` and `ResponseQueue` generic, indicated with a `<T>` (see figure 14.9).

You drop the `Response` and `Request` names to gain a `Queue` and `Cache` type for elements outside of the network domain, and you would also refactor these types to make them generic in functionality (see figure 14.10).

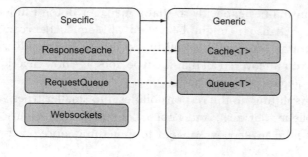

Figure 14.9   Making types generic

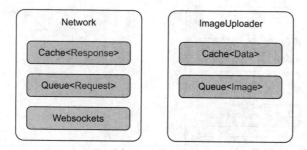

Figure 14.10   Reusing generic types

This time you can use the generic Queue and Cache types to queue and cache network requests and responses. But in some other part of your application, thanks to generics, you can use a queue and cache for storing and uploading image data, for example.

Having smaller types with a clear responsibility makes building larger types easier. Add generics on top of that and you have a Swifty approach to deal with core functionality inside an application.

As a counterpoint to generics, creating a generic type from the start isn't always fruitful. You might look at a chair and a couch and think "I only need a generic Seat type." It's okay to resist *DRY* (Don't Repeat Yourself) once in a while. Sometimes duplication is a fine choice when you're not sure which direction your project is going.

14.5   Naming abstractions

Naming your classes, variables, and files in programming can be harder than naming a firstborn baby or your pets, especially when you're giving names to things that are intricate and encompass several different behaviors.

This section shows how you can name types closer to the abstract while considering some as generic candidates as well.

14.5.1   Generic versus specific

If you give a programmer the task of creating a button to submit a registration form inside a program, I think it would be fair to assume that you don't want them to create an abstract Something class to represent this button. Neither would an oddly overspecific name such as CommonRegistrationButtonUsedInFourthScreen be favorable.

Given this example, I hope you can agree that the fitting name is most likely somewhere between the abstract and specific examples.

14.5.2 Good names don't change

What can happen in software development is a mismatch between what a type can do versus how it's used.

Imagine that you're creating an app that displays the top five coffee places. The app reads a user's past locations and figures out where the user visited most often.

A first thought may be to create a FavoritePlaces type. You feed this type a large number of locations, and it returns the five most-visited places. Then you can filter on the coffee types, as shown in this example.

Listing 14.6 Getting important places

```
let locations = ... // extracted locations.
let favoritePlaces = FavoritePlaces(locations: locations)
let topFiveFavoritePlaces = favoritePlaces.calculateMostCommonPlaces()

let coffeePlaces = topFiveFavoritePlaces.filter { place in place.type ==
    "Coffee" }
```

But now the client calls and wants to add new functionality to the application. They also want the app to show which coffee places the user has visited the least, so that they can encourage the user to revisit these places.

Unfortunately, you can't use the FavoritePlaces type again. The type does have all the inner workings to group locations and fulfill this new requirement, but the name specifically mentions that it uses favorite places only, not the least-visited places.

What happened is that the type's name is overspecified. The type is named after how it is used, which is to find the favorite places. But the type's name would be better if you can name it after what it does, which is find and group occurrences of places (see figure 14.11).

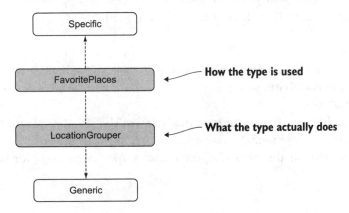

Figure 14.11 Naming a type after what it does

The point is that good names don't change. If you started with a `LocationGrouper` type, you could use it directly for both scenarios by adding a `leastVisitedPlaces` property; this would have prevented a naming refactor or a new type.

Ending up with a bad name is a small point, but it can happen effortlessly and subtly. Before you know it, you might have too many brittle names in a codebase. For example, don't use something like `redColor` as a button's property for a warning state; a `warning` property might be better because the warning's design might change, but a warning's purpose won't. Alternatively, when creating a `UserheaderView`—which is nothing more than an image and label you can reuse as something else—perhaps `ImageDescriptionView` would be more fitting as well as reusable.

14.5.3 *Generic naming*

The more abstract you make your types, the easier it is to make them generic. For example, a `LocationGrouper` is not too far removed from a `Grouper<T>` type, in which `T` could represent `CLLocation` such as `Grouper<CLLocation>`. But `Grouper` as a generic type can also be used to group something else, perhaps ratings for places, in which case you'd be reusing the type as `Grouper<Rating>`.

Making a type generic should not be the goal. The more specific you can make a type, the easier it is to understand. The more generic a type is, the more reusable (but harder to grasp) it can be. But as long as the type's name fits a type's purpose, you've hit the sweet spot.

14.6 *Checklist*

Next time you create a project, see if you can follow a short checklist to bump the quality of your deliverables:

- Quick Help documentation
- Sparse but useful comments explaining the *why*
- Adding SwiftLint to your project
- Cutting classes with too many responsibilities
- Naming types after what they do, not how they are used

14.7 *Closing thoughts*

Even though this wasn't a code-centric chapter, its ideas are still valuable. When you keep a consistent, clean codebase, you may make lives more comfortable for yourself and developers around you.

If you liked this chapter, I recommend reading Swift's API design guidelines (http://mng.bz/XAMG). It's jam-packed with useful naming conventions.

You're almost finished; in the next chapter I have some suggestions for you on what you can do next.

Summary

- Quick Help documentation is a fruitful way to add small snippets of documentation to your codebase.
- Quick Help documentation is especially valuable to public and internal elements offered inside a project and framework.
- Quick Help supports many useful callouts that enrich documentation.
- You can use Jazzy to generate Quick Help documentation.
- Comments explain the "why," not the "what".
- Be stingy with comments.
- Comments are no bandage for bad naming.
- There's no need to let commented-out code, aka Zombie Code, linger around.
- Code consistency is more important than code style.
- Consistency can be enforced by installing SwiftLint.
- SwiftLint supports configurations that you can let your team decide, which helps eliminate style discussions and disagreements.
- Manager classes can drop the `-Manager` suffix and still convey the same meaning.
- A large type can be composed of smaller types with focused responsibilities.
- Smaller components are good candidates to make generic.
- Name your types after what they do, not how they are used.
- The more abstract a type is, the more easily you can make it generic and reusable.

Where to Swift from here

You've made it to the end; it's time to give yourself a big pat on the back! You've touched upon many language-specific points and best practices, and you've expanded your technical arsenal to attack many different problems in a Swifty way. Even better, you have seen how Swift is a collection of modern and not-so-modern concepts wearing a modern coat. These concepts will stay with you in your programming career. Next time you see an exciting new framework or even a new language you want to learn, you may recognize generics, map, flatMap, sum types, and optionals and apply the concepts straight away. Understanding these core concepts carries more weight than a neat Swift trick or a shiny framework.

I hope that you embraced these concepts and that your day-to-day work has gotten a big quality bump. And I hope that helps you get that interesting job or exciting promotion, or it allows you to get those pull requests merged quicker while teaching others powerful ways to write Swift code.

But what should you do next? Read on for some ideas.

15.1 Build frameworks that build on Linux

At the time of writing, Swift has a strong focus on Apple's OS frameworks, such as iOS, tvOS, and MacOS. These platforms already have tons of frameworks. But the Swift community could use some help in making sure that frameworks also build on Linux. Having Swift code compile for Linux projects will help the community on the server side of things, such as command-line tools, web frameworks, and others. If you're an iOS developer, creating Linux tools will open up a new world of programming and you'll touch different concepts. A good start is to make your code work with the Swift Package Manager.

15.2   Explore the Swift Package Manager

The Swift Package Manager helps you get up and running and building quickly. First, take a look at the Getting Started guide (http://mng.bz/XAMG).

I also recommend exploring the Package Manager source (https://github.com/apple/swift-package-manager). The Utility and Basic folders especially have some useful extensions and types you may want to use to speed up your development. One of them is `Result`, which we've covered already. Other interesting types are `OrderedSet`, `Version`, or helpers to write command-line tools, such as `Argument-Parser` or `ProgressBar`.

You may also find useful extensions (http://mng.bz/MWP7), such as `flatMap-Value` on `Dictionary`, which transforms a value if it's not nil.

Unfortunately, the Swift Package Manager is not without its problems. At the time of writing, it doesn't support iOS for dependency management, and it doesn't play too well with Xcode. Over time, creating systems applications will get easier and more appealing with the evolution of Package Manager and more frameworks being offered by the community.

15.3   Explore frameworks

Another learning exercise is to play with or look inside specific frameworks:

- Kitura—(https://github.com/IBM-Swift/Kitura)
- Vapor—(https://github.com/vapor/vapor)
- SwiftNIO — For low-level networking (https://github.com/apple/swift-nio)
- TensorFlow for Swift—For machine learning (https://github.com/tensorflow/swift)

If you're more interested in metaprogramming, I suggest taking a look at Sourcery (https://github.com/krzysztofzablocki/Sourcery), which is a powerful tool to get rid of boilerplate in your codebase, amongst other things.

15.4   Challenge yourself

If you've always approached a new application a certain way, perhaps it's a good time to challenge yourself to try a completely different approach.

For instance, try out true protocol-oriented programming, where you model your applications by starting with protocols. See how far you can get without creating concrete types. You'll enter the world of abstracts and tricky generic constraints. In the end, you will need a concrete type—such as a class or struct—but perhaps you can make the most of the default implementations on a protocol.

See if you can challenge yourself by using protocols, but at compile time only, which means you'll be using generics and associated types. It will be harder to work with, but seeing your code compile and watching everything work is very rewarding. Taking a protocol-oriented approach may feel like you're programming with handcuffs on, but it'll stretch your thinking and be a fruitful exercise.

Another idea is to avoid protocols altogether. See how far you can get with nothing but enums, structs, and higher-order functions.

15.4.1 *Join the Swift evolution*

It's great to see Swift progress every few months with fancy new updates. But you don't have to watch from the sidelines. You can be part of the conversation of Swift's evolution and even submit your own proposals for change. It all starts at the Swift evolution Github page (https://github.com/apple/swift-evolution).

15.4.2 *Final words*

Thank you so much for purchasing and reading this book. I hope your Swift skills have gotten a good boost. Feel free to contact me on Twitter at @tjeerdintveen. See you there!

index

iOS Development with Swift
by Craig Grummitt

> ISBN: 9781617294075
> 568 pages
> $49.99
> November 2017

iOS Development with Swift in Motion
by Craig Grummitt

> Course duration: 8h 3m
> $39.99
> November 2018

Classic Computer Science Problems in Swift
Essential techniques for practicing programmers
by David Kopec

> ISBN: 9781617294891
> 224 pages
> $39.99
> March 2018

For ordering information go to www.manning.com

MORE TITLES FROM MANNING

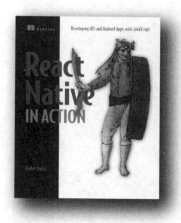

React Native in Action
Developing iOS and Android apps with JavaScript
by Nader Dabit

ISBN: 9781617294051
300 pages
$49.99
January 2019

Hello Swift!
iOS app programming for kids and other beginners
by Tanmay Bakshi with Lynn Beighley

ISBN: 9781617292620
350 pages
$34.99
January 2019

Anyone Can Create an App
Beginning iPhone and iPad programming
by Wendy L. Wise

ISBN: 9781617292651
336 pages
$29.99
March 2017

For ordering information go to www.manning.com